Improbable Heroes

The True Story of How Clergy and Ordinary Citizens Risked Their Lives to Save Jews in Italy

by

Carl L. Steinhouse

authorHOUSE™
1663 LIBERTY DRIVE, SUITE 200
BLOOMINGTON, INDIANA 47403
(800) 839-8640
WWW.AUTHORHOUSE.COM

© *2005 Carl L. Steinhouse. All Rights Reserved.*

No part of this book may be reproduced, stored in a retrieval system, or transmitted by any means without the written permission of the author.

First published by AuthorHouse 10/27/05

ISBN: 1-4208-6838-1 (sc)

Library of Congress Control Number: 2005905833

Printed in the United States of America
Bloomington, Indiana

This book is printed on acid-free paper.

After supervising the loading of the Jews into waiting cattle cars, SS Captain Dannecker was not in good humor. Of the estimated 8,000 Jews in the Rome ghetto and the adjoining area of Trastevere, his troops had been able to round up only 1,239 of them. So much for his proud report to the Führer! Colonel Kappler gloated to himself.

"I will get the rest of them," he growled to Kappler.

The SS colonel fixed Dannecker with a steely gaze. "I'm afraid you underestimate the enemy, Captain. You're fighting the most improbable heroes—ordinary Italians, priests and nuns who won't give up the Jews so easily. Oh, you'll get a few of them; there are always careless ones, but face it, your *razzia* is basically *kaput*."

Dedicated to the memory Findlay C. Penix, a friend and one of the unsung heroes who contributed to the liberation of millions under the thumb of Hitler and to the ultimate defeat of the Nazis on the battlefields of Europe as an officer in the United States Army infantry and suffered as a POW before going on to a distinguished career in education at the University of Michigan

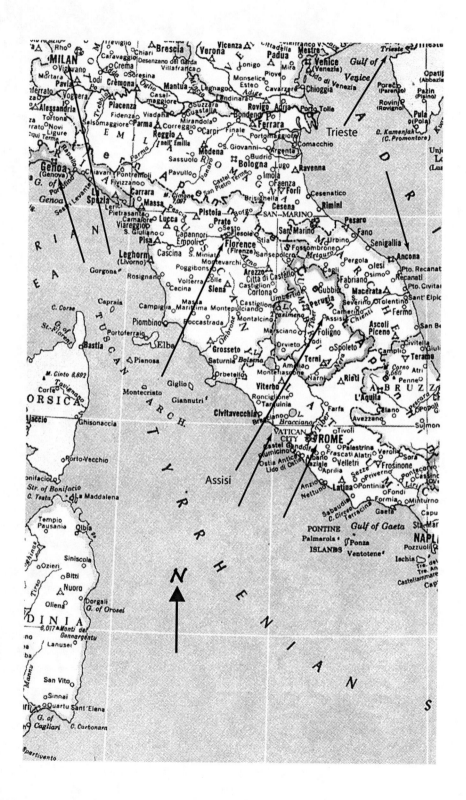

PREFACE

The horrors inflicted on the Jews by the Germans and their sympathizers during the Adolf Hitler years are well documented. The actions and heroics of ordinary Italians and the clergy to frustrate the German SS attempts to round up the Jews in Italy is not so well known. Too much focus has been on what Pope Pius XII did or not do, and not enough on the real heroes. The entire true story deserves to be told.

For continuity, certain events are not in exact chronological order and others are combined. Unless otherwise noted, all of the German Nazi characters are real, as are the Italian government officials and military officers, the Allied Forces officials and the clergy in Italy. The stories and agonies of many of the refugee and Italian victims of the Holocaust portrayed here have been told, handed down, and recorded in history, but whose names remain unknown. I have given them names and, at times, to keep the book length manageable, combined the experiences of several such victims into one character or family, experiences that themselves were very real and suffered by far too many Jews. Among the major unidentified characters and families to whom I have given names are the Divis family, Lidia Fiano, the Attilio Nathan family, the Davide Nathan family, Ester Piperno, Cesare Rabello, the David Schwartz family, the Joseph Schwartz family and Augusto Sonnino. For the reader's convenience, I have included a Cast of Characters with those given fictional names set forth in **boldface**.

I am indebted to my editor, Susan Converse Winslow, whose tough love approach to my manuscript and attention to detail was invaluable. I am grateful to for the encouragement given to me by Professor Nancy Shuster, Author Hollis Alpert and Janine Warsaw. I valued the comments of my children who read early drafts of my manuscript. Above all, I owe more than I can express to my wife, Diana, who suffered through all of the drafts, reading most of them and providing valuable insights. She bore many of my frustrations with understanding and love.

CAST OF CHARACTERS
(Fictional characters are shown in **boldface**)

Almansi, Dante, president of the Union of Italian Jewish Communities
Ambrosio, Vittorio, Italian general, field commander in Croatia
Anticoli, Lazzaro, the prizefighter called Bucefalo
Attolico, Bernardo, Italian ambassador to Germany
Avidabile, Dr., Italian commandant of Fossoli Prison Camp in Italy
Badoglio, Pietro, Italian general, succeeded Mussolini as Prime Minister
Balbo, Italo, Italian general and military governor of Libya
Baquis, Giorgio, secretary of a Genoa synagogue
Beetz, Hildegard, SS operative
Benedetto, Maria, Capuchin monk, also know in France as Father Pierre-Marie Benoît
Benoît, Pierre Marie, see Benedetto
Bergen, Diego von, German ambassador to Vatican under Pius XI and the beginning of the reign of Pius XII
Bertolucci, chief of police in Assisi
Bismarck, Prince Otto von, German ministerial counselor in Rome
Bocchini, Arturo, head of police and OVRA, the Italian secret police
Boetto, Pietro Cardinal, Archbishop of Genoa
Bosshammer, Friedrich, SS colonel; Adolph Eichmann's expert on Italian affairs

Boyd, Dennis W., Captain, commander of the British aircraft carrier *Illustrious*
Brizi, Luigi, printer who made false IDs in Assisi for Father Niccacci
Brunacci, Aldo, professor canon of San Rufino Cathedral, Assisi
Bucefalo, see Anticoli
Buffarini,-Guidi, Guido, Salò government minister of interior
Candotti, Arturo, Christian friend of Davide Nathan whom he took into his home
Cantoni, Raffaele, DELASEM leader in Florence and Venice
Carboni, Giacomo Italian general, Rome commander of Italian forces during the takeover by Germans
Carlità, Mario, head of Fascist gang arresting and killing anti-Fascists and Jews
Casini, Leto, priest in Florence assisting Father Cipriano Ricotti
Cassutto, Anna, wife of Nathan Cassutto
Cassutto, David, rabbi, father of Nathan Cassutto
Cassutto, Nathan, chief rabbi of Milan
Castellano, Giuseppe, Italian general, negotiated with the Allies for Italy's surrender
Cavallero, Ugo, Italian general
Celli, Emo, shopkeeper in Rome who helped Jews with food ration cards.
Cerica, Angelo, commander of the Italian military police
Chevalier, Adrienne, daughter of Madame Chevalier
Chevalier, Madame, gave shelter to Jews and Allied POWs in her Rome apartment
Ciano, Edda, daughter of Mussolini and wife of Galeazzo Ciano
Ciano, Galeazzo (Gallo), Mussolini's foreign minister and son-in-law
Cochis, Arnaldo, proprietor of Hotel Lyskamm, Gressoney, Italy
Coen, rescued from Servigliano Camp
Cunningham, Andrew, British admiral who conceived and carried out the attack on Taranto
Dalla Costa, Elia Cardinal, Florence
Dannecker, Theodor, SS captain, reported to Adolph Eichmann.
De Bono, Emilio, Italian general executed by Mussolini

De Grenet, Filippo, Italian consul killed at the Ardeatine Caves
De Vecchi, Cesare, Grand Council member
Degler, Grechen, also known as Sister Agnes, aliases of Dora Schwartz
Di Castro, Pacifico, nephew of Rabello, prisoner at Fossoli beaten to death by SS Sergeant-Major Haage
Di Porto, Celeste, the Black Panther
Divis, Bela, daughter of Lev Divis
Divis, Lev, Dr., fled Prague with family in March 1939 after German invasion of Czechoslovakia
Divis, Zophie, wife of Lev Divis
Dobbrick, Hellmuth, SS major, refused orders to participate in the Ardeatine Caves executions
Donatelli, Sebastiano, alias of Father Francesco Repetto
Donati, Angelo, helped Jews escape to and from France
Eichmann, Adolph, German SS colonel, in charge of the deportation of Jews in Europe
Faggini, Adriana, Gentile friend of Joseph Schwartz, helped hide his family in Italy
Fahrener, Alfred, Swiss citizen connected with the League of Nations
Fatucci, Renzo, Jewish typographer assisting Benedetto
Fermi, Enrico, Italian physicist who escaped to the United States with his Jewish wife
Fernando, Giorgi, priest serving in a church near Ardeatine Caves
Fiano, Lidia, inmate at Fossoli Prison Camp, befriended Ester Piperno
Filippo, Prince, see Pamphili, Prince Filippo Doria
Foà, Beppe, a Jew and an Italian aircraft designer who escaped from Italy after racial laws enacted
Foà, Ugo, leader of the Rome Jewish community
Fortini, Arnaldo, mayor of Assisi
Frascati, Dino, professor from Florence
Giuseppina, Mother Abbess, Sisters of the Poor Clares, Convent of St. Quirico, Assisi
Goebbels, Josef, Dr., propaganda minister of Germany

Goering, Hermann, field marshal, German Air Force chief, second in authority to Hitler
Gottardi, Luciano, labor leader executed by Mussolini
Grandi, Dino, Grand Council Member
Grosser, Bernard, DELASEM leader from Genoa
Haage, Hans, German SS sergeant major who took over control of Fossoli Prison Camp
Hauser, Wolfgang, German colonel, General Mackensen's adjutant
Hess, Rudolph, Hitler's secretary in early years; later, vice chancellor
Hesse, Philip von, Prince, a Hitler diplomatic representative in Italy
Himmler, Heinrich, *Reichsführer,* Head of all German security services
Hitler, Adolf, German dictator
Höss, Rudolph, German commandant, Auschwitz Concentration Camp
Ischia, Mario, secretary to a clandestine Jew in Florence
Jodl, Alfred, German general, chief of operations staff
Jozsa, Paolo, Hungarian Jewish refugee in Italy, artist, and expert forger
Kaltenbrunner, Ernst, chief of the Reich Central Security Office (RSHA)
Kappler, Herbert, German colonel, chief of SS in Rome
Keitel, Wilhelm, German general, negotiated surrender of France
Kessel, Albrecht von, German embassy secretary in the Vatican, assistant to Consul Weizsäcker
Kesselring, Albert, German field marshal, commander of German forces in Italy and North Africa
Koch, Pietro, head of Fascist gang arresting and killing anti-Fascists and Jews
Krumey, Hermann, German major, assistant of Adolph Eichmann
Lächert, Elsa, German SS sergeant at Fossoli Prison Camp
LaFarge, John, American priest who helped prepare draft encyclical for Pius XI
Legnano, the marshal in the police in Ancona
Lemp, Fritz Julius, German captain of U boat
Lercoz, Rudy, Italian border guide

Levi, Gino, Jewish inmate in Servigliano
Levi, Renzo, DELASEM leader in Rome
Levine, Avram, captain in the British Jewish Brigade from Palestine
Liuzzi, Guido, Italian general fired because he was a Jew
Lospinoso, Guido, sent to Nice by Mussolini to assist Germans in deporting Jews
Mackensen, Baron Han Georg von, German ambassador to Italy
Maelzer, Kurt, German general, military commander in Rome; took over from General Stahel
Maglione, Luigi Cardinal, secretary of state of the Vatican under Pope Pius XII
Malcovati, Achille, Christian truck driver working for Massimo Teglio, delivering arms to partisans
Marinelli, Giovanni, administrative secretary, executed by Mussolini
Matteotti, Giacomo, Socialist in the Italian Parliament, slain by Fascists
May, John, butler to British Ambassador Osborne; helped Jews and POWs
Mazzolini, Count Serafini, foreign minister in Salò government
Möllhausen, Eitel Friedrich, a German consul to the Vatican
Montini, Giovanni Battista, monsignor (future Pope Paul VI), assistant secretary of state, Vatican
Morosini, Francesco, priest who helped Jews, worked with Fathers O'Flaherty and Benedetto
Moscati, Mino, Rome Jewish boy
Müller, Valentin, German colonel, commandant in Assisi
Mussolini, Benito, Italian dictator
Mussolini, Edvige, sister of Mussolini
Mussolini, Rachele, wife of Mussolini
Naito, Takeshi, Japanese army lieutenant, assistant air attaché in Berlin, investigated the British raid on Taranto
Nathan, Attilio, Italian Jew living in Rome ghetto
Nathan, Davide, Italian Jew living in Rome ghetto
Nathan, Elena, daughter of Davide and Olga Nathan
Nathan, Michele, son of Attilio and Rosa Nathan

Nathan, Olga, wife of Davide Nathan
Nathan, Rosa, wife of Attilio Nathan
Niccacci, Rufino, friar in Assisi
Nicolini, Giuseppe Placido, bishop in Assisi
O'Flaherty, Hugh Joseph, Irish monsignor in the Vatican
Orsenigo, Cesare, monsignor, papal nuncio in Berlin
Osborne, Sir Francis D'Arcy, British ambassador to Vatican
Ovazza, Elena, daughter of Ettore and Nella Ovazza
Ovazza, Ettore, Fascist Jew from Turin
Ovazza, Nella, wife of Ettore Ovazza
Ovazza, Riccardo, son of Ettore and Nella Ovazza
Pacelli, Eugenio, see Pope Pius XII
Pacifici, Riccardo, rabbi in Genoa
Pamphili, Prince Filippo Doria, Italian Prince, funded rescue of Jews in Rome
Papen, Franz von, vice chancellor of Germany until 1938, signed concordat with Vatican
Pareschi, Carlo, Italian agriculture minister executed by Mussolini
Pariani, Alberto, Italian general, chief of staff in 1940
Petacci, Clara, one of Mussolini's mistresses; executed with him
Pièche, Giuseppe, general, head of Italian Intelligence
Piperno, Ester, Jewess from Florence, sent to Fossoli Prison Camp
Polacco, Bino, janitor of the Genoa synagogue
Pope Pius XI, Achille Ratti
Pope Pius XII, Eugenio Pacelli
Preysing, Konrad von, monsignor, archbishop of Berlin, and later, cardinal
Preziosi, Giovanni, renegade priest, anti-Semite and later, minister of race in Salò government
Pugliese, Umberto, former Inspector General of Navy, fired because he was a Jew
Putoni, general, king's military aide
Nelson, Gordon, captain, British Intelligence
Rabello, Cesare, deaf prisoner killed at Fossoli Prison Camp by SS Sergeant Major Haage
Rafanelli, Enrico, a Jewish Fascist in Rome
Raganalla, Libero, Rome priest

Rahn, Rudolph von, German ambassador to Italy
Ratti, Achille, see Pope Pius XI
Repetto, Father Francesco, priest in Genoa, working with DELASEM
Ribbentrop, Joachim von, German foreign minister
Riccardi, Arturo, Italian admiral commanding the Taranto Naval Base
Ricotti, Cipriano, a Dominican monk in Florence helping DELASEM
Roatta, Mario, Italian general, commander in Yugoslavia, then chief of staff
Robotti, Mario, Italian general, succeeded General Roatta in Yugoslavia
Roey, Joseph-Ernst Cardinal, in Belgium
Rommel, Erwin, German general, commander of Afrika Korps; later, commander of Army B in Northern Italy
Roncalli, Angelo Giuseppe, monsignor, papal nuncio in Turkey (future Pope John XXIII)
Ronga, Carmen, alias of Professor Frascati
Roosevelt, Franklin Delano, President of the United States
Rosa, Enrico, priest who died before he could edit the encyclical for Pius XI
Rossi, Mario, partisan
Sarfatti, Cesare, husband of Margherita Sarfatti
Sarfatti, Margherita, Italian Jew, a Mussolini confidant and mistress
Sarfatti, Roberto, son of Cesare and Margherita Sarfatti
Schuster, Idlefonso Cardinal, archbishop of Milan
Schwamm, Stefan, Viennese Jewish lawyer, posing as International Red Cross representative in Italy
Schwartz, Dora, wife of Joseph Schwartz
Schwartz, Fredrick, son of Joseph and Dora Schwartz
Schwartz, Joseph, a tailor who fled Vienna with his family in 1938
Schwartz, Karl, brother of Joseph, fled Vienna, escaped Italy on the ship, *Athenia*
Schwartz, Sophia, daughter of Joseph and Dora Schwartz

Scorza, Carlo, Fascist Party secretary
Senise, Carmen, chief of police in the 30s
Sereni, Enzo, Italian Jew who emigrated to Palestine in 1927; joined the British Intelligence Service and parachuted into Italy in 1944 to assist partisans
Skorzeny, Otto, colonel, rescued Mussolini
Smith, Walter Bedell, American general
Sonnino, Augusto, Jew from Ancona who became a partisan
Sorani, Rosina, sister of Settimio Sorani
Sorani, Settimio, DELASEM leader in Rome
Stahel, Rainer, German general, Rome Military Command
Stalin, Soviet dictator
Starace, Achille, secretary of Fascist Party, 1931-1939
Stoppa, Mario, Pius XII's chauffeur
Strong, Kenneth, British general
Supino, Luigi, Italian army colonel stationed in Croatia
Tamburini, Tullio, Salò government chief of police
Tardini, Domenica Cardinal, Rome
Taylor, Maxwell, American general, a negotiator in the surrender of Italy
Taylor, Myron, President Roosevelt's representative to the Vatican
Teglio, Massimo, aviator/playboy from Genoa who became a lynchpin of DELASEM
Tisserant, Eugene Cardinal, of France
Tittmann, Harold, American charge d'affaires to the Vatican
Triberti, Giobatta, alias of Massimo Teglio
Valobra, Lelio, attorney from Genoa, president of DELASEM
Velde, Ernst von den, German captain, Gestapo
Victor Emmanuel III, King of Italy
Vincenti, Federico, parish priest in Porta de Santa Susanna, San Andrea Church
Viterbi, Emilio, Jewish professor, colleague of Enrico Fermi
Volterra, Vito, Jewish partisan
Wachsberger, Arminio, a Jew picked up in the Rome ghetto during the roundup, served as an interpreter in Auschwitz
Weiss, Clara, Jewish refugee who died after illness in Assisi
Weizsäcker, Eitel von, German consul to the Vatican

Wolff, Karl, German general, liaison officer of Himmler until 1943; later, military governor of north Italy and plenipotentiary to Mussolini's Salò government

Yamamoto, Isoroku, Japanese admiral who planned the attack on Pearl Harbor

Zolli, Israel, chief rabbi of Rome

PROLOGUE

The year was 1924. Adolf Hitler, a convicted criminal despised by those in power, found himself in prison in Germany. In Italy, another Fascist already had been head of state for two years, rapidly consolidating his power as dictator of a grateful nation that was tired of strikes and the internecine warfare between the Socialists and the Fascists. Hitler admired Benito Mussolini and looked to him as a model for his own aspirations. Mussolini, by contrast, looked upon Hitler as an uncouth, unemployed, Austrian rabble-rouser.

In one of the ironies of history, less than twenty years later, their positions—and their attitudes toward each other—would be reversed, with the potential for a catastrophe for the Jews in Italy like that inflicted on the Jews in Germany. But Italy was not Germany. Many of Italy's brave citizens refused to give up their fellow countrymen singled out for extermination simply because they were Jews; and together with a group of clergy, colluded, at the risk of their lives, to hide Jews and spirit many of them out of the country, thus frustrating Hitler's murderous intentions. The result: over 80% percent of the Jews in Italy survived the Holocaust, a situation not experienced in most other European countries under the domination of the Nazis. This, then, is the story of their survival.

March 1924, Munich, Fortress of Landsberg am Lech Prison

A criminal prisoner like no other ever incarcerated in the fortress of Landsberg, Adolf Hitler, the führer, the leader of the National Socialist German Workers' Party, had a loyal following made up of a substantial number of prisoners and some of the prison guards. The prison authorities were unusually accommodating to Hitler's needs. His followers were permitted to clean his cell every day, a task they considered an honor.

Every day, before breakfast, Hitler took his solitary walk in the garden of the warden, the only prisoner allowed to do so.

As he paced up and down, he mulled over the attempted putsch of November 1923. During that disastrous Munich march led by Hitler and his armed followers, someone in the group, he did not know who, had fired a shot, whereupon the police opened fire. Max Ervin von Scheubner-Richter, standing next to Hitler, fell, becoming the first fatality. Gunfire wounded Hermann Göring, marching behind Hitler.

Reading an opinion piece on page one of a Munich newspaper he carried out with him into the garden, Hitler tugged angrily on his moustache. The columnist had branded him a coward for crawling off the street and running away, abandoning his trapped comrades. He sighed. Unfortunately, it was true; he'd panicked, something he admitted only to himself. This mental admission lasted only as long as it took him to rationalize that, as führer, he had to survive to lead his party to victory on another day. He had the uncanny ability to abandon unpleasant truths, readily adopting more acceptable rationalizations and firmly believing them—and then convincing his followers in the prison.

He realized he would have to come out of this mess looking like a strongman, not a weakling, so he concocted a story of valor—that he had dragged a child to safety during the melee, a good reason for leaving the scene. He so firmly convinced himself of the truth of that heroic scenario that it became an indisputable fact in his mind. Eventually, he would find a child willing to verify his story.

Finishing the offensive newspaper article, Hitler ripped the page to sheds, crushed the strips and threw them down, grinding the newsprint under his heel. Looking around, he decided he'd better not abuse his garden privileges. He picked up the pieces and deposited them in a trash receptacle.

In a sour mood, he reached into his inner jacket pocket for more pleasant reading, pulling out a tattered envelope, one of the hundreds of pieces of mail he received each week. He re-read it for the fourth time.

> What you stated there is the catechism of a new political creed coming to birth in the midst of a collapsing, secularized world. To you a god has given the tongue with which to express our sufferings. You formulated our agony in words that promise salvation.

It was signed "Joseph Goebbels, Ph.D. philology."

This man has a way with words, he thought. I must see him when I get out of prison. He stuffed back into his jacket pocket the letter and the envelope with the return address. He looked at his watch—breakfast time.

The prison officials permitted Hitler to take his meals with his followers in the large common room. They sat at a long table with Hitler at its head. He sat under a swastika banner, yet another privilege afforded to him. After breakfast, the prisoner-followers reported to Hitler for a daily conference with their chief. The führer's deputy, Rudolph Hess, sat to his immediate right, taking notes of his leader's utterances. Hitler later used these notes to dictate to Hess the manuscript of *Mein Kampf* ("My Struggle").

Precisely at ten o'clock, Hitler stood up, leaning his hands on the table. The noise of dozens of conversations slowly diminished as prisoner-followers hushed their comrades until the quiet seemed almost to create a vacuum. Satisfied, Hitler began speaking. "I would divide mankind into three species, the culture creators, the culture bearers and the culture destroyers. In the first category are you and me, the Aryans, who have built the foundations of civilization. At the other end of the spectrum is the Jew, a parasite that will eventually kill off the host nation. The Jew has no culture-creating ability whatsoever and his intellect will never act as a constructive force." Hitler's voice rose to an almost hysterical crescendo, his fist pounding the table and spittle flying in all directions. "One of our primary goals is to totally eliminate this Jewish sponger, this malign bacillus that spreads more and more through its host nation. We must save the world from such vermin!"

The room erupted in cheers, causing Hitler to pause. He folded his arms tightly to his chest. If he enjoyed or appreciated this affirmation, his face did not show it. He maintained his scowl. The audience became quiet.

"The coercive Jewish hold on our state can be broken only by terror and counter-coercion and, above all, by the elimination of their presence. Only then can we construct the new, ideal state. If at the beginning of the Great War, the Jewish corrupters had been poison gassed, as happened to hundreds of thousands of our best German workers in the field, the sacrifice of millions would not have been in vain. The elimination of such scoundrels, such international poisoners, would have saved the lives of countless real Germans, so valuable for our future."

The room erupted again, with followers standing, raising their fists in the air, shouting, "Kill the Jews."

Hitler waited, glaring straight ahead without acknowledging their support. He lowered his voice, almost to a growl. Followers leaned forward to hear every word. "One is either a hammer or an anvil. The only choice is between me and death, victory or destruction, glory or ignominy. We shall be rich or poor." His voice rose. "We shall be conquering heroes or sacrificial lambs. We shall be hot or cold, but those who are lukewarm shall be damned.

"We can prevail. Look at the great dictator in the south, Benito Mussolini. He has created an efficient Fascist state in Italy. He has led the way; he has been our teacher. We shall follow his example!"

Hitler nodded to Hess, who rose. Both of them left the meeting without another word, to the shouts of "*Ja, Mein* Führer."

Back in his comfortably furnished prison cell, the führer flopped onto the sofa while Hess sat at the table, poised with his pad and pencil, ready to go to work. Hitler immediately jumped off the sofa and paced up and down. "I have learned from the disaster of the attempted putsch. It is hopeless to try to overthrow a modern state by violent means. Our struggle will succeed only from within the system. We must pervert the constitution to our needs and cloak our acts under the guise of legality. But have no doubt, Rudolph; I will become the sole leader of a new Reich. Now, let's get to work."

Hess flipped through the pages of his pad and read aloud his notes of the morning's conferences. The führer nodded and began dictating the next chapter of *Mein Kampf.*

Same Year, Rome, a Room in the Continental Hotel

Margherita Sarfatti, daughter of the wealthy Grassini family, Jews from Venice, waited for the arrival of Mussolini, the Duce, the leader of Italy. They had met when he was editor of Avanti and she was a reporter working for him. They had hit it off almost immediately and joined forces. Her education, wealth and social advantages provided the young, peasant-born Mussolini with everything he was not, as they moved from Socialism to Fascism. Her money, ideas and passion had sustained him though his violent struggle for power. Much of his Fascist philosophy and programs came from her. They shared sexual, emotional, intellectual and political intimacies. She filled a need that Mussolini's wife, Rachele, could not or would not provide. Rachele, a frump of a woman, with no social grace, no interest in politics and no original thoughts, had remained behind in Milan with her children after Mussolini came to Rome to assume the leadership of Italy.

Sarfatti and Mussolini made a formidable team. As his trusted confidante and intellectual mentor, Sarfatti became one of the most influential women in Italy, if not Europe.

Sarfatti had no illusions about the Duce's faithfulness. He was an unreformed womanizer and proud of it. She had no need to make discreet inquiries because he bragged of his conquests often enough. She had to admit that his sexual exploits were impressive. Every day, late in the afternoon, his secretary would interview and select an attractive woman, drawn usually from correspondence he received from adoring females. She would be led up the back stairs for a "private audience." Mussolini wasted no time with preliminaries, pulling down the day's liaison onto the thick carpet and taking his pleasure, removing neither his trousers nor his shoes. The tryst rarely lasted more than ten minutes. When Sarfatti once questioned him about these dalliances, he replied, "Would you like to eat the same dish every day?" She never asked again—and it never seemed to affect his ability to satisfy her sexually. She marveled at his stamina, but he'd never hear it from her.

Mussolini, however, had no monopoly on faithlessness. Sarfatti's husband, lawyer Cesare Sarfatti, profited handsomely from his wife's association with Italy's leader. At the same time, while Cesare loved Margherita dearly, he was considerably older, so that her relationship with Mussolini relieved him of performing his sexual obligations. Two years ago, Cesare had suffered a burst appendix, widowing Margherita.

The great dictator of Italy had taken to sneaking out of his room at the Grand Hotel, down the service stairs, and out the side entrance. He walked to the Continental Hotel. While he was not yet prepared to give up his mistress and Fascist collaborator, he did accede to the wishes of his aides to be more discreet concerning the Jewess.

Margherita Sarfatti heard the light tapping and opened the door to her suite. Mussolini stood there in his typical pose, hands on hips, large square chin jutting out; his large bulging eyes looked at and then past her, making sure no one else was in the room. The Duce's eyes, "eagle eyes," she called them, were like those of that bird of prey; they mesmerized her.

Sarfatti did not consider Mussolini a tender lover, but he did take more time making love to her than to his parade of one-afternoon stands. For her, he even took off his trousers and shoes. Sitting up in bed, she lit a cigarette and watched the Duce get dressed. "I have some concerns about that Hitler fellow in Germany. I certainly support at least part of what he stands for—Fascism for Germany."

Mussolini looked at her. "So?"

"So, I don't like his statements about the Jews and the Aryan race. If he comes to power, it could mean serious trouble for Jews, including me."

Mussolini snorted and with a wave of his arm, he swept away her concerns. "The man's an uncouth peasant from Austria. He's doing a Teutonic imitation of me and making a poor job of it. Unless the National Socialists get another leader, they'll never enjoy the success of the Italian Fascist Party. Did you see what happened to them in Munich? Pure stupidity! They're buffoons."

Sarfatti shook her head. "Still, as a Jew, I . . ."

Mussolini seated himself on the bed, slipping on his shoes. He hushed her. "Hitler's Nordic mythology and theories of a German master race are pure claptrap. After all, their blue-eyed, blond-haired dogma of racial superiority would leave most Italians out of the master race. Did you know that one authority on racial biology described Hitler's facial and head characteristics—low receding forehead, ugly nose, broad cheekbones, small eyes and dark hair—as those of a Mongol?" Mussolini laughed harshly. "He's hardly one to preach of a master race. Ha! I am more of an Aryan than he is! As a matter of fact, not one of his deputies—Göring, Himmler or Roehm—can claim to be a Teuton."

Sarfatti, not responding, hugged her knees, which were drawn up to her bare chest.

Mussolini gently touched her bare shoulder. "Look, Margherita. A Jewish problem doesn't exist in Italy and never will while I am in power. The Jews in Italy have always shown themselves to be good and loyal citizens on the battlefields and in the universities. Many have been early supporters of the Fascist Party. But if it concerns you so, why don't you convert to Catholicism? Become one of the Italian majority!"

She frowned. "*My* beliefs certainly would not prevent me from that, but with my husband not so long in his grave, I don't think now is the time."

Mussolini stood with his hands on his hips. "If Cesare was such a loyal Italian, why did he embrace Zionism? Didn't he want to stay in Italy?"

Sarfatti shrugged. "He would have certainly never have left his beloved Italy, but he felt that Jews should have the *choice* of returning to their biblical homeland if they so wished."

Mussolini shook his head. "Cesare's dead. You, of all people know that you must get on with your life and not be burdened with dead memories."

She sighed. "You may be right. But his death is still too fresh in my mind."

Mussolini shook on his jacket. She knew something was wrong when he spoke in a low voice, without looking at her—quite uncharacteristic for him.

"Things are getting touchy in Rome. It would be better if you returned to Milan."

"Just what does that mean?" she flared.

Not accustomed to being challenged, Mussolini glared at her, raising his head and thrusting his jaw out, as he usually did when about to make a pronouncement. "It means, my dear, that you will go back to Milan without delay and stay there until I call for you." Not waiting for a reply, he turned on his heel and strode out, slamming the door behind him.

"So much for being Jewish not meaning a thing in Italy," she shouted after him, trying to make herself heard through the closed door.

July 10, 1933, Berlin, the Chancellery

In power as Germany's chancellor for five months, Hitler had invited his closest National Socialist cronies to a small reception to celebrate his first diplomatic triumph, the signing of a concordat with the Vatican. Sipping mineral water, he smiled at his vice-chancellor, Franz von Papen. "Congratulations on getting Pacelli to sign the concordat."

Papen nodded. "Thank you *Mein* Führer. It was extremely fortunate that Cardinal Pacelli, the nuncio to Germany for many years, had been appointed Vatican secretary of state. He's been a good friend of the Reich—almost as German as we are."

Goebbels, now propaganda minister of the Reich, listening in on the conversation, interjected, "The concordat was a masterful stroke, *Mein* Führer. Your insistence on depoliticizing the Catholic clergy and disbanding the Catholic Center, the last democratic party in Germany, in return for safeguarding the religious rights of Catholics, was simply brilliant."

Hitler snorted. "That Pacelli thinks this agreement will make the church an integral part of German life, but he will find out in good time that I will completely eradicate Christianity from Germany. You are either Christian or German, you cannot be both."

"A profound observation," Papen offered.

Hitler ignored the flattery. He sipped his mineral water, looking past the small group crowded around him, studying the red, black and white swastika banner hanging from the ceiling. "With the clergy categorically forbidden to engage in political activity, we can go ahead with laws for euthanasia and sterilization of the mentally and physically handicapped." He spoke to no one in particular.

Papen nodded. "My thinking exactly."

Goebbels could barely repress a sarcastic comment about Papen's fawning. Instead he turned his back on the vice-chancellor, as though he wasn't there, and spoke directly to Hitler. "In a sense, the Catholic Church has given moral recognition to our persecutions of the Jews. Now that it is state policy, the church is legally bound by the concordat to silence on the matter."

Hitler wagged his index finger at Goebbels. "That, Doctor, is why I insisted on that provision. The concordat demonstrates the Catholic Church's acknowledgment of our National Socialist state. The treaty shows the whole world that the assertion that we are hostile to religion is a lie. An atmosphere of confidence has been created that will be especially significant in the urgent struggle against international Jewry. Now, we must begin planning the next step, their eradication."

Papen raised his glass of champagne. "Here's to Cardinal Pacelli. May he become the next pope!"

Hitler raised his glass of mineral water. "I'll certainly drink to that."

Morning of the Same Day, Rome, The Vatican, Study of Pope Pius XI

Ambrogio Damiano Achille Ratti, Pope Pius XI, sat at his desk, reflecting on his earlier years before ascending to the papal throne, years when he had been a keen mountaineer. He liked to think of himself as a social activist. As archbishop of Lepanto in the 1920s, the then reigning pope sent him on a difficult diplomatic mission to Poland. Despite a threatened Bolshevik attack, he had refused to leave his post there. Later, as pope, he had addressed the issues of unemployment and the arms race. Now, he faced another great challenge, the threat to humanity presented by the racial and radical dogmas of the new chancellor of Germany, Adolph Hitler, and his National Socialist Party. Ten years ago, before the rise of

Nazism, Ratti had, with great patience, pursued a concordat with the Bolshevik government in order to secure a measure of protection for the Catholics in the Soviet Union, but he had encountered nothing but bitter hostility. He had come to realize there could never be any accommodation with the Soviets while Stalin was in power. The anti-religious excesses of Stalin in 1930 had confirmed his worst fears. Bolshevism represented the greatest threat to the church in this century. Now, he faced this new threat—Hitler.

A series of light raps interrupted the pope's reminisces. The door opened slowly. Eugenio Cardinal Pacelli stood, ramrod straight, on the threshold. The pope greeted his thin, six-foot-tall secretary of state, bidding him enter. The cardinal approached, dressed in a long black cassock with scarlet buttons, a short black cape trimmed in scarlet, a broad sash of the same color worn high up on his chest, and a small scarlet zucchetto (skullcap) on his head. Pius XI presented a stark contrast, dressed entirely in white. The Holy Father extended his hand and the cardinal kissed his ring.

The pontiff waved Pacelli to a chair in front of his desk. Pacelli was his first visitor this morning, the time of day when he met with Vatican officials in the plainly furnished study just off his bedroom. Later in the morning, the pope would descend to the floor below and spend many hours in the much more elaborate rooms where he granted individual audiences to diplomats and important people passing through Rome, or in the auditorium, the Hall of Benedictions, for audiences of larger groups.

The short, rotund, slow-moving pope with his large, round face and steely gaze through small, round spectacles, watched the tall, spare cardinal with the sharp, narrow nose, thin lips and high cheekbones move with almost feminine grace to the chair. He's more like a Hindu mystic than a cardinal, Pius thought irreverently. The differences between the two churchmen were not limited merely to dress and looks. Pacelli was the consummate diplomat, but too often, he was indecisive and hesitant—the cardinal would never develop a fighter's temperament. Pius XI liked to think of himself as a fighter. And indeed he was. As solitary and strong-willed as Mussolini, he had an authoritarian streak and favored what he called Catholic totalitarianism. Pius XI was uncompromising. He demanded obedience and subordination, not collaboration, for those who toiled under him.

The pope picked up the concordat document. "Good morning, Eminence. I know I approved this treaty, but I must tell you I am not happy with it. I think we gave away too much, especially in view of the actions of Hitler's government."

Pacelli pressed his already thin lips together—they almost disappeared. "Good morning, Your Holiness. Indeed, Consul Kirkpatrick of Britain is already on my back saying the treaty constituted an approval of Nazism by the Holy See. Any day now, I expect to hear similar comments from the Americans and the French."

The pontiff frowned. "I'm not so sure they're wrong."

Pacelli squeezed the corners of his eyes with his thumb and forefinger, then looked up at the pope. "The stark fact is, Holiness, that it is Germany, not the Western democracies, that is the greatest bulwark against the biggest threat facing the church, the spread of Bolshevism in Europe."

"I agree that the Bolsheviks must be stopped, but at what cost? By allying ourselves with that German megalomaniac?"

Pacelli let out a long sigh. "The chancellor's statements so far have not been unfriendly to the church but have been blatantly hostile to Communism. Look, I detest Hitler's reign of terror as much as anyone, Your Holiness, but we had to choose between a treaty proposed by them or having their hostility turned against us, threatening the virtual elimination of the Catholic Church in Germany. Like a pistol pointed at my head, they gave me—and you—only a week to decide. It came down to selecting whether to protect the Catholic faithful in the Reich or have them persecuted like the Jews. Our cardinals in Germany are of one mind. Cardinal Faulhaber in Munich felt that protesting Nazi attacks on the Jews—even those who have been baptized for many years and are good Catholics—was pointless since it could only extend the struggle to those born Catholic. Cardinal Bertram in Berlin was most insistent that there were more immediate issues of importance than defending the Jews."

The pope leaned on his chin and looked at Pacelli. "Such as?"

"Such as the maintaining of Catholic associations, charities and education. Bertram assures me that the Jews are fully capable of helping themselves."

The pontiff straightened up in his chair, shaking his head. "*That* I sincerely doubt."

The cardinal paused, studying his own long, slender fingers. "Perhaps, but our first obligation, after all, is to our flock. Bertram tells me if the Catholics of Germany are forced to choose between the church and Hitler, we'll lose our faithful."

The pope snorted. "Or our not-so-faithful. Did you hear what Hitler said at a meeting with our German bishops?" The pontiff searched his desk and found what he was looking for. He picked up a report, waving it at Pacelli. "Defending his treatment of the Jews, Hitler said, and I quote," the pope began to read, "'For 1,500 years the Catholic Church has considered Jews as parasites and has banished them to the ghetto. They knew the Jews for what they are. I join myself to what was done for 1,500 years. I am perhaps rendering the greatest service to Christianity.' Can you believe that man?"

Pacelli shrugged. "At least, if the German government violates the concordat, we have a treaty on which to base a protest."

The pope emitted a harsh laugh. "You think a protest will do much good with a man like Hitler? Not likely. No, my dear Cardinal, I fear that somewhere down the road, we'll have to take a strong stand. I cannot and will not sit by idly if the situation of the Jews gets much worse."

Pacelli nodded. "Let's hope it doesn't come to that—or forget that our first obligation is to protect our flock in Germany. I know the German mind. We can make things much worse for both the Catholics and the Jews in Germany if we take too aggressive a posture."

The pope stood, indicating the meeting was over. "You can't say we weren't warned by that German Carmelite nun about what our silence would mean."

"You mean that converted Jew, Edith Stein?" Pacelli interjected.

Pius nodded. "She warned that we cannot be silent at the destruction of Jewish blood for that would be a silence regarding a profanation of the most holy humanity of our Savior. Well, I agree and I, for one, will not be silenced by that thug in Berlin who called Christianity 'an Oriental and Semitic product that should be replaced by a pagan religion.' I am thinking about issuing an encyclical condemning the superstitious doctrine of race and blood."

Pacelli rose. "Please, Your Holiness, let us move slowly and carefully until we have a better idea of what we are facing. When you decide, I shall be happy to do the drafting."

The pope nodded his dismissal.

March 3, 1938, Rome, The Vatican, Study of Pope Pius XI
Over the next five years, Pius was not a happy pontiff. He had permitted Cardinal Pacelli to edit and water down *his* encyclical, *Mit brennender Sorge* (With Burning Anxiety), issued a year ago. Although the encyclical condemned racism generally, it did not refer to the Jews or anti-Semitism specifically, nor did it condemn the political and social totalitarianism of Germany. He read the pertinent language again.

> Whoever takes the race or the people, or the state or the form of the state, or the repositories of power, or any other fundamental value of the human community—all things which occupy a necessary and honorable place in the earthly order—whoever takes these notions and removes them from this scale of values, not excluding even religious values, and defies them through an idolatrous cult, inverts and falsifies the order of things as created and ordained by God. Such a man is far removed from true belief in God and from a conception of life in keeping with that faith."

The encyclical had pleased no one. Hitler called every sentence an insult to new German nation and called the pope, "deputy of the Jew-God in Rome." The enemies of the Reich called the encyclical's vague condemnation woefully deficient in a situation that required the church to deal in specifics—namely, the persecution of Jews in Nazi Germany.

□□□

For days, Pius XI had prayed for guidance; today he knew what he had to do. After a group audience with a multitude of Jesuits, as the group was filing out, he stopped a very surprised American Jesuit, Father John LaFarge, and asked him to remain behind. After leading the young Jesuit upstairs to his study, he motioned him to chair. The thoroughly confused priest sat down.

The pontiff smiled. "I understand your bewilderment, Father. We are quite alone because that is my wish."

LaFarge nodded. "Yes, Your Holiness." His reply came out more like a squeak. The young priest blushed with embarrassment.

"Relax, my son. You are here because of your work on the Jesuit publication *America*. I have received excellent reports about your writing and have personally read some of your work."

"Th-thank you, Your Holiness, but I . . ."

The pope put up his hand. "Please, to alleviate your discomfort, let me come right to the point. First, though, I must swear you to secrecy. It is vital for this project."

LaFarge frowned. "Of course, Your Holiness."

"I am most concerned about radicalism in both Germany and Italy. I have read your book, *Interracial Justice*. It was one of the best things written on the subject."

LaFarge smiled for the first time. "Thank you, Your Holiness."

"You may not thank me when you hear what I want you to do."

LaFarge gripped the arms of his chair tightly, as if they were the only thing between him and the abyss.

"I am asking you to draft the text of an encyclical for the universal church on a topic that I consider one of the most pressing of our times, racism. I have been praying and thinking about this for some years."

LaFarge finally released the arms of the chair and leaned forward in rapt attention.

Pius put on his reading glasses and briefly checked some notes. "I would like to include in the encyclical a historical perspective of the totalitarian concept of human society and its effect on such a society, the unity of humanity including all races and religions, the immorality of racism and its destruction of the fabric of society, the importance of Judaism as the religion of the people chosen by

Almighty God to prepare the way for the incarnation of God's Only-Begotten Son, the evils of anti-Semitism and persecution of the Jews, and the task of the church to show the way by education and example." Pius XI leaned back in his chair and waited for the Jesuit's reaction.

LaFarge shook his head slowly. "Why me, Holiness? With all the eminent church scholars at your command, surely there must be those far more competent to carry out your wishes."

"As I was looking for someone to write on these topics, God has sent you to me. I considered many 'eminent scholars' as you put it, but on reflection, I am convinced that you are the most competent, and here you showed up at just the right time."

LaFarge bowed his head, in shock. The pope said nothing, simply watching the young priest. LaFarge, uncomfortable with the silence, finally cleared his throat. "The project is too colossal. Where shall I begin? What shall I write? I will need much guidance."

The pope leaned forward, looking into the priest's eyes. "Have faith in yourself, Father LaFarge. Say simply what you would say if you yourself were pope. Select two or three scholars to assist you. And remember, secrecy is essential."

"Holiness, do you have a title for the encyclical?"

The pontiff nodded. *"Humani Generis Unitas."*

LaFarge automatically translated the Latin: "The Unity of the Human Race."

After LaFarge left, the pontiff leaned back in his chair, thinking. He said aloud, but softly, "No, my encyclical won't be watered down again. I'll see to that."

PART I

The Deepening Shadows

CHAPTER ONE

March 11, 1938, Vienna, Apartment of Joseph Schwartz

Joseph Schwartz arrived home from his tailor shop early, as he usually did on Friday afternoon, in time to greet Queen Sabbath. His wife, Dora, was busy preparing the family dinner. Cooking had to be completed before sundown. Once the Sabbath had begun, no labor, including cooking, was permitted until sundown on Saturday.

He wandered into the kitchen, lifted the lid on the pot and ladled some soup into a small cup. Dora turned from the counter. "How many times must I tell you, no noshing before dinner; the soup isn't even ready yet."

"But it's delicious!"

"Enough with the flattery. Out of my kitchen! Go read the newspaper."

He smiled. It was the same every week. Or was it? Through the sitting room window, opened a crack to let in the early spring air, he heard the lusty singing of a song that chilled his blood—the words of the "Horst Wessel" song: *Wenn das Judenblut vom Messer spritz, dann geht's nochmal so gut* . . .("Let Jewish blood squirt from your knife and see how good it feels . . . .")

With great reluctance, he looked out of the window. Marching down the street were German soldiers followed by tanks and armored vehicles. *Germans? Here?*

He ran back into the kitchen.

"What did I tell you?" Dora began to scold.

"Never mind that," he said a little too loudly. "The Germans have invaded Austria. My God, Dora, we are in trouble. We must consider leaving Vienna. I shall talk to my brother Karl and his family."

"Joseph, you are overreacting."

He pounded the table with his fist. "Am I? Just look what's happened to the German Jews. You will see, the Germans will make Austria part of Greater Germany and the same thing will happen to us. If it were just us alone, perhaps I would chance it. But I have to think of Sophia and Fredrick. I can't risk our children's lives."

March 14, 1938, Rome, Palazzo Venezia, Office of Mussolini

Mussolini had chosen for his office the *Sala del Mappamondo,* the largest of the ballrooms, on the second floor of the Palazzo Venezia. Named the Hall of the Globe after the ancient map of the world prominently displayed there, the room was two stories high, with a tall window-door onto a balcony overlooking the huge piazza below. The Duce had had two mosaics laid on the floor at the entrance to his office, one depicting himself saving the Princess Europa from the bull of Bolshevism, the other showing him as a sea god embracing a sea nymph, symbolic of the Mediterranean. A huge chandelier lit the office, sparsely furnished with a thirteen-foot desk and three chairs in front of a monumental fireplace on the wall opposite the entrance. A small door next to the fireplace led to the Duce's private apartment. Behind the desk hung a large calendar showing Anno XV, fifteenth year. In his egocentricity, Mussolini had ordered that the years of the calendar be counted from the day of the Fascist March on Rome that had put him in power.

Inspector General of the Navy Admiral Umberto Pugliese had just entered and stood at rigid attention, next to the more relaxed Foreign Minister Galeazzo Ciano, Mussolini's son-in-law.

The Duce looked up from his desk. "At ease, Admiral. I understand you have some proposals for increasing the combat effectiveness of our navy."

Pugliese came with impressive credentials. Italy's leading naval designer, he created and oversaw the construction of warships that were the envy of other navies. High-powered vessels with lightweight hulls, they were unrivaled for speed and maneuverability. He had developed the still secret "Pugliese bulge," an underwater outer hull design enabling the ship to absorb much of the energy of a torpedo explosion, thus protecting the main armored hull behind the bulge. Many considered him to be the father of the modern Italian Navy.

Pugliese nodded. "It is my opinion, Duce, that we should embark on a crash program to built at least two aircraft carriers. I have prepared plans to convert some of our older battleships for that purpose."

Mussolini puckered his lips and crossed his arms across his chest. "And give up the most important part of my navy? Never! The battleships are the backbone of our fleet."

Pugliese knew that the firepower and the range of a battleship's guns were miniscule compared to a carrier with a full complement of aircraft loaded with bombs or torpedoes. "The British have several carriers and that will give them a significant advantage in the Mediterranean . . ."

"Not so!" Mussolini thundered as he stood, his fists leaning on his desk. "With all our land air bases we can adequately cover the Mediterranean." Chin jutting out, he began chopping the air with his right arm. "Italy and Sicily are one, huge, unsinkable aircraft carrier. We don't need the floating kind with airplanes."

"But with all due respect, Duce, we have no naval scout planes capable of finding an enemy at sea and staying airborne long enough to report the discovery. Our land-based planes possess neither the speed nor range for effective reconnaissance."

Mussolini sighed. "Admiral, you stick to designing cruisers and battleships. Leave the rest of the armaments up to me. That will be all."

Pugliese saluted sharply, did an about face and marched out of the office, closing the door behind him.

Mussolini looked at his foreign minister. "That Jew thinks he's a know-it-all because he has designed a few warships. I don't appreciate his questioning my judgment on armaments. Just who does he think he is? He'll be gone by the end of the year after I institute the racial laws against the Jews."

Ciano shrugged. "He is, Duce, one of our leading naval designers—perhaps you should make an exception . . ."

"For that cheeky Pugliese? I will not!"

March 20, 1938, A Road out of Rome
In their on-again-off-again relationship, Mussolini took up with Sarfatti once more. They sped out of Rome east on Via Tiburtina towards Tivoli and into the countryside. Sarfatti, her hair flowing behind her in the open convertible, shouted above the roar of the engine and the wind, "I think you can slow down now."

Mussolini looked in the rearview mirror of his Alfa Romeo, easing his foot off the accelerator pedal. "Ha, I lost them again," referring to his security detail. "Those clowns can never drive as well, or as fast, as I can."

"Benito, I am frightened about Hitler. He'll do the same things to the Jews in Austria that he did to the Jews in Germany. Now, he's right on Italy's northern doorstep. It makes me *very* uneasy."

Mussolini shook his head. "First of all, you're Catholic, and have been since 1928."

"That doesn't mean a thing to Hitler. He treats all converted Jews as Jews and nothing more."

"You're safe in Italy. Hitler won't attack us; we are his Fascist allies. He thinks the sun rises and sets around me."

"That, I doubt," continued Sarfatti dryly. "It is you who are more and more trying to emulate Hitler. I have been hearing that laws that may be passed restricting the rights of Jews in Italy. I couldn't live here under those conditions."

"That's ridiculous. I'm the Duce, not you. I should know and I'm telling you that you have nothing to worry about."

She nodded. "I truly hope so." Her face brightened. "I want to tell you about my trip to America. I had a personal meeting with President Roosevelt. You should find it very interesting."

Mussolini frowned. "If you must."

"He's an amazing man, Benito. His personality and intelligence more than make up for his paralysis. He knows a lot about Italy and admires some of your economic programs."

"Enough," he growled. "I am really not interested. What matters is military force, which Germany has and the United States does not!"

"But you always admired the men and resources America brought to bear in the Great War."

He pounded the steering wheel and thrust his chin out. "It means nothing. In any future war, things would go differently and the United States would not be able to stop Germany."

Sarfatti stared straight ahead as Mussolini slammed his foot down on the gas pedal, causing the souped-up Alfa to leap forward. Determined not to be intimidated by the Duce, she continued. "For the past year, ever since you visited Berlin, you have been toadying up to that maniac. It won't be long before you'll do anything Hitler wants, simply to please him."

"I am the Duce," he roared above the noise of the revved-up engine as the speedometer hovered at 170 kph, "and I toady up to no man. I should throw you out of the car for that insult!" He slowed the car. "Germany is the most powerful military force in the world. The future of Italy is tied to an alliance with Hitler, not Roosevelt. When war comes, Italy shall sit at the table of the victors along with Germany and dictate terms to the pathetic Western democracies."

"War?" she exclaimed, turning to look at him. "You would tempt fate by engulfing Italy in a war to please Hitler? What about the Jews? What will you do to them in order to ingratiate yourself to that murderer?"

Mussolini stiffened. "Tempting fate! Ha! Statesmen only talk of fate when they have blundered! I will make my own fate with war. War will ennoble the people of Italy if we have the courage to face it. Like Caesar and Napoleon, I will instill in our nation such courage and make Italy a conqueror. We shall be unstoppable!" again pounding the steering wheel with his fist.

My God, Sarfatti thought, the man's gone over the edge and really believes the Fascist Party propaganda nonsense that he is invincible. She shouldn't have been surprised. He'd shown evidence of delusional behavior for years. She recalled that when he went to visit Sicily, a newspaper reported that a violent eruption of Mount Etna had miraculously stopped upon his arrival on the scene. She had read the newspaper account to him, thinking he would be amused. To her surprise, he had found the story nothing out of the ordinary.

He had actually thought it was reasonable that he had stemmed the flow of lava by the force of his personality.

Sarfatti sighed. "Don't think I haven't noticed the increased Jewish smear campaign in the press that you control—the constant references to the threat of Jewish Bolshevism, the Jews representing English Zionism—things like that. When are you going to institute anti-Jewish laws as part of your rapprochement with Hitler?"

"I have decided no such thing. Moreover, whatever I do will be political strategy to benefit Italy and not necessarily out of principle or conviction. This is my obligation—and my right—as a world leader."

She watched him sitting in the driver's seat in his already famous pose of defiance—head up, jutting jaw, pouting mouth. Had he not been driving, he'd have had his arms folded tightly across his chest. "Oh, I know you, Benito, and I have no doubt you've already decided to attack the Jews. You will lose the respect of important leaders like Roosevelt."

He braked the car and put it into a swift, squealing U-turn. "I don't want to hear another word about the Jews or that paralytic Roosevelt, who needs someone to wipe his ass when he shits. America is a country of niggers and Jews who will destroy civilization if we let them."

The Alfa Romero, now turned around, picked up speed. "We will return to Rome now," the Duce growled.

Hurt and frightened, Sarfatti sat staring straight ahead, her arms close to her sides. The Duce would continue to cater to the führer. That much was clear. She was finished with him—and probably with Italy, as well. She prided herself on her political astuteness, and the warning bells were going off loud and clear. As a Jew, she'd better be clearing out of her mother country.

June 20, 1938, Rome, Palazzo Venezia, Mussolini's Office

At the light rapping on the door, Mussolini laid aside his newspaper and picked up some official papers. "Come in," he bellowed. Foreign Minister Ciano stuck his head in the door. "I am here with General Balbo and Marshal De Bono, as you requested."

Mussolini waved his arm. "Bring them in." The three ran the twenty yards to the front of Mussolini's desk—a requirement instituted by the Duce to "keep his deputies in shape." No one sat down. That was another rule. Only important foreign dignitaries were invited to sit in the chairs—all others with business in Mussolini's office had to snap to attention in front of his desk and give the Roman salute, another Mussolini innovation. The Duce had banned the handshake, which, he maintained, was an effete bourgeois custom that through its physical, human contact, made Italians softer and friendlier. The Roman salute, the bent elbow and lifting of the right hand at a seventy-five-degree angle, promoted the bellicose virtues of what Mussolini referred to as the Second Roman Empire. One had to be careful not to use foreign phrases in front of the Duce, because he had banned them as "un-Italian."

Mussolini's new appearance still gave Ciano a start. The Duce had taken to shaving his head to hide his graying and receding hair. The dictator developed a high sensitivity to exhibiting any physical weakness to his people, such as aging. He'd rationalized to Ciano how important the strongman look was to inspire the confidence of the Italian citizenry.

Mussolini looked up from his papers. "Gentlemen, I have two important matters to discuss. First, I plan to introduce a new military march step, the *passo romano*. He leaped out of his chair and began parading around the large room. "Watch, as I demonstrate."

To General Emilio De Bono, it looked like a mixture of the Nazi goose step and the slow march of English guards regiments. "With all due respect, Duce, I don't see why we have to imitate Hitler."

Mussolini stopped parading around and faced De Bono. "This step, for your information, was that of the ancient Roman legions." He looked his general. "Those who object to it do so merely because it requires effort; they are men who cannot see over their stomachs, men who are always left behind."

General Italo Balbo, a popular war hero and flying ace in the Italian Air force who had risen to the heights of power, just under the Duce, shook his head. "I agree with General De Bono. You are merely shining Hitler's boots by imitating him."

Mussolini thrust his face into De Bono's. "You are an old idiot who should be put out to pasture. I am tired of keeping you around for old time's sake." Whirling around to face General Balbo, he continued, "Italo, you'd better watch out. I know you're really a democratic swine who used to be an orator at the Masonic lodge in Ferrara."

"Duce," Balbo stammered, "you have no right . . ."

"I have every right," Mussolini stormed, causing Balbo to back up a few steps. "Both of you will keep your opinions to yourselves." Walking to the window, he stared out on the piazza. His visitors waited until he turned to face them again. "The second matter is the introduction of the racist ideology to Fascist Italy. Hitler has become too powerful to oppose. The Western democracies do not stand a chance against Germany. It is better for Italy if we are on the winning side—and that means allying ourselves with Germany. Hitler has made it quite clear that he will not collaborate with us unless we deal with the Jewish question in Italy. If we ally ourselves with Hitler we can't expect the loyalty of Italian Jews anyway. Therefore, we have nothing to lose. Accordingly, I have decided we need a racial policy for Fascist Italy—to preserve her purity."

Ciano nodded. "If I understand you correctly, Duce, once Jewish blood is declared to be a threat to the purity of the Italian race, it would follow that ultimately, we will rid Italy of the Jews."

Mussolini drew himself up, chin jutting out. "Eventually, yes."

Balbo shook his head. "The purity of Mediterranean Italians as an Aryan race." He uttered a harsh laugh. "That should be news to the Italians!"

De Bono snickered. "No more so than the German leaders can lay claim to Aryan purity. You know what they say in Germany? 'The true Aryan must be as blond as Hitler, as tall as Goebbels, as slender as Göring, and his name must be Rosenberg.'" He laughed.

Mussolini went back to his desk and leaned his fists on it. "Enough of this carping! I am declaring there now exists an Italian race and that the Jews do not belong to it. Do I believe it? Of course not! I do it for reasons of state—to achieve total solidarity with our ally Germany. This, then, transcends all your arguments."

Ciano frowned. "But, Duce, what are you going do with all the Jews in Italy?"

It was Mussolini's turn to laugh. "How about sending them all to Italian Somaliland, which has many resources, including a shark fishery. It has the advantage that, to begin with, many Jews would be eaten."

Ciano laughed politely. The military men stood there stone-faced.

Mussolini sat down. "First things first. Next month, the newspapers will publish a 'Manifesto of Race' endorsed by Italian racist scientists stating that the European Mediterranean is an Aryan whose race must be preserved by prohibiting intermingling with Jews. Then we will enact racial laws to isolate the Jews from the Italian population, socially and economically, including restrictions on education, employment and service in the military. That is all. You may leave now." Grabbing some papers from the desk, he swiveled his chair so that his back was to his visitors.

A Few Minutes Later, Piazza Venezia, Just Outside of Mussolini's Office

Balbo straightened his hat, pulling down the brim to shade his eyes from the glare of the sun in the huge square. "The man's become a raving lunatic—race manifestos, Italian goosesteps and the Roman version of '*Heil* Hitler'. . ."

"The Fascist Party has taken to calling Mussolini the 'divine Caesar,' 'another St. Francis' and 'spiritual father of the Italian people,'" De Bono put in.

Balbo sighed. "I know. He now puts himself on the level of Julius Caesar and Napoleon. It would be laughable if it weren't so embarrassing in dealing with foreign diplomats."

"It will get worse," De Bono added gloomily. "The party has ordered that, like God, all pronouns referring to the Duce have to be capitalized because he has done as much for Italy as Napoleon did for France—but with greater vision, courage and originality."

"So much courage," Balbo scoffed, "that he hides under the skirts of Hitler and disenfranchises loyal Italian citizens to impress that German tyrant."

"I just hope," De Bono added, "that our military is not put to the test in a wide war with the Western democracies—we are woefully unprepared."

"Of course we are. That's why he's cuddling up to the Nazis for protection."

DeBono patted his colleague on the back. "My friend, Italy is in trouble. Either Germany or the Western powers will devour us, depending on who wins the upcoming war."

Balbo looked at the marshal. "Do you think there will be another world war?"

De Bono sighed. "No doubt about it, General, absolutely none. And our military will be no more ready than we were entering the Great War in 1915."

CHAPTER TWO

July 1, 1938, Vienna, Apartment of Joseph Schwartz
On Friday evening, at sundown, Dora Schwartz followed the Fourth Commandment and Exodus 20:8 to remember and observe the Sabbath.

Carefully removing the candelabra from its storage place in the closet in the dining room, she gently placed it on a silver tray resting on the table and inserted the candles.

Joseph and the two children gathered around for the weekly ritual to welcome the Sabbath.

She lit the candles and held her hands over them to form a canopy, closed her eyes and chanted the blessing. "Blessed are you, Lord, our God, King of the Universe who has sanctified us by His Commandments and commanded us to kindle the Sabbath light."

Then, Joseph Schwartz, continuing the Sabbath ritual, recited the sanctification, the *Kiddush*. A moment later, slicing the *challa*, the traditional Sabbath loaf, he dropped the bomb. "This will probably be our last *Shabbos* in Vienna."

Startled as she entered from the kitchen carrying a tray of steaming dishes, Dora hastily set down it on the nearest table. "What did you say?"

"You heard me, Dora, we have to leave our home."

"We can't just up and leave our home. What would happen to our things?" She picked up a silver platter her mother had given her and held it lovingly.

Schwartz shrugged. "What we can't carry, we'll have to leave behind."

"I simply won't leave my heirlooms," Dora declared firmly. "Why are you doing this?" She suddenly began to cry.

"Dora, Dora, it's not as if we have a choice. If we stay, we will lose everything, not just our furniture but maybe even our lives and those of Sophia and Fredrick."

"I can't believe that," she sobbed.

"Colonel Eichmann, the head of the Nazi's Jewish Department, is here in Vienna," her husband explained. "He has set up a very efficient assembly line to strip Jews of all their assets and issue them papers, supposedly to permit them to emigrate."

"At least they are not killing us. I still don't see why we have to go."

"No, Dora, you don't understand. It is a ruse to seize our valuables. People go from window to window in the Gestapo processing center where they are progressively stripped of their money, goods, property and political rights. Then they are given permission to leave Austria, but they are told they must emigrate within two weeks or they will be sent to concentration camps. The conditions the Germans impose to obtain visas and transportation are, of course, quite impossible within that time. And how could we buy tickets when they have taken our money? No, no. If we go through that process, we—and our children—will be trapped here; eventually we'll perish."

"But the Germans are civilized, Joseph. They would not simply murder innocent civilians," she cried.

Schwartz felt sorry for his wife, but he had to be firm. "The Nazis are doing that very thing to their own Jews in Germany. I see no reason why they won't do it to us here. They've already announced that every Jewish male will be given the middle name of 'Israel' and every Jewish female, 'Sarah,' for easy identification of us. You know what that will mean, since Hitler has declared that Austria is now part of Greater Germany."

Schwartz viciously slashed a slice off the *challa*. "It doesn't matter. I am not going to risk the lives of my children on the chance that the Germans will show us some benevolence—end of argument."

Dora crushed the table napkin she had picked up. "But what happens if we don't report for processing? The Gestapo will come for us."

"Right, and if we do report for Eichmann's processing, they will take all our money and we'll never get out. So we must act quickly! We'll leave Sunday and, God willing, be safely across the border and out of Austria with all the possessions we can carry."

"Where will we go?"

"To Italy—over the Brenner Pass. I understand the border guards there are still Austrians, not Germans. They'll accept bribes and will permit us to cross into Italy—the Alto Adige Province. There, we can make our way to one of the large northern Italian cities."

"How will we get by in a foreign country?"

"Dora, I'm a tailor. Every society needs tailors and Italy is no exception. I will be able to support us—and more to the point, our children will be able to grow up in safety. Mussolini has said repeatedly there is no Jewish problem in his country and never will be."

Dora frowned. "*Nu*, another dictator—and you believe him?"

"We must," her husband sighed. "We've run out of options, Dora dear."

July 15, 1938, Rome, the Vatican, Study of Pope Pius XI

In his morning conference with his cardinal secretary of state, Pius XI pounded the front pages of two Rome dailies lying on his desk. "Did you read this morning's newspapers, Eminence? Outrageous, absolutely outrageous." Pacelli nodded somberly.

"This 'Manifesto of the Racist Scientists' repeats the German racial theories," the pope thundered on. "Can you imagine? These imbeciles have constructed a theory of *Italian* Aryans—the term itself an oxymoron! If there is such a thing as an 'Aryan race,' most Italians are the farthest thing from the blue-eyed, blond Nordic model. Worse, these fools talk about the Jews not belonging to the Italian race and the need to preserve the *purity* of the Italians. What, I ask you, is the biological difference between a Jewish Italian and a Christian one? What ridiculous and hateful garbage! Mussolini has adopted a disgraceful imitation of Hitler's Nordic mythology that runs counter to the great traditions of the Roman Empire that the Duce purportedly seeks to emulate."

Pacelli had rarely seen the pope in such a state. "I agree, Holiness, it is disingenuous and very disappointing," he said soothingly.

"It is more than disingenuous; it is sinful and we must not countenance the Manifesto by silence. I shall speak out in no uncertain terms, against this abomination."

Pacelli put up a cautionary hand. "Holiness, I recommend restraint in the language we use; keep it general. We have a favorable treaty with Mussolini that has effectively protected the church for the last nine years. We don't want to burn our bridges . . ."

The frustrated pontiff interrupted, letting out a long breath. "With all due respect, Cardinal Pacelli, we do not need clichés."

"Of course, Your Holiness. You are correct and I apologize."

Pius XI waved away the statement. "No need to apologize. Let us concentrate our efforts on sending Italy and the world a strong message of condemnation—and make sure our words are published in both the Vatican's *L'Osservatore Romano* and the Jesuit's, *La Civiltà Cattolica*. I am sure coverage will be sparse in the Mussolini-controlled newspapers."

After Pacelli excused himself, the pontiff leaned back in his chair composing in his head the words of the statement he would make. Suddenly a new thought intruded, the encyclical drafted by Father LaFarge is becoming more urgent. He must speed up the process.

July 15-20, 1938, Milan and the Swiss Border Near Como

The publication of the "Manifesto of the Racial Scientists" moved Sarfatti, in Milan, to a decision—she would leave immediately for Switzerland and from there, travel to Paris, to wait out Mussolini's reign—or return to his senses. She saw clearly from the Manifesto, undoubtedly drafted by the Duce himself, that declaring Jewish blood a threat to the purity of the Italian race meant that no Jew would be spared. That included Sarfatti herself and other original, still faithful supporters of the Fascist Party. However much she wanted to continue to believe in Fascism, she could not accept the explanation that things would return to normal after the war.

Sarfatti felt sure Mussolini would have her arrested if he caught her leaving Italy. Her years of intimacy, both on personal and political levels, meant potential embarrassment for the Duce if she were away from his control. Therefore, she would have to escape by subterfuge.

With the rise of Hitler, perceptive Jews in Milan and Genoa had set up the Committee to Assist Jewish Refugees, COMASEBIT. Funded by Jewish agencies such as the Joint Distribution Committee (JDC) in the United States, COMASEBIT helped Jews fleeing Germany and Eastern Europe. After the issuance of the Italian Manifesto, it broadened its task to aid Jews seeking, legally or illegally, to leave Italy. Such work was dangerous and therefore would be appealing to Massimo Teglio, a Jew from Genoa whose taste for derring-do made him a better stunt pilot than part-time participant in his father's business of importing dried fish. One day he received a visit from his friend and fellow aviator, General Italo Balbo, who had been made governor of Libya, one of Italy's African colonies, because Mussolini had felt threatened by the general's popularity. Balbo, one of the few Fascist leaders brave enough to oppose the Manifesto, warned Teglio of what Mussolini's racial laws would mean for Jews. That was enough to involve Teglio in the work of COMASEBIT.

Through her family connections in Milan, Sarfatti met Teglio. She was one of the first people he helped. With the false identification papers he obtained for her, she crossed the border into Switzerland on July 20 without being recognized as Margherita Sarfatti, Mussolini's well-known Fascist collaborator and mistress.

On the same day that Sarfatti escaped Italy to avoid persecution as a Jew, a hundred kilometers to the east, the families Joseph and Karl Schwartz successfully bribed the Austrian border guards at the Brenner Pass and escaped *into* Italy—also to avoid persecution as Jews. The exquisite irony of their opposing actions was lost on them since neither Sarfatti nor the Schwartzes knew of each other's existence.

October 26, 1938, Rome, Office of the Minister of the Navy

The minister of the navy did not relish what he was about to do. The racial laws required him to fire Admiral Umberto Pugliese, inspector general of the Naval Engineering Corps, simply because he was a Jew. It didn't matter that the brilliant Pugliese, in charge of all naval construction, had built a fleet that Italy could be proud of; indeed, the Navy was probably the only branch of service of which that could be said. There was no one to take his place. Yet the bureaucrats in the Fascist government had insisted he be fired. *How in hell am I supposed to run an effective navy with such idiots in power?*

A buzzer sounded and his secretary announced, "Minister, Admiral Pugliese is here."

"Send him in."

Admiral Pugliese entered and saluted smartly.

"Sit down, Admiral. What I have to say, I say with a heavy heart."

Pugliese frowned. "Yes, Minister?"

"I'm afraid you will have to retire from the Naval Engineer Corps."

"But, Minister, I'm only fifty-seven."

"I'm sorry, I have no choice. It's disgraceful and I despise myself for having to do it, but it's the law. No Jews may remain in the military."

"So I'm being fired. Is that what you're saying?"

"I prefer to call it the retirement of a fine officer."

"Sugar coat it all you want," Pugliese replied bitterly. "What you are doing is nothing less than destroying my career."

"It is not I, Admiral, I assure you."

"Minister, I'm no politician, but it is clear to me that if people like you do not stand up to these ridiculous racist laws, Italy will go down the path of Nazi Germany. Here," he declared in a rasping tone, "do you want my medals for heroism in the Great War?" He detached them from his chest and threw them on the desk. "For the Ethiopian War?" He threw those on the desk also. "Apparently they count for nothing."

Under the Admiral's withering gaze, the minister pushed the decorations back to Pugliese. "Please, Admiral, keep them. This has been the hardest thing I have ever had to do in this damn job." He sounded on the verge of tears.

Nodding briefly, Pugliese scooped up his medals and thrust them in his pocket. It had been a grand gesture, but he hadn't really wanted to part with them. They were a proud part of his life. "Will that be all, Minister?"

The minister nodded.

Pugliese saluted smartly, did an about-face and marched out of the room—and out of the Italian military.

November 13, 1938, Rome, Palazzo Venezia; Mussolini's Office, and Villa Savoia, Drawing Room of the King

Routinely, Mussolini met with Foreign Minister Ciano and Arturo Bocchini, head of OVRA, the secret police, every morning at ten o'clock to start his business day. Today was no exception, but Mussolini's foul temper toward his two top deputies was unusual. He would not listen to their usual daily reports.

"I am not interested in that garbage today," Mussolini railed.

The two officials stood uneasily in front of Mussolini's desk, shifting from foot to foot, enduring his blazing invective. "How did Sarfatti get out of the country?" the Duce thundered. "I issued specific orders to detain her."

Bocchini frowned. "I know, Duce, and we had the border police looking out for her. We learned later, however, that she crossed the border to Switzerland under a false passport and identity."

"When?"

"Only a few days after we published the Manifesto."

"Where is she now?"

Bocchini read from a small notebook. "My operatives have traced her to Paris, where she has rented an apartment."

Mussolini shook his head. "That Sarfatti is one smart bitch. We must lure her back to Italy."

"We can kidnap her and bring her back," Bocchini suggested helpfully.

Mussolini frowned. "No, I want no violence whatsoever used against her. I only want her under my watchful eye, not harmed physically in any way. Do I make myself clear?"

"I understand, Duce," the secret service chief replied.

Ciano cleared his throat. Mussolini looked up at him. "Yes, Minister, what is it?"

"The racial laws we enacted in September and this month have sparked an international outcry, especially from the Western democracies. I explained to the American ambassador that the laws were a reaction to the mass migration of Jews into Italy from Central and Eastern Europe. Without the racial laws, we would be powerless to prevent it and in five years we would be harboring a half million foreign Jews."

"From now on," the Duce growled, "no more explanations to those pathetic democracies. It's none of their business what we do in Italy and I don't give a damn what they think or say."

Ciano nodded.

"What makes me furious is that old, fat fool of a pontiff rotting in the Vatican. Do you remember what he said after the Manifesto?" Mussolini picked up a paper and began reading. "'The entire human race is but a single and universal race of men. There is no room for special races. We may ask ourselves why Italy should have felt a disgraceful need to imitate Germany.'"

"I warned the nuncio," Ciano cut in, "that if the Vatican continues on this path, a clash is inevitable because you now regard the racial question as constituting the fundamental basis of the Italian State."

Mussolini laughed harshly. "A lot of good it did. Did you hear the pope's latest radio broadcast to the Italian people? He told them that anti-Semitism is a deplorable movement in which Christians must have no part. 'Anti-Semitism,' he said, 'is inadmissible. We are spiritually Semites.'" The Duce slammed his open palm on the desk. "I will not let that senile old bastard stop me from getting rid of the Jews. It is a matter of state, not a religious policy. We shall defend ourselves against the villainous collusion of Jewry, Bolshevism and Freemasonry, pope or no pope."

Mussolini looked at the clock. "I must leave now. I have an appointment with the king."

◻◻◻

Half an hour later, a guard at the magnificent Villa Savoia ushered Mussolini into the drawing room of Victor Emmanuel III.

Silently, the Duce watched the king approach to greet him. Only five feet tall, Victor Emmanuel had, in proportion to the rest of his body, grotesquely short legs. He looked as if he were standing in a hole. A long, narrow nose and sharp protruding jaw completed his unhandsome features. The monarch was an embarrassment to Mussolini and Italy, but there was nothing the Duce could do about it now. The highly popular king enjoyed the loyalty of the Italian people—why, the Duce could not fathom. Ironically, although Mussolini desperately wanted his soldiers to have Nordic features, much to his annoyance, this ugly, blue-eyed king, with so much Austrian and German blood, looked far more Nordic than most of them.

The despicable little coward was arguing against Italy's military adventures in Ethiopia and Albania, Mussolini mused. If Hitler had had to deal with such an idiot of a monarch, he could have never conquered Austria.

The king greeted the dictator, motioned him to an armchair and sat down himself, facing his visitor. "Prime Minister, these new racial laws distress me," he began. "I have here a letter from General Guido Liuzzi, a famous and highly decorated officer, who writes me that he has been dismissed simply because he is Jewish. I'll read it to you because I think he makes some good points. 'Today, our fault seems to be our nonbelonging to a presumed Italian Aryan race. But this guilty situation apparently does not exist for other Italians who also belong to a foreign race, such as the Arabs, Slavs, Albanians, Armenians, and so on. This means that Italian racism is hiding behind a mask, in order to give anti-Semitism the appearance of having a logical foundation.'"

The king stopped reading and looked directly at Mussolini. "Frankly, I don't understand how a leader of your stature can copy such racial nonsense from a thug like Hitler." The king spit out the German dictator's name with obvious disgust. He hadn't forgotten the rudeness Hitler had displayed to him during the führer's recent state visit to Rome last April. It had also been reported to him that Hitler had called him King Nutcracker behind his back and instructed his deputies, with great glee, not to laugh at the small kneeling figure greeting them on the station platform—that was the king standing to his full height.

Mussolini thrust forward his square jaw and stared at the king. "I take vigorous exception to Your Majesty's comments." The Duce's voice began rising. He could no longer sit. Jumping up, he strutted around the drawing room. "The Manifesto and the racial laws were not instituted at the instigation or on the orders of the German government." Now Mussolini was fairly shouting. "They are Italian laws, created by an Italian for the benefit of Italians." He paused, collecting his thoughts. "We are not Hamites, we are not Semites and we are not Mongols. If we are none of these races, then we must obviously be Aryans who have come from across the Alps from the north."

The king frowned and shook his head in disbelief and disapproval.

Ignoring the gesture, Mussolini continued. "Thus, we are Aryans of the Mediterranean type—pure!"

The king's eyes followed the still marching Duce around the room. "Pray listen to yourself Prime Minister. 'Aryans of the Mediterranean type.' You hear how ridiculous that sounds? I am disappointed that you have chosen to emulate the worst features of the German government. I have infinite pity for the Jews who are as Italian as you and your deputies."

With his hands on his hips, Mussolini declared, "The trouble with Italy is that there are twenty thousand spineless Italians who are moved by the fate of the Jews."

Overlooking Mussolini's disrespectful tone and aggressive stance, the king replied softly but with conviction, "My dear Mussolini, I must inform you that *I* am one of those spineless Italians."

December 13, 1938, Turin, Office of the Chief Rabbi

On his arrival in Turin from Austria, Joseph Schwartz sought assistance in setting up a small tailor shop. The chief rabbi of Turin took the Austrian immigrant under his wing. He suggested that he see the Jewish banker and publisher Ettore Ovazza.

"You must understand, however," the rabbi said, "that Signore Ovazza has been a Fascist Party leader and still claims undying loyalty to the Duce, the anti-Jewish racial laws, notwithstanding."

Schwartz frowned, noting in broken Italian, "How can that be? Can't he see what's happening?"

The rabbi shrugged. "That, you will have to ask him. But one suggestion. Don't exhibit any Zionist sympathies. If he suspects you have the slightest leaning in that direction he may beat you up. He is definitely violently anti-Zionist."

"Violently?"

The rabbi lowered his voice conspiratorially even though only the two of them were in the room. "After the first set of racial laws, Ovazza became furious, not with the Duce but with the Zionists, whom he blamed for everything. He was very bitter, accusing the Zionists of disloyalty, which, he said, forced Mussolini to promulgate the racial laws. It is common knowledge that Ovazza and his gang burned down the Zionist press office in this city."

"Is he blind?" asked Schwartz, uncomprehendingly. Then he shrugged.. "Fascist or not, if he can help . . ."

The rabbi interrupted. "Just be thankful you are not a professor, doctor or lawyer. They have lost their right to a livelihood. But so far, they haven't bothered tailors."

December 15, 1938, Late Morning, Turin, Café Torino

Schwartz crossed the impressive Piazza San Carlo, the extravagant bronze statute of Duke Emanuele Filiberto, the "Iron Head," sheathing his sword overlooking the large square. Glancing around, he spotted his destination, the Café Torino and headed for it at a rapid pace, not wanting to be late.

As prearranged, the Austrian was carrying an umbrella and wearing a feathered Tyrolean hat, a unique costume on this sunny day. Ettore Ovazza waved Schwartz over to his table. As Schwartz looked at the elegant chandeliers and frescoed ceilings, he fervently hoped Ovazza would pick up the check—the nineteenth century Café Torino, one of the most elegant in the city, appeared to be well beyond the immigrant tailor's budget.

Ovazza stood to greet his guest. They shook hands and sat down. Schwartz ordered the same thing as Ovazza, a double cappuccino.

The banker looked at his guest. "So, Signore Schwartz, I understand you want to go into business here in Turin."

"Well, Sir, I escaped recently from Vienna, and that was my intention—to go into the tailoring business. But to be quite honest, I'm not so sure anymore."

"Come, come, Signore Schwartz. If you are a good tailor, there is a great need in Turin."

Schwartz shook his head. "It's not that—it's the recent racial laws. As foreign Jews, my children are not allowed to go to school in Turin. The same thing is happening here that happened in Germany and Austria. I don't think it is wise to stay in Italy, but I do not know how to get a visa to go elsewhere, possibly America or Palestine."

Ovazza's face darkened. "Palestine? You're not one of those Zionists, are you?"

Schwartz realized his mistake as soon as it was out of his mouth. He'd forgotten the rabbi's warning. "No indeed, Signore Ovazza. But to save my family I would consider moving to any country outside of Europe that will accept us."

"Outside of Europe? I think you are overreacting. You're perfectly safe here in Italy. I guarantee it. After the war, things will return to normal—the Duce has assured me. I wrote to him and told him we have built a wall between the Jewish Italian Fascists and the international, Masonic and democratic Jews. The damn Union of Jewish Communities brought this law down on themselves for their disloyalty by supporting international Judaism."

"With all due respect, Signore Ovazza," protested Schwartz, "you are deluding yourself if you think you are safe. You will see: the situations of *all Jews* will become progressively worse until it is too late to do anything. Relying on being a loyal Fascist is a trap, even if it seems like a lifeline now."

He could see growing rage in Ovazza's face.

"You're a damn Bolshevik, aren't you?" Ovazza declared in a voice loud enough to attract the attention of patrons at the adjoining tables.

Schwartz got up from his chair. "If you will excuse me, Signore Ovazza, I don't think we have anything further to say to each other." He headed out the café into Piazza San Carlo. Behind him he heard Ovazza shouting, "Mussolini is a friend of the Jews. It's you Zionists that caused all this trouble. The Duce will restore our rights after the crisis passes, you . . ."

The glass doors of the café swung shut behind him. Of one thing he was certain. Even if Ovazza had been willing to help him, he, Joseph, would never set up a tailor shop in Turin. As a Jew and a foreigner, he'd stand out in this small city. No, until he could work out a way to emigrate, his family's immediate needs were the anonymity of a big city. They could lose themselves more effectively in the large population of Rome.

◻◻◻

"Joseph, we will not be going to Rome with you," Karl Schwartz informed his brother when they met later that day in Joseph's apartment.

"But you will be safer in a big city like Rome."

"Undoubtedly, big brother, but we have other plans."

Schwartz looked at him suspiciously. "Such as . . .?"

Karl broke out in a big grin. "Such as going to America." He waved some papers in front of Joseph's nose. "These are affidavits from my wife's cousins in America. With these, my family can obtain visas at the United States legation."

"That is very good news, but how are you going to get to the United States?"

"By booking passage on a ship out of Genoa. That's why I want to go there. The port is only 140 kilometers from here." Karl's smile turned into an expression of great sadness. "I just wish I could have included you and your family also."

Schwartz patted his brother on the back. "It's good—at least *you're* getting out. Don't worry, we'll figure something out. When will you be leaving?"

Karl shrugged. "Who knows? I understand it's very difficult to book space on the ships sailing to America. It may take a while, but we'll just keep trying."

For a few moments the two brothers looked at each other silently. Then Karl hugged Joseph. His voice broke. "Thank you, Joseph, for insisting that we flee Austria. I was terrified of crossing the border illegally, but you managed it for all of us—and we got out with most of our money and valuables intact." Briefly he tightened his hold. "I shall miss you, big brother." Karl relaxed his bear hug.

Schwartz stepped back one pace and patted Karl on the shoulder. "And I, you."

CHAPTER THREE

February 9, 1939, the Vatican, Bedroom of the Pope

Pius XI, mortally ill, lay in bed, attempting to read the draft encyclical. Wearily, he dropped it on the edge of the white blanket and picked up the script of his planned broadcast. The encyclical slipped down to the floor, the pope too weak to retrieve it. His deteriorating physical condition overwhelmed his famous iron will. LaFarge had completed a draft of the encyclical last summer. The burden of reviewing the draft for the pontiff had fallen upon the broad shoulders of Father Enrico Rosa, chief editor of the Jesuit publication, *La Civiltà Cattolica*. Rosa was uniquely qualified for the task for many reasons, two of the most important being the pope's complete faith in his discretion, judgment and loyalty, and Rosa's professional writing abilities. Rosa had seemed the ideal solution for the ailing pontiff. But Providence had stepped in and dealt a fatal blow to the plans of His Holiness and—not incidentally—to Father Rosa, who succumbed to a massive heart attack. Pius, with heavy heart, assumed the burden himself; he ordered his doctors to keep him alive until he could complete the encyclical.

First though, he had prepared a speech for radio broadcast condemning Nazi anti-Semitism, Germany's treatment of the Jews and others, and Hitler. Enough was enough. He could no longer stand silently by. Incapacitated or not, he planned to broadcast the speech tomorrow—after he made a few changes—even if he had to speak from his bed. Before he died, he had to commit the future pope, whomever he might be, to action. His determined effort this day was his last. The speech slipped off the bed to the floor, landing on top of the encyclical, as his valiant heart finally gave up the struggle.

□□□

The pope's housekeeper discovered the body, called the doctors and informed Pacelli, who rushed to the pope's bedroom. As cardinal camerlengo, it was up to him to summon the College of Cardinals to Rome to elect a successor. The burden of making the funeral arrangements also fell on him. From the time the pope's physicians officially announce "The Holy Father is dead," until the election of a new pope, the cardinal camerlengo is a virtual dictator with absolute power over the church hierarchy.

In the bedroom, the housekeeper approached the cardinal. "Your Eminence?"

Pacelli, busy gathering the papers on the pope's desk, impatiently looked up. "Yes, Sister, what is it?" He did not bother to mask his annoyance at the interruption.

"I am sorry for the bother, Your Eminence, but I found these on the floor under the bed of His Holiness. I think he was reading these when, when . . ." She began weeping, unable to finish her sentence but still holding out the documents in her hand.

The cardinal nodded and took the papers from her. He scanned the speech and frowned. A brief glance at the other paper told him this was the one he was looking for. He'd known about the encyclical but not about the speech. He gave a brief silent prayer of thanks that it hadn't been delivered. Following tradition, he ordered the room locked and sealed after removal of the pope's body. Then he hastened to his own office, clutching the draft of *Humani Generis Unitas* and the never-to-be-delivered radio speech.

Later the Same Day, Rome, Palazzo Venezia, Mussolini's Office

The telephone operator was finally able to put Mussolini through to Hitler. "Good news, Chancellor, the Pope is dead. Thank the Lord the stubborn old man is gone!" *The gods must have been smiling on me today,* Mussolini thought. *Even the telephone connection was static-free and Hitler came through with unaccustomed clarity.*

"That is excellent news, Duce. I do hope they elect Pacelli. He is a good friend of Germany and our preferred candidate."

Mussolini smiled. "I agree. Unlike Pius XI, he won't rock the boat—he likes to maintain the status quo. He won't give us the trouble the old pope did."

March 2 and 3, 1939, the Vatican

Twenty days after the death of Pius XI, the College of Cardinals gathered in the Pauline Chapel for the Mass of the Holy Spirit. The cardinals then retired to the Sistine Chapel for the election of a new pope. Nearby rooms were converted into dormitories, and the assemblage was locked in the area. They would have no contact with the outside world until a new pope was elected; even food was passed through a window to the princes of the church.

The election of Pacelli was not without opposition. Eugene Cardinal Tisserant of France was unalterably opposed to Pacelli because, as he asserted, "He is indecisive, hesitant, a man more designed to obey orders than give them." Domenico Cardinal Tardini, who came from a working-class district in Rome, observed that Pacelli, unlike Pius XI, was not born with the temperament of a fighter. Tardini spoke bluntly of Hitler as "a motorized Attila" and noted that while the powerful nations remained quiet, Pius XI had not hesitated to protest Hitler's racist excesses. Left unsaid was the comparison to Pacelli, but the inference was clear.

On March 3, 1938, on the third ballot, one by one, each cardinal approached the altar in the Sistine Chapel, holding his ballot with two fingers of his right hand. Kneeling at the altar, in a loud voice, each cardinal intoned, "I call to witness Christ the Lord, my judge, that I am electing him who I believe should be elected by God's Will," and then placed his ballot on the paten.

□□□

Late in the afternoon, the secretary of the College of Cardinals stood before Eugenio Cardinal Pacelli in the hall of elections. "Do you accept your canonical election as supreme pontiff?"

"I accept," replied Pacelli.

"By which name do you wish to be called?"

"Pius, in grateful memory of Pope Pius XI."

At approximately six that evening, a cardinal stepped out onto the central loggia of St. Peter's Basilica and announced to crowds gathered in the square, "It is with great joy that I announce to you that we have a new pope. It is Eugenio Cardinal Pacelli, who has taken the name of Pius XII." It had taken just one day to elect Pacelli to St. Peter's throne.

In one of his first acts after his coronation, the new pope sent certain papers of Pius XI to the Vatican Archives. Then he sent Hitler a letter:

> To the Illustrious Herr Adolf Hitler, Führer and Chancellor of the German Reich! Here at the beginning of Our Pontificate We wish to assure you that We remain devoted to the spiritual welfare of the German people entrusted to your leadership . . . During the many years we spent in Germany, We did all in Our power to establish harmonious relations between Church and State. Now that the responsibilities of Our pastoral function have increased Our opportunities, how much more ardently do We pray to reach that goal. May the prosperity of the German people and their progress in every domain come, with God's help, to fruition!

The pontiff, in turn, received a communication offering "the warmest congratulations of the Führer and the German Government."

March 10, 1939, Rome, Office of the Foreign Minister

It was a busy day for Italian Foreign Minister Ciano. This morning he had heard from his ambassador to Germany, Bernardo Attolico. German Foreign Minister Joachim von Ribbentrop advised Attolico that Germany planned to march on Czechoslovakia and incorporate it into the Third Reich. Ciano immediately telephoned the new cardinal secretary of state, Luigi Maglione, who called back later to advise Ciano that the Holy Father planned no public protest of the takeover. Ciano passed that information on to Ribbentrop.

Mussolini's reaction, however, was another matter. With one stroke, the Germans planned to annul the Munich Treaty of 1938 guaranteeing the independence of Czechoslovakia, a treaty for which Mussolini took full credit. "The Italians will laugh at me," the Duce groaned in one of their daily morning meetings. "Germany acts with little regard for us. It seems that the Axis functions to serve only one of its partners." Ciano listened but knew there was nothing Mussolini could do about it. Germany was too powerful to oppose and the Duce wanted desperately to be on the winning side of the coming war—and that meant sticking with Hitler.

March 15, 1939, Milan, United States Consulate

Beppe Foà, a leading aircraft designer for the largest Italian aircraft manufacturer, Piaggio, had been shocked when he read the "Manifesto of the Racist Scientists," published in the newspapers in July 1938, but he had never feared for his position at Piaggio—after all, he was their best aircraft designer. He had just completed the production of an airplane that could fly nonstop from Rome to San Francisco. Oh, he'd been harassed and even jailed in 1933 for his anti-Fascist leanings, but his employer had stood steadfastly by him and given him his job back on release from prison. Now, on the eve of the test of *his* airplane, the government had forced the company to fire him—because he was a Jew—or face prosecution under the racial laws.

His dismissal convinced Foà that Italy would soon be no safer for Jews than Hitler's Germany. He reached a previously unthinkable decision—he would leave his beloved Italy. On a visit to Rome, he tried to convince his cousin, Ugo Foà, a leader of the Jewish community in Rome, to leave as well, but Ugo had just become angry. "We must submit to the racial laws, obey the rules and become model citizens," he'd told Beppe. "Then, nothing will happen to us. After the war, all the restrictions will be lifted. Beppe, by being a disloyal Jew, you will make things harder for the rest of us."

Today, as he sat in the reception room of the U.S. consulate in Milan, Beppe Foà thought again his unspoken reply to Ugo's advice. *Disloyal? Why shouldn't I be, after being stripped of my rights as a citizen, fired from my job and threatened with confiscation of my property?*

Foà watched a man, he'd guess in his early thirties, sit down next to him. The man looked as if he was about to speak, then hesitated.

"Yes?" Foà inquired.

"Are you applying for a visa?" the man asked in a thick German accent that immediately set Foà on edge. It was none of this German's business, but he answered anyway.

"Yes, I am. But why are *you* leaving?" After all, you're German, was left unsaid.

The man caught Foà's accusatory tone. "I'm a Jew from Austria—just escaped from Vienna. I think the same thing will happen to the Jews here."

Foà realized he'd jumped to the wrong conclusion. He relaxed. "Yes, I agree. That's why I'm leaving too."

"You're a Jew?"

Foà nodded. He put out his right hand. "Beppe Foà, and you are . . . ?"

The man shook Foà's hand. "Karl, Karl Schwartz."

"You have relatives in America, Signore Schwartz?"

"I do, and I have their affidavits right here." He patted the envelope in his pocket.

"I do too, I'm going to America."

Karl Schwartz knitted his brow. "You think that's the right thing to do?"

"Of course. There's no future for the Jews in Italy and a lot of danger."

Schwartz rubbed his chin. "You know that publisher in Turin, I think his name is Ovazza?"

Foà's face turned dark. "Yes, I know Ettore Ovazza," he growled.

"Yes, that's the one. Anyway, he says as soon as the war is over, all this will go away. Jews that abandon the Duce, he says, are traitors. A great new world under fascism is around the corner."

Foà shook his head. "He's a pompous ass—so Fascist that he'll be saluting *Il Duce* when his Gentile fellow Fascists come to shoot him. He's been an apologist for Mussolini since 1922 and every time the Fascists visit another outrage on the Jews, he's right there with some rationalization of why it's really good for us. He's a dangerous man to listen to, Schwartz, don't do it. You get yourself and your family to America. Not so many Jews in Europe have that opportunity—make the most of it."

His companion nodded. "I guess so."

"Good, I'm glad we got that out of the way. Now, how are you planning to get to America, once you obtain the visa?"

"I haven't given that much thought yet. I suppose I'll have to book passage on a ship."

"Go to Genoa. There are several lines sailing to the United States. But space on the ships is very scarce; you may have to wait for a long time to obtain a reservation. You best not delay booking your tickets. You never know when the ax will fall and trap you here."

The Austrian nodded. "I went through the same thing in Vienna and almost left too late. If we hadn't bribed a border guard . . ." He shook his head.

Same Day, Prague
Dr. Lev Divis left his office in the late afternoon, strolling home at a leisurely pace. Dinner would not be for another two hours, so he had time to enjoy the early spring in his much loved Prague. The tall, thin physician, with long strides, headed for the Charles Bridge. He would watch the street vendors plying their trades; then he'd stand at the railing to watch the Danube traffic flow by, a welcome respite from the misery and sickness he had to deal with every day.

Before he could reach the bridge, the loud rumble of what could only be heavy military vehicles assaulted his ears. Far down the broad avenue, he could see a long line of traffic approaching. Curious, he stopped and waited. When they were a block away, he could see the flags on the front fenders—the all-too-familiar black swastika on a red and white background.

Divis forgot about his daily trip to the Charles Bridge and rushed home to his family. He had a lot to do and not much time to do it in.

March 16, 1939, Rome, Palazzo Venezia, Mussolini's Office
Foreign Minister Ciano ushered Prince Philip von Hesse, Hitler's personal representative, into the Duce's large office. The prince, a

nephew of Kaiser Wilhelm, had married the Italian king's second daughter, making him a natural link between the German and Italian leaders. Hitler was quick to make use of the relationship, and Prince Philip became the führer's "mailman" to Italy.

The prince opened the discussion. "The führer wanted you to know that he moved against Czechoslovakia because the Prague government would not demobilize its military forces, thus constituting an unacceptable danger on Germany's flank. Also, the Third Reich could not continue to permit the Czechs to mistreat their German citizens. The führer wishes to advise you that his actions in no way reflect on your fine efforts to find a peaceful resolution in Munich. Matters simply began to get out of hand and we had to act."

"Such pretexts are fine for Herr Doctor Goebbels's propaganda machine," protested Ciano, "but you should not use them on us, your allies. And furthermore . . ."

"Be quiet," Mussolini barked. He turned to Prince Philip. "The takeover made me look foolish. I don't appreciate that. At the very least, the führer could have given me sufficient notice to prepare the Italian people."

The prince nodded. "Perhaps that is true and I apologize for the position our actions put you in. But let me add that the führer asked me personally to assure you that he will support your efforts to assert your rights to the Mediterranean Sea, the Adriatic and adjacent zones. Germany has no intention of making its power felt in those areas."

Mussolini leaned back in his chair, deep in thought. Both his guests waited; neither spoke. Finally the Duce sat up straight. "For your information, President Roosevelt offered me a ten-year truce."

Philip looked up. "And . . .?"

Mussolini laughed. "And I told the American ambassador that the proposal must have been the result of Roosevelt's progressive paralysis. Never in the course of history has a nation been guided a paralytic. There have been bald kings, fat kings, handsome and stupid kings, but never a king who, in order to go to the bathroom and eat at the dinner table, needed the support of other men."

Mussolini's scatological outburst against the American president appeared to have embarrassed the German diplomat. The prince pressed his lips together. "Our government is not anxious to provoke the Americans at this time. It's a mistake to underestimate them."

"The Americans," Mussolini scoffed, "are basically stupid and uncultured, living in a country of Negroes and Jews. With the two Fascist nations moving hand in hand, no one can stop us; not the British, not the French and certainly not the Americans. As far as the Czechs are concerned, they have only themselves to thank for the loss of their independence, having failed to free themselves from the influence of the Jews, Freemasons, Democrats and Bolsheviks."

Ciano blinked. Mussolini had come full circle, accepting—and rationalizing—the fait accompli with which Hitler had presented him. The great Duce had slid further under the thumb of Adolph Hitler.

CHAPTER FOUR

July 6, 1939, Karlovac, Yugoslavia

Dr. Lev Divis did not wait for the German roundup of Jews in Prague to begin. Within a week of the takeover, he packed all the valuables he could carry and with his wife, Zophie, and daughter, Bela, made his way across Czechoslovakia to the city of Bratislava on the Hungarian border. He didn't dare take the train because the Germans and their Nazi sympathizers carefully checked the papers of railroad passengers. Much of the Divis money—much more than expected—had gone for hiring taxis and then a boat to take them across the Danube into Hungary. They'd finally worked their way down to Yugoslavia, settling in the town of Karlovac, about 60 kilometers southwest of Zagreb.

August 31, 1939, Genoa, Anchor-Donaldson Lines Ticket Office

Karl Schwartz sat in the outer office of the British Anchor-Donaldson Steamship Line, waiting for his tickets for America aboard the *Athenia*, scheduled to make one stop in England en route. He spotted a familiar face leaving the inner office. "Beppe Foà, *Ciao*! Karl Schwartz here."

Foà extended his hand. "Ah, Milan, yes, of course, I remember. You took my advice—good for you."

Schwartz smiled. "I did indeed—and it was excellent advice! I sail later today aboard the *Athenia*. How about you, are you ticketed for this sailing?"

Foà sighed. "I wish I were. I decided to save a little money and booked instead aboard an Italian rust-bucket, also leaving today. But we won't get to America for two weeks. I was stupid. Just now I tried one last time to get on the *Athenia*, but they're booked solid for the next two months. So I'm stuck."

"Relax, my friend," said Schwartz, patting the other on the back. "You waited this long, another week won't hurt. The main thing is that you are getting out of Europe. I wish my brother, Joseph, and his family could have left, too. The entire continent, I'm sure, will be engulfed in war very soon with that Austrian paperhanger going crazy in Germany."

The two men shook hands. "Good luck, my friend. Perhaps we shall meet again in America."

Schwartz nodded. "And good luck to you. We will put in a good word for you with American Immigration."

September 3, 1939, Rome, Palazzo Venezia, Mussolini's Office

Mussolini looked up from his desk at Ciano, standing there waiting patiently for the Duce to address him. "He's a madman!" Mussolini roared. "I told him we wouldn't be ready to fight a war for another year or two and still he goes ahead and invades Poland. It's treachery. Perhaps that exonerates us from any treaty obligations to the Germans."

Ciano frowned. "Hitler already told me he didn't need our help and would overrun Poland in three or four weeks. However distasteful it is, we must stay with Hitler—he will be on the winning side."

"Distasteful?" Mussolini nodded, waving a telegram at Ciano "You haven't heard the latest. Let me read part of this message I just received from Hitler. 'The Poles, in direct contrast to our German workmen, are especially born for hard labor. There can be no question of improvement for them. On the contrary, it is necessary to keep the standard of life low in Poland and it must not be permitted to rise. The Polish landlords must cease to exit. They must be exterminated wherever they are. There should be only one master for the Poles—the Germans. Therefore, all representatives of the Polish intelligentsia are to be exterminated; such is the law of life. The lowest German workman and the lowest German peasant must always stand economically 10 per cent above any Pole.' "

"All I can say is I hope he never comes after us," said Ciano, shaking his head.

Mussolini just grunted.

Ciano smiled. "Yesterday, Ribbentrop assured me that Britain and France would never declare war over Poland. I disagreed and we made a wager."

Mussolini looked at his foreign minister. "But Britain and France today did declare war on Germany."

Ciano nodded sadly. "And also today I am the proud owner of a collection of antique armor."

Mussolini snorted. "Don't expect to collect from that double-dealer."

Same Day, at Sea in the Mediterranean

German submarine U-30 surfaced somewhere off the coast of Spain enabling its captain, Fritz Julius Lemp, to receive the coded message that the Fatherland was now at war with the British and the French. He dismissed as ludicrous another message from Admiral Doenitz not to attack shipping until things were clarified. We are at war! I shall not stand down if enemy targets of opportunity present themselves, thought Lemp as he took his submarine down to periscope depth and began the hunt. A target was not long in presenting itself. Staring intently through the raised periscope, Lemp moved U-30 in for a closer look. "Load torpedoes in the forward tubes," he barked.

The first officer repeated the order, then turned to face the captain. "Sir, Admiral Doenitz's communication said no hostilities were to commence until we receive further orders. Besides, it appears to be a civilian passenger ship."

Lemp waved the first officer away. "It doesn't matter—it's a Britisher. It's our sacred duty to engage the *enemy,* and that is precisely what I intend to do."

"But Captain . . ."

"Prepare to fire the torpedoes," he shouted, leaving his second in command no choice but to repeat the order to the men in the torpedo room.

September 4, 1939, at Sea in the Mediterranean

Beppe Foà stood at the railing of the lumbering old Italian freighter. The officers and crew suddenly started rushing around the deck. Curious, Foà stopped one of the deck hands. "What's going on? Is there some sort of emergency?"

"A ship has been torpedoed and we are changing course to pick up survivors. We should reach the area of the sinking in about an hour."

Foà had a bad feeling. He left the deck and descended to his cabin to fetch his field glasses. Returning to the deck, he leaned on the railing, scanning the horizon. Finally, in the distance, he made out some small boats in the water—they looked like lifeboats.

"Do you happen to know the name of the ship that was torpedoed?" he shouted to a deck officer.

Without looking up, and continuing to perform his task, the man shouted back, "The *Athenia*, I believe."

Foà bit his lip. *And to think I was envious of their booking on that fast, modern liner. God, I hope they were in one of those lifeboats.* He kept his eyes glued to the field glasses, lowering them occasionally to wipe away a tear. Several hours later, after the survivors had been picked up, he did not find the Karl Schwartz family among them.

September 10, 1939, Rome, Home of Italian Foreign Minister Galeazzo Ciano, Early Afternoon

Edda Ciano put down the newspaper and looked at her husband, sitting at his desk on the other side of the wood paneled study. "What will happen under the 'Pact of Steel?' Will it require Italy to enter this war against Britain and France?"

Mussolini had labeled last May's treaty with Hitler the "Pact of Steel." It obligated each partner to provide military support to the other upon the outbreak of *any* hostilities.

Ciano put down the pen and closed the diary he'd been keeping since becoming foreign minister. The Duce had requested it in order to create a historical record of the Mussolini achievements on behalf of the "new Roman Empire," as the Duce had phrased it. Ciano rubbed his eyes and gave careful thought to his wife's question before answering. "Technically, it will. The pact, unfortunately, makes no distinction between the attacked and the attacker. It's simply an unconditional pledge of military aid."

"How could you, as foreign minister, have permitted my father to enter such a treaty?"

Ciano emitted a short, harsh laugh. "I? *Permit* the Duce? You must be joking! Without consulting me or any of his other advisers, your father gave the Germans free rein to draft the entire treaty; he wanted an alliance, he didn't care about its terms. I was just the messenger. To be quite frank, I can't recall ever reading a treaty like this one. It's a very dangerous one." He opened the diary and flipped the pages to the May entries. "This is what your father told me." He poked the page several times with his forefinger for emphasis before he began reading. " 'A bloc of 150 million men will be formed, against which nothing can be done. This bloc, a formidable array of men and weapons, wants peace, but it is ready to impose its will should the great conservative and reactionary democracies try to stop our irresistible march.' You know your father, when he sets his mind on something . . ."

Edda nodded understandingly without having to hear the rest of the sentence. "What will happen, now, Gallo?"

"Who knows?" shrugged her husband. "Fortunately, Hitler let your father off the hook in Poland, saying he didn't need help. But with Britain and France coming to Poland's aid, I think your father now realizes that he's given Hitler carte blanche to start the next world war."

"I hear my father has just ordered the dissolution of all Jewish organizations including the Union of Jewish Communities. Why is he doing that? He's made so many statements earlier that the Jews would never be a problem in Italy."

"It's quite simple. An alliance with Hitler, which your father desperately desires, was not possible without his making some move against the Jews. And I'm afraid it's going to get progressively worse for the Jews in Italy."

"Well, I'm going to speak to him about this," declared Edda angrily. "Such actions do not befit the great leader that he is."

"Go right ahead, my dear, but don't expect to change his mind. To him, the alliance will make Italy a world power and a force in the council of nations. He's determined and is not about to let any Jews stand in his way."

Later the Same Day, Rome, Palazzo Venezia, Mussolini's Office

That afternoon, Edda showed up unannounced at Palazzo Venezia. For support she brought along her aunt, Mussolini's sister, Edvige. Mussolini could never turn away his favorite—and strong-willed—child. *Just like me,* he thought proudly as he motioned her and his sister to chairs.

"What can I do for you, my dear?" There was a definite edge to his voice. "You know my days are very busy."

Critical rejoinders ran through Edda's mind. *You can fool the citizens about how hard you work, but not me. If you put in more than four hours a day, I'd be surprised. No doubt we're probably interrupting your liaison with the slut of the day.* She did not voice them, of course, especially those concerning the sexual liaisons that her father thought were such a great secret. *Poor Mama, suffering in silence!* Instead Edda begged, "Papa, you must show some mercy to the Jews. Don't become another Hitler—you've never been an anti-Semite before this, you've never believed that Aryan Race garbage. According to your racial proclamations, our swarthy southern Catholics are Aryans whereas a blond and blue-eyed Triestino Jew is not. It makes you look silly."

"And don't forget how much you cared for that Jewess, Margherita Sarfatti," Edvige added. "Would you visit all that misery on her and her people?"

Mussolini rubbed his cheek, then raised his head, thrusting out his chin. "Sarfatti has already fled the country and is quite safe. Of course, I don't believe this nonsense of Italian racial purity or that there is a Jewish menace. It's simply state policy to assure Italy her empire, a strategy to benefit our government. It's the only way to be certain that we will be on the winning side of the coming war."

"By getting into bed with Hitler?" Edda interjected, her tone dripping with its usual sarcasm. "At what moral cost, Father?"

"Morals have nothing to do with it, my dear. Great leaders cannot and do not have such a luxury. To benefit Italy, I must run this country as I see fit. You think I like Hitler, that sexual pervert, who deflowered his own niece? He rode to power using violence against his own people. I told him not to invade Poland and he ignored me. It would serve him right if the British and French inflicted a few defeats on him—that would take him down a peg or two. But that's not likely to happen and we are dependent on the Third Reich for military help. That, dear ladies, calls for a state policy against the Jews—and I will continue to impose more restrictions in the future. I must protect the true Italians, not Jews."

The Duce stood. "Now, I have to get back to work." He ushered the two frustrated women out of his office.

PART II

War!
The Net Closes on the Jews

CHAPTER FIVE

June 10, 1940, Morning, Rome, Palazzo Venezia, Mussolini's Office and the Balcony

On Mussolini's orders, Ciano, Marshals De Bono and Pietro Badoglio, and General Balbo, recalled from Libya, gathered in the dictator's office. There was little to prepare for since the Duce had refused to tell them the subject of the conference.

Mussolini looked at his wall clock—10 o'clock. He rose from his desk and strode over to the balcony looking out on Piazza Venezia. People packed the square. Pleased, he smiled, then stepped out and assumed his habitual scowl.

Flanked by the two symbols of fascism on the stone wall behind him, the ax and the lictor's rods, Mussolini, in his battle uniform, gray with a black Sam Browne belt, jodhpurs with wide black stripes and high black boots, put both hands on the balcony railing, his body straight and rigid and his head held high, his square chin thrust out. "Fellow Italians, this is an hour of irrevocable decisions; fate strikes the skies of our country." He paused, looking out over the crowd, now murmuring nervously. Jabbing his fist into the air, he shouted, "On this day, Italy has declared war on Great Britain and France in accordance with our obligations under the 'Pact of Steel!' The great Italian people are resolved to meet the risks and sacrifices of war because our honor, interests and future demand it! We shall join our ally, the Third Reich, which has already achieved gigantic victories against our decadent enemies."

Standing in the office behind the Duce, Ciano looked questioningly over to Badoglio, Balbo and De Bono. They all shrugged. It dawned on Ciano that the Italian dictator had committed Italy to a world war without consulting or notifying any of his cabinet or military leaders.

Ciano couldn't concentrate on the Duce's speech. He shook his head. *May God help Italy. This is insane!*

The dictator's belligerent shouts caught Ciano's attention again. ". . . a gigantic struggle of poor and countless people against the plutocratic and reactionary democracies of the West—the starvers who ferociously hold the monopoly on all the riches and all the gold of the earth, enemies who have become sterile and are in the process of decline . . ."

Ciano looked over to Badoglio. The marshal looked angry, his eyes shooting daggers at Ciano.

Did Badoglio think this was my idea? Ciano signaled his ignorance by shrugging and spreading out his arms, palms up.

". . . to win shall be our password! And win we will, in order at last to give us a long period of peace with justice to Italy, to Europe, and to the world. Italian people! Take up arms! Show your tenacity and courage! Fight with valor!" Mussolini ended his speech and with his arms crossed over his chest. He waited, scowling in his usual fashion, nodding his head and pouting defiantly. There was some polite cheering, but none of the crowd hysteria he had expected from his fiery words.

Ciano frowned. *What did the man expect? War was last thing the Italian people wanted.*

□□□

Stepping back into his office, Mussolini faced three very unhappy military subordinates, who looked on the verge of rebellion. He spoke before they could voice objections. "I have an appointment with history and can no longer remain passive. France is on her knees, almost defeated." He smirked, rubbing his hands together. "Consider me like a cat watching its prey and choosing precisely the right moment to jump—the moment when it has an almost mathematical certainty of victory. This is that time."

Improbable Heroes

The three military leaders and Ciano looked at the Duce in frosty silence. Mussolini scowled. "You are angry because you weren't consulted. So be it. For your information, the secret of Hitler's success has been that he, not his generals, makes the decisions and dictates the strategy. I intend to be the same kind of victorious commander-in-chief. Now that war is declared, I shall mount my horse and take command in the field of battle!"

Badoglio could contain himself no longer. "This is suicide, Duce. Before you get your ass shot off on a white horse, you'd better realize that we have few arms, tanks or airplanes—not even shirts and shoes for our soldiers!"

Mussolini slammed his fist on the desk. "Enough!" he shouted. Then lowering his voice to a growl, he continued, "You are not calm enough to judge the situation. By September, this whole thing will be over. If I can have a few thousand dead Italians, then I will be able to sit at the peace conference as one of the victorious belligerents."

De Bono waded into the argument. "And just what are we going to fight with? Our ammunition depots are almost depleted and have not been restocked since the Ethiopian war. Our antiaircraft and antitank weapons are ancient, decrepit, and almost depleted and we don't have enough fuel to power our fleet."

"You are a bunch of cowards and liars," Mussolini shouted, jabbing his finger at his subordinates. "We have thousands of tanks—haven't you seen them parading down the avenues of Rome? General Valle has advised me that we have 3,006 first-class fighter planes. We shall use our air superiority to great advantage!"

Balbo, the former ace aviator, broke his silence. "General Valle is an idiot! Superiority, you say? We are lucky if we can get a few hundred planes into the air. Just because a few thousand of them sit lined up neatly at our military bases doesn't mean they can fly in combat. Most of them lack replacement parts and are not airworthy. Our artillerymen are firing old Austrian guns built in 1908, while the British have the very latest models. As far as those thousands of tanks are concerned, you chose to build those weak, slow, tinny affairs instead of fast, heavy tanks so you could have more of them for the same cost. Well, Duce, those tanks are next to useless because their armor can be pierced by rifle or machine gun fire. They are nothing more than rolling coffins for our soldiers."

Mussolini stubbornly folded his arms. "It doesn't matter. We can always use poison gas to make up for any armament deficiencies."

Balbo rolled his eyes. "We are not fighting backward Ethiopia now, a country that had few arms and no exotic weapons. Your enemies in this war have the ability to retaliate in kind with dire consequences for our soldiers and for Italy."

Badoglio leaned forward on the desk. "Calling us cowards, Duce, will not solve our lack of raw materials and food supplies to wage a long war. We are not self-sufficient in so many things—fuel, iron ore, and coal to mention a few. We lack the merchant ships with which to supply the far-flung theaters you want Italy to fight in."

"Speaking of merchant ships," De Bono interjected, "by not consulting us before you declared war without warning, many of our ships are probably trapped in foreign ports and will be impounded. Had our merchant fleet been alerted, it would have been simple to put out to sea before war was declared. But . . ."

"That's enough," Mussolini shouted. "I told Hitler at our last meeting in Berlin that according to the laws of Fascist morality, when one has a friend, one marches with him to the very end. We will do this with Germany and her people. One thing you defeatists forget is that we are allied with the finest army in the world, the Wehrmacht. My chief of staff, General Pariani, assures me that with Germany's help, Italy can win a lightning war, that we are fully equipped for a war against Britain and France. Now get out of my sight!" Mussolini turned to Ciano. "Gallo, you remain."

Ciano watched Italy's best military leaders leave the room. He couldn't believe that the Duce was placing the fate of Italy in the hands of Alberto Pariani, who was nothing more that an old Fascist hack and crony with no military abilities whatsoever. Ciano agreed wholeheartedly with what De Bono, Balbo and Badoglio told the Duce. But what good would it do to join in the attack on his father-in-law? He'd only create problems for himself, his family and his marriage. And for what? The Duce was a stubborn old man who did not listen to advice anyway.

Mussolini waited until the three military leaders had closed the door behind them. "Well, you were the quiet one. I expected that at least you would stand by me."

Ciano shrugged. "What was there to say? I am only a diplomat, not a military man. My views on military preparedness are irrelevant."

Mussolini grunted. "I shall show those weaklings that I can mastermind battle strategy and win this war."

"I do have one concern," Ciano offered. "I was disturbed by the lack of enthusiastic reaction to your speech by the crowd in the square."

"What do the people know?" Mussolini scoffed. "They are dirty, stupid and do not work hard enough. They are content with their little movie shows."

Mussolini got out of his chair and began marching around the large room smacking the palm of his left hand with the fist of his right. "Governing the Italians is not difficult—only useless. The only things I need to govern them are policemen and bands playing in the streets. Only by accepting obedience will they learn to grow; and when they do learn, then they must believe what I tell them. I will be satisfied when I can march the crowd past a military cap stuck on a pole and have them salute it!"

Mussolini sat down again. Ciano took this as his cue to leave. "Will that be all, Duce?"

Mussolini looked up at his son-in-law. "Just one more thing. With the war on, I have prepared the latest round of restrictions on the Jews. Here." He held out a sheet of paper.

Ciano had to walk around the large desk to reach and take the paper. He scanned it. "Are these restrictions really necessary? These people present no danger to us and many of them have been our firmest supporters."

Mussolini shook his head. "Sometimes you are so dense, Gallo! Are they a danger to us? Of course not! Are the restrictions necessary? Of course, since it will please our German ally. As foreign minister, you should appreciate the importance of keeping Hitler happy."

Ciano started walking toward the door.

"One moment, Gallo. Here, take these and deal with them. They are petitions from Ettore Ovazza for exemption from the racial laws on the grounds of his dedicated service to the Fascist Party and his undying loyalty to me. I am tired of answering his entreaties. You do it."

"Shall I exempt him?"

'Not any more. We've got to set an example. If he's strutting around unfettered, it will be difficult to apply the racial laws to other Jews. I know Ovazza from the old days; he's a braggart who'll crow about his special status and we can't have that."

June 12, 1940, Berlin, Conference Room in the Chancellery

General Wilhelm Keitel, Heinrich Himmler and Hermann Göring watched the führer pace excitedly around the room. They remained quiet, waiting for their commander-in-chief to speak.

"The French are suing for peace," Hitler said softly. He turned to face General Keitel. "You will be responsible for concluding the armistice. Give the terms of surrender to the French delegation and permit no discussion. The terms must be accepted as submitted."

Göring cleared his throat. *"Mein* Führer, do you plan to attend the signing ceremony?"

"Oh yes, I wouldn't miss it. We will sign the surrender at the Compiègne railroad station. Keitel, you must make sure that the signing will take place in the very same railroad car that was used to sign the armistice when our cowardly leaders surrendered in 1918."

Keitel looked puzzled. "How can I find . . .?"

Hitler, smiling, interrupted his general. "It's quite simple. The railroad car in question resides in a museum in Compiègne. The French have preserved the carriage in its condition at the time of the 1918 armistice and proudly display it, rubbing salt in our wounds all these years. You will have it pulled out of the museum to the same siding." Hitler squeezed his hands together. "I have looked forward to this day for a long time."

"Shall I consult the Italians?"

Hitler snorted, "They left us in the lurch in September 1939. I feel no obligation to them now. Only after we conquered Poland, Norway, Holland and Denmark—and now have France on its knees—did those 'brave' Italians decide to join the war. The Duce reminds me of the circus clown who rolled up the mats after the

Improbable Heroes

acrobats completed their death-defying performance and demanded that the audience applaud *him*. I am willing to humor Mussolini for now, but under no circumstances are you and your staff to reveal any of our military plans to them."

"I spoke to Mussolini," Göring interjected. "He has put in a claim for Nice, Corsica, Tunisia and French Somaliland."

Hitler laughed harshly. "He hasn't fired a shot yet and he acts as if he won the war single-handedly—Alexander the Great and Julius Caesar all rolled into one."

Hitler paused, then shook his head vigorously. "He'll get no territory from France. I have the French where I want them—I don't want to drive their government into the arms of the British. Besides, the Italians are useless. Mussolini has sent me an urgent message requesting merchant ships. The fool lost a third of his fleet because he did not order them out of enemy ports before he declared war. Can you believe that?"

Hitler excused General Keitel. He ordered Himmler and Göring to remain. "Now that the war is in full swing, we must avoid internal dissension."

Himmler looked up. "What are you thinking of?"

"We will stop, until further notice, confiscation of the property of all Christian churches."

Himmler jumped up. "But, *Mein* Führer . . ."

Hitler interrupted the head of the security police with a wave of his hand. "I know those traitorous Catholic bishops have openly opposed euthanasia of the mentally ill, but I will not be provoked just now. While the war is in progress, we will try to be conciliatory."

Himmler sighed. This was not what he wanted. It would only delay the inevitable and make things more difficult. "Very well, Führer, I will instruct the Gestapo to ease its harassment of Catholic Church officials."

Hitler frowned. "*All* Christian churches. Don't misunderstand me. I know I have numerous accounts to settle with the churches. We will not deal with Christians now, but rest assured, I have not forgotten about them. In due time I will bring out the big book, and after the war ends, my final great contribution to the Third Reich will be to solve the religious problem because our nation will become secure only with the eradication of Christianity."

"What about the Jews in Italy?" Himmler inquired. "While the Italian government has enacted some anti-Jewish laws, the Jews still live a fairly good life in Italy. I've talked and talked to the Duce, and I must say, he doesn't seem serious about solving Italy's Jewish problem."

Hitler rubbed his chin. "My patience is not unlimited, but still, Italy is our ally, however unreliable. We will do nothing concerning Italy without the Duce's acquiescence. I am scheduled to meet with Mussolini next week. I will pressure him regarding his Jews."

June 14, 1940, Rome, the Ghetto

"Stand still, so I can finish pinning the cuffs of the trousers—you're so fidgety." Notwithstanding the pins in Joseph Schwartz's mouth and his thick Teutonic accent, Davide Nathan understood his tailor perfectly.

"Who wouldn't be? I'm a Jew, no? And you're a foreign Jew, so you should be even more worried. Did you read today's paper? Mussolini has heeded the calls of the Fascist press for more punitive measures against the Jews."

"Stay still, I'm almost finished—unless you want one leg shorter than the other," Schwartz grumped.

But an agitated Nathan continued. "All radios owned by Jews will be confiscated. Can you imagine? All Jewish bank accounts have been frozen. How will I get my money? How will you get your money?"

Schwartz stood up and stretched his legs, shaking out the stiffness in his knees from squatting. He took the pins out of his mouth. "I didn't put my money in the bank. I learned from my experiences in Vienna."

Nathan looked at his reflection in the full-length mirror, concluding that the tailor knew what he was doing. "So far, I've been lucky. When the racial laws required me to sell my wholesale textile business to a Gentile, I found a *goy* friend to whom I turned over the business. It is in his name but I still run it and keep the profits, less a five percent commission to him. But who knows? Several of my friends did the same thing and were kicked out by the new owners, who kept the businesses for themselves."

Schwartz bent down again, working on one cuff. "I'm glad I'm in a service business—I have nothing anyone wants—just my needles, thread and talents as a tailor. Listen to me, I know, it will get worse, a lot worse."

"And what we see is just the tip of the iceberg," Nathan added. "Now, Jews have been expelled from Sicily and Sardinia, as well as the mountain and seaside areas—they claim we are security risks. My father was a hero in the Great War, for God's sake!"

Schwartz slipped the jacket on Nathan. "Hmm, it doesn't look as if it needs much alteration."

"Have you heard anything I've just said?" Nathan asked in exasperation.

The tailor nodded. "Look, I have no plans to visit the mountains or seashore. But I can tell you this. The anti-Semites have short memories. My father also was a decorated and respected soldier—Austrian general—in the last war and it didn't help me one bit, not one bit. It won't help you either." He chalk-marked the shoulders.

"Schwartz, you should be more worried than the Italian Jews. They are threatening to take all foreign Jews into custody. You're like my brother, Attilio. He has three children and blithely insists everything will be all right."

Schwartz sighed. "Listen, my friend, I was worried about that long before this proclamation was issued today. That's why I moved my family to Rome and the ghetto. It is easier to get lost here, especially when they have no record of us in Rome. I'm on the list of no synagogue or Jewish organization."

Nathan picked up the newspaper and slapped it. "They are shutting down all Jewish organizations, even the charitable ones. The Union of Jewish Communities, which oversees all the Jewish organizations and synagogues in Italy, has been disbanded."

"What about that committee to help Jewish refugees?"

"COMASEBIT? It's gone too."

Schwartz shook his head. "That's the worst news I've heard today. Its representative in Rome, Settimio Sorani, has been trying to help me to get out of Europe." He shrugged. "I suppose I can live with the restrictions. I don't think they'll ever find me here in Rome. But I have one word of advice for you and other Italian Jews. If the Germans ever march in here, go into hiding. Don't wait, not even a day."

"Ah, Schwartz, it will never happen here. The Germans are our allies."

Schwartz frowned. "Forget that. They were saying the same thing in Austria."

Nathan looked at his tailor. "Have you had any word from your brother yet?"

"Not a peep. I don't know if he reached America. I just hope he wasn't on that torpedoed ship, the *Athenia*."

"Ah, that's not likely, Schwartz. You worry too much. With this war, I'm sure it's just the mails."

Early July, 1940, Genoa, Office of Attorney Lelio Valobra

The portly lawyer Lelio Vittorio Valobra looked out the window facing the busy port on the Gulf of Genoa. His secretary stuck her head in the door.

"They're here."

Valobra nodded. "Send them in, please."

He watched the Jewish leaders of the now defunct COMASEBIT file into the conference room for the emergency meeting he'd called: Bernard Grosser from Genoa and Raffaele Cantoni from Venice and Florence, and from Rome, Renzo Levi and Settimio Sorani. They all greeted Valobra warmly.

"Gentlemen," Valobra began, pacing around the room, his fingers firmly hooked into his suspenders, "we must reconstitute COMASEBIT. Its mission is too important, not only to the Jews of Italy but to Jews from all over Europe who are flooding into this area."

Grosser looked at Valobra. "What, precisely, does that mean? Why won't the government be just as hostile to a successor organization? Or are we going to go underground?"

Valobra paused, stopped pacing and flopped into a chair, formulating the answer in his mind. "Good questions, Grosser. My thought is to move the headquarters of COMASEBIT from Milan and set up the new organization here in Genoa."

Grosser nodded. "It certainly appears the Genoa has the most friendly-to-the-Jews police force here—they're highly sympathetic to our plight."

"My thought exactly," concurred Valobra. "Also, Genoa is a large entry point for Jews fleeing from German-occupied territory."

"It will be a lot easier if we don't have to operate underground," Sorani posited. "We are too widespread to coordinate everything we have to do if we have to act clandestinely."

Valobra stood up again and moved to the window, then turned back. "I have an idea. I think I can convince the Fascist government that it will benefit from the new organization since it will help relocate the thousands of foreign Jews that the Italian leaders don't want in this country. At the same time, through the Joint Distribution Committee in the United States, considerable foreign currency—American dollars—will flow into the country to assist these Jews. The government desperately needs foreign currency. I think they'll go for it, but only if Cantoni lies low and does not have any obvious connection to us."

"I know, I know, said Cantoni, waving his arms. "It was probably my anti-Fascist reputation the caused the government to close down COMASEBIT in the first place."

Sorani looked at him. "We still need your considerable skills, Cantoni, but they'll have to be behind the scenes."

Cantoni nodded. "It'll make life a lot safer both for both of us."

Valobra smiled. "Good. I propose to call the new entity DELASEM, the Delegation for Assistance to Jewish Emigrants."

Grosser smiled. "DELASEM? It has a nice ring to it."

CHAPTER SIX

November 11, 1940, Bay of Taranto

A British destroyer, several miles offshore to avoid detection, steamed past the inside of the heel of the Italian boot. The captain swept the area with his binoculars for the umpteenth time; he could find no Italian picket ships patrolling the approaches to the Bay of Taranto, where the cream of the Italian fleet rode peacefully at anchor. He preferred good old eyesight to that newly installed gismo, radar, which he didn't trust. The gadget had shown no blips indicating Italian ships at sea; it had to be wrong. The Italians would never leave the naval base unguarded like that.

The second-in-command joined the captain on the bridge. "Anything yet, Sir?"

The captain shook his head. "I'll be damned; the radar isn't lying. No ships out there patrolling. Admiral Cunningham should have a field day with that major concentration of ships in the harbor."

The second-in-command smiled. "I'm certainly glad the Eye-talians don't have radar. They'd be at battle stations by now."

Meanwhile, the British flagship, the aircraft carrier *H.M.S. Illustrious,* circled the Greek Island of Cephalonia, two hundred miles southeast of Taranto. Aboard, Admiral Sir Andrew B. Cunningham pored over the high-altitude reconnaissance photos taken by the speedy Martin Maryland aircraft, capable of outrunning the Italian Arrow fighters. The latest photos confirmed that the Italian fleet was still at anchor in the Taranto harbor—battleships, cruisers and destroyers. Cunningham knew that without radar, the Italians would

Improbable Heroes

not be aware of the presence of the British fleet two hundred miles away unless an Italian ship happened to spot it, and as far as he knew, that hadn't happened.

The planning hadn't been easy. Torpedoes had to be devised that would not run deep and thus bury themselves harmlessly in the mud in the shallow bottom of Taranto's harbor. The defenses at the base included dozens of antiaircraft batteries, barrage balloons, metal nets and powerful listening devices. The listening devices would pick up the drone of the attacking airplanes, which would be the first warning of the raid. Cunningham had thirty Farley Swordfish biplanes to launch. They were slow but highly reliable and capable of taking plenty of punishment. Moreover, it was highly unlikely they would encounter any Italian fighters, which did not fly at night. The Swordfish would go out in two waves, an hour apart. Two of the planes carried magnesium parachute flares to illuminate the harbor for the attackers.

As the sun set, Admiral Cunningham ordered Captain Dennis Boyd, commander of the *Illustrious,* to prepare for the attack, to commence at 2100 hours.

Shortly before the attack hour, the *Illustrious* and several escorting cruisers and destroyers began turning slowly into the wind. The carrier launched the first wave of Swordfish, armed with either 18-inch Mark XII torpedoes or bombs.

□□□

Italian admiral, Arturo Riccardi, looked with dismay at the sight in the harbor. He'd had warning of the approach of the enemy aircraft from his massive sound-detection equipment. His frantic calls to his counterparts in the air force were to no avail. They refused to send up interceptors at night. The antiaircraft batteries were not very effective, shooting down only two of the dozens of slow-flying attacking aircraft. The battleship *Conte de Cavour*, hit by one damn torpedo, had sunk and settled onto the bottom of the harbor with only its big guns and superstructure showing, blocking much of the harbor channel. Neither the *Littorio,* struck by three torpedoes, nor the *Ciao Duilio,* hit by one torpedo, had sunk, but they were damaged so badly they had to be grounded in the shallows.

Riccardi knew he'd have to raise the *Cavour* and, together with the *Littorio* and the *Duilio,* repair and refit them to fight another day. He sighed. Though there was not much he could do considering the sorry state of Italian preparedness and the interservice rivalries, he'd be lucky not to be imprisoned by the Duce. Riccardi telephoned his staff officer. "Get our best salvage expert here right away. We have to clear the harbor and get these ships back in action before summer!"

"Admiral?"

"Yes, what is it?"

"There is only one person capable of doing all that in the time you require."

"Well, who is it? Order him to Taranto—immediately!"

Silence at the other end of the line.

"What?" the admiral grumbled.

"Sir, that will be difficult. The person is . . . former Inspector General of the Navy Umberto Pugliese. You remember, the one the Duce fired because he was a Jew."

"*Marronne*," the admiral groaned, then mumbled, half under his breath, "The idiot."

"What was that, Sir?"

"Nothing. Nothing." The admiral hung up, thought a minute, then telephoned the minister of the navy.

Same Day, Early Afternoon, Rome, Apartment of Umberto Pugliese

Pugliese sank down in his favorite chair. He'd had too much to drink for lunch and he wasn't used to it. It had been, however, a welcome diversion from the boredom he had been experiencing since being dismissed from active service.

The ex-admiral enjoyed having lunch company, a rare treat these days, and he welcomed the invitation to dine with Renzo Levi and Settimio Sorani, two Jewish activists in Rome. They'd been anxious, it turned out, to recruit him for DELASEM, to help Jews to emigrate. A person of his stature, they said, would give the organization a big boost in morale. He had objected that he was just a military man and not into politics. But, they had pointed out, there was no escaping that he was also a Jew.

He had told them he would think about it, but if the truth were known, he really did not want to get involved in such activities. His interest and passion was quite narrow—the military. If he couldn't do that, well . . .

The telephone rang, interrupting his train of thought.

"*Ciao.*"

It was the minister of the navy. Would the admiral be home for the next hour? Pugliese acknowledged that he would be. Then the minister would be right over.

That puzzled Pugliese. He'd heard from none of his naval cronies, including some close friends, since being unceremoniously cashiered by the minister, as if he had a highly communicable disease. Now, all of a sudden, the minister himself wanted to see him. He wondered if they'd seen the error of their ways. He shook his head. Not likely, he thought. He gave up trying to speculate and devoted his energies to straightening up his living room for the distinguished visitor.

Twenty minutes later the bell rang. The minister of the navy stood at the door.

"Come in, come in, Minister. This is quite an honor."

The minister smiled. "I truly wondered whether I'd be welcomed here after . . ."

"I hold no grudge. I know who caused me to be dismissed, and it was no one from the navy. But tell me, to what do I owe this visit?"

"I'll get straight to the point, Admiral."

Pugliese's eyes widened as the minister addressed him by his former rank. "That's always the best way, Minister."

"I am here, hat in hand, because we need you back. We've had a disaster of catastrophic proportions at the Bay of Taranto. While our ships were at anchor, the British launched a surprise attack. Their torpedo planes sunk the *Cavour* and badly damaged the *Littorio* and other ships."

Pugliese shook his head sadly. "I designed and built the *Littorio*, you know," he said softly. Then in a louder voice, "How in heaven's name could the British have gotten in so close without being detected?

The *Littorio*'s big guns should have been able to rain destruction on the enemy ships miles from the harbor!"

"We are looking into that now—heads will probably roll. We returned fire with our shore and ship antiaircraft batteries. But that is for later consideration. We have more pressing problems. The pride of our fleet is now a scrap heap in the bottom of the bay. Right now we need someone able to raise the *Cavour*, refloat and refit it and repair the other badly damaged ships that were not sunk. You are the only one who can restore the fleet and clear the harbor."

Pugliese, looked at the ceiling, deep in thought. Then he looked across at the minister. "Very well, I will assume the responsibility."

The minister smiled. "Wonderful, Admiral. How much do you want for the job?"

Pugliese's forehead creased in anger. "I won't do this for money. I am, and always will be, a loyal and patriotic Italian military officer. I only require the cost of transportation to Taranto and return."

"Well, we'll certainly pay your living expenses in Taranto."

"Thank you, Minister, but no, all I require is transportation."

The minister shook his hand vigorously. "Thank you, Admiral Pugliese, the nation owes you a debt."

Pugliese said nothing. He simply shrugged.

When the minister departed, Pugliese went to the bedroom and found his white admiral's uniform, for a long time hanging mute and unused in the closet. He took it out, carefully and lovingly. He removed the protective cover, shook out the mothballs and checked the garment—it was spotlessly clean. Satisfied, he donned the dress uniform, the jacket emblazoned on the chest with the myriad of colorful awards and medals he'd accumulated over the years of his naval career. He stood ramrod straight and looked himself over in the mirror. Seeing himself in uniform again felt good. The image pleased him. He'd kept in good physical shape and the uniform fit as well today as the day he left the navy. He would not wear civilian clothes again until his tasks were completed. He knew that once the job was done he'd not be welcomed back to the navy. But that didn't matter. He'd do his duty. He pulled down an old, battered suitcase and began packing.

November 14, 1940, Taranto, Office of Admiral Riccardi

Lieutenant Takeshi Naito, the Japanese assistant air attaché in Berlin, introduced himself to Admiral Riccardi. The admiral did not have time for such visitors, but since Japan was an ally, he listened politely and answered the lieutenant's questions concerning the British attack, depth and size of the harbor and the ability of the British to use, so effectively, torpedoes in the shallow water.

Riccardi wondered at the Japanese interest in an event so far from the Pacific, but he didn't dwell on it. He had too much work to do.

November 20, 1940, Tokyo, Office of Admiral Yamamoto

Six days later, Admiral Isoroku Yamamoto reviewed Lieutenant Naito's meticulous notes again. He smiled and silently thanked the British. For years, Yamamoto had planned and proposed an attack on the United States naval base at Pearl Harbor in Hawaii. He considered that to go to war with the United States, as his superiors were determined to do, was unwise, but if it was to have any chance of success, Japan would have to knock out the American fleet in the Pacific right at the beginning. Pearl Harbor presented such an opportunity, but he'd been unable to convince his superiors of its feasibility.

If the British could successfully launch torpedoes in shallow harbor waters, the Japanese could find a way to do it also. Japanese planes, he knew, were vastly superior to the antiquated Swordfish, and the navy could mount an attack with ten times the number of aircraft. The harbor at Taranto was not dissimilar to Pearl Harbor, and if the British could do it against an enemy with which it was already at war and which was on its guard, surely Japan would have even greater chances of success against a country at peace, with few defenses manned, especially on Sunday mornings. He put down Lieutenant Naito's report. Now he had the ammunition to convince his superiors that if they insisted on war, a surprise attack on Pearl Harbor was both feasible and imperative.

June 21, 1941, Taranto, Office of Admiral Riccardi

From the window, Admiral Riccardi looked over his command, floating in the Bay of Taranto. Pugliese stood next to him, watching the *Cavour* steam out of the harbor, refitted and on her shakedown cruise. The *Littorio* and the *Ciao Duilio* had left the same harbor two months earlier, ready for combat.

The admiral looked at Pugliese. "Inspector, no one else could have accomplished what you have done in just eight months. The Italian Navy owes you an immense debt of gratitude. Indeed, all of Italy does."

Pugliese made a deprecating gesture, not turning to the admiral, but preferring to watch the *Cavour* make its way out to the open sea. "It was nothing, Admiral, just doing my duty."

"Nothing, you say? My God, man, when I looked at those destroyed ships, I thought there was no way they'd ever fight for Italy again. But here we are, just eight months later, restored to the position we were in before the British attack. I'm sure our grateful nation will amply reward you for your heroic efforts."

Now Pugliese turned and faced Riccardi. "Apparently, being a Jew did not affect my ability to do something you superior 'Aryans' could not."

"Inspector, you know I don't believe all that garbage. No one in the fleet really does."

Pugliese's gaze bore into the admiral. "That doesn't mean much to me, unless, of course, you are saying I can return to active duty?"

Riccardi, frowning, bit his lips. "You know I can't do that. I'd be violating the law—and the orders of Il Duce."

"That's what I thought," Pugliese said with some venom. "I require no rewards for my service—except to be left in peace in my exile."

"But Inspector . . ."

Pugliese picked up his suitcase and stalked out of the office, and headed for the railway station.

□□□

Ex-Admiral Umberto Pugliese arrived back in Rome later that day. In his apartment he put down his suitcase, walked over to the full-length mirror and looked at himself, resplendent in his admiral's uniform. He thought of all the Jewish military officers, including admirals and generals, whose numbers were well out of proportion to the Jewish population in Italy, all unceremoniously fired, even those awarded Italy's highest medals for valor and heroism. He shucked his jacket and removed the rest of his uniform. Gathering up the garments with loving care, he took them to the closet. He hung them on hangers, seeing that all creases were properly maintained. He ran his hand gently over the cloth of the jacket one last time, then slipped on its protective cover, sliding the uniform to the back of the closet.

Still in his underwear, he looked over his civilian clothes, indecisive as to what to wear. He wouldn't choose now. Instead, he stretched out on the bed for a nap—but sleep would not come.

CHAPTER SEVEN

June 23, 1941, Genoa, the Office of Cardinal Boetto

After a lengthy debate at DELASEM, the directors had decided that the best person to approach in the Catholic hierarchy was Pietro Cardinal Boetto, archbishop of Genoa. There were good reasons for DELASEM's choice: Pope Pius XI had promoted Boetto on April 24, 1938 to archbishop. A Jesuit known for his anti-Fascist sentiments, Boetto had received the appointment to provide leadership in the Catholic Church at a time when Hitler was beginning to be more of an influence in Italy. Pius XI had the reputation of being a staunch opponent of Germany's racial policies and reported atrocities. Boetto, it was said, had the qualifications and outlook the pontiff wanted in a man in that position. With the German invasion of the Soviet Union, joined by 250,000 Italian troops sent by Mussolini, DELASEM had decided the time was ripe to explore enlisting the assistance of non-Jews ready and willing to assume the functions of DELASEM if and when its Jewish leaders were no longer able to act. DELASEM expected a large increase of refugees from a new group—Soviet Jews now fleeing the Germans.

Accordingly, on this June morning, Don Francesco Repetto ushered Lelio Valobra and two other DELASEM directors, Raffaele Cantoni and Settimio Sorani, into the resplendent Archbishop's Palace in the shadow of the medieval Cathedral of San Lorenzo and then to the office of Cardinal Boetto. The cardinal motioned his guests and Repetto to chairs around a low table and joined them. "You are most welcome, gentlemen. What can I do for you?"

"We seek your help, Eminence," Valobra began. "With the increasingly restrictive racial laws in Italy, it's becoming more difficult for our organization, DELASEM, to help Italian Jews to emigrate to countries not under the heel of the Germans, or threatened by them. We have also assumed responsibility for aiding foreign Jews—those from Poland and other German-occupied territories—to escape Europe. Now, we have them coming from Russia as well. For the present at least, we can provide funding, which comes from various relief agencies in the United States."

Boetto paused before answering. He stared down at the thick carpet and fingered his large crucifix. His guests waited. Finally he looked up. "I pledge you my wholehearted support. I believe we can arrange sanctuaries for those poor people, if that becomes necessary. What kind of assistance do you provide to the refugees now?"

Valobra glanced at Sorani, who nodded imperceptibly. "We provide false documents to hide their Jewish identity, help them cross into Switzerland, find them ships heading for Palestine and obtain guides to sneak them out of Poland, France and other occupied territories and into—or out of—Italy. Things like that. Your Eminence, even baptized Jews . . ."

The cardinal put up his hand. "Signore Valobra, we will help whether or not the Jews are baptized. It is our God-given duty to do so."

"We are overwhelmed by your generosity," Cantoni said. "While we can still function, we had hoped to set up a liaison with your office to acquaint whomever you appoint with our operations."

Boetto nodded. "By all means. I had a feeling that's what you needed. That's why I invited Father Repetto to sit in today. He will be my representative, with instructions to give you whatever assistance you require. We can provide some funds, as well. To start, we can put five million lire at Father Repetto's disposal."

□□□

After Repetto had shown the appreciative visitors out, Cardinal Boetto called him back into his office. The priest stood in front of the archbishop's desk, his hands folded behind his back.

"Sit, sit, Father."

Repetto took a seat. "Your Eminence, these people approached me and asked for an audience with you. I . . ."

"You did the right thing, Don Francesco. As long as a year ago, I received reports from Italian officers on the Eastern Front of the terrible things they had witnessed in Poland, Russia and Yugoslavia. These Jews are innocents and in real danger. We must help them at whatever cost to ourselves."

"Thank you, Your Eminence."

"No thanks are necessary for involving me in this project. But to extend *effective* help to these poor people we must expand our efforts beyond Genoa."

"I certainly agree, Your Eminence. What do you have in mind?"

"I'm going to send you, as my emissary, to enlist the efforts of Cardinal Dalla Costa in Florence, Cardinal Schuster in Milan and Cardinal Fossati in Turin. I know these prelates are highly sympathetic to the agonies of the Jewish people; I'm sure they'll help any way they can."

"That seems to be a good start," Repetto replied. "I could learn a lot from Father Benedetto in Marseilles. He's been a whirlwind, helping Jews in occupied France, supplying them with false identity papers, hiding them with the Capuchin friars in Marseilles and assisting hundreds to escape into Spain or Switzerland."

"Then do it." The cardinal's eyes momentarily misted. He sat quiet for a few moments and then he looked at Repetto. "How could they? How could the people of Germany, a country with so many Catholics, permit acts of such unparalleled depravity? Sodom and Gomorra all over again. We should be thankful that God has revealed to us our divine Christian mission. We can no more let the Jews down than we can let Him down."

Repetto nodded. "I felt God's calling for this mission, too, Your Eminence." He paused, looking at the cardinal. "I may be out of place to ask but . . ." Again, he paused.

Boetto looked at the priest questioningly. "Please, Don Francesco, if you have something on your mind, let me hear it."

Repetto looked down at his highly polished shoes then back at the cardinal. He took a deep breath. "Do you plan to discuss this project with the Holy Father."

Cardinal Boetto's face briefly flashed a frown. "Not yet, Don Repetto, not just yet. When I decide it is necessary, he will know."

July 11, 1941, Rome, Palazzo Venezia, Mussolini's Office

Ciano waved the requested document at the Duce during their usual morning meeting. "I have the report. British Wellington bombers have stuck Naples again. There has been a serious loss of civilian life and considerable damage has been done to our refineries and fuel storage depots. We lost at least six thousand tons of fuel oil."

Mussolini smiled. "I am not too disturbed. It is a good thing that Naples is having such severe war experiences. The bombings will harden the citizens; it will make the Neapolitans a Nordic race."

Ciano thought about the promise that Il Duce had conveniently forgotten, his promise to the people that bombs would never fall on Italy. The foreign minister wanted to express his outrage at such callousness but thought better of it. It wouldn't move the stubborn old goat, anyway. Without commenting, he continued. "False air raid alarms in Rome are wreaking havoc on the economy and the nerves of the citizens. The Rome air defense officials have asked for a cancellation of your order that the alarms in the capital be set off every time there is an alarm in Naples. The comments on the street are quite negative."

Mussolini stood up. "Absolutely not!" he roared. "The Romans are shamefully soft and cowardly. They must be given the impression there's a war on. I am issuing another order: After the alarms go off, the anti-aircraft gunners, at the first opportunity, should fire in order to make things more interesting." He stood there, arms folded across his chest, chin jutting out, challenging his foreign minister to object.

Ciano merely shrugged. "One more thing, Duce. There is news on the Eastern Front. The Axis forces are advancing on Leningrad, Moscow and Kiev but at a very heavy price in casualties."

Mussolini sat down heavily. "This is war. We can't get away from casualties, so Italians will have to get used to it. I am sick of negative comments about the war in our own press. It must stop!" He picked up a newspaper from his desk and slapped it. "Here's an article by someone named Ansaldo that refers to the war in Russia . . ." scanning the newspaper page and finding the offending passage, " '. . . as under the direction of Hitler.' "

The Duce tossed the newspaper at Ciano. The foreign minister picked it up off the carpet.

Mussolini leaned back in his chair. "Because of such tripe, the Italian people are beginning to believe that it is only Hitler who directs the war." He raised his voice and waved his arms. "This is unacceptable. Do they think we are playing tiddlywinks in Russia? I want Pavolini to get rid of that journalist!"

As secretary of the Fascist Party, Alessandro Pavolini was technically second in command in the Italian government. Ciano looked upon Pavolini as a thug who believed in fierce retaliation against anti-Fascists. Pavolini had created his own independent militia, the Republican Guard, which visited violence on Italian citizens, acting under its own rules. Thanks to the Duce, the militia was not answerable to the courts. Squads, funded by the government, ran protection rackets, private prisons and torture chambers. Mussolini did not want to seem weak, so he turned a blind eye to such excesses. Well, Ciano would be damned if he'd tell Pavolini. Ansaldo would lose not only his job but in likelihood his life. Ciano didn't need that on his conscience.

August 12, 1941, Marseilles, the Capuchin Friary

Father Pierre-Marie Benoît, a French national, had lived for many years in the Capuchin friary in Rome, where he was known as Father Benedetto. He'd returned to his homeland in 1940, when war with Germany was imminent, and entered the Capuchin community in Marseilles. The slight, balding, Father Benedetto greeted the much taller Don Francesco Repetto and led him to the rear of the small chapel, where they could escape the clusters of people who seemed to be everywhere. The French friar motioned his guest to sit next to him in the rear-most pew. Father Benedetto hiked up his robe slightly as he sat down. His mild exterior hid his passion and courage—Father Benedetto, the fearless, innovative fighter for the oppressed. Now, the oppressed were the Jews in France.

The friar smiled, "It is good to see you, Don Francesco. What brings you to Marseilles during these turbulent times?"

The cardinal's emissary looked grave. "I'm afraid that Italy will be going the way of the rest of Europe. Some Jewish leaders, in anticipation, have asked our assistance should they have to go underground. I know you have had experience helping the Jews to blend into the local population or to escape to friendlier countries. Angelo Donati, a Jewish leader in Rome, urged me to see you."

Benedetto nodded. "I know him well. As you are aware, after France's surrender last year, the Germans occupied the northern half of the country and the Vichy government, sympathetic to the Nazis, controlled the south. That's why I returned to Marseilles. Sure enough, Vichy officials enacted anti-Jewish legislation, similar to that of the Third Reich. While Jews flowed in here, fleeing not only from the north of France but from other occupied territories and from Germany itself, the Vichy government began arresting and incarcerating foreign Jews. By the end of 1940, some thirty thousand foreign Jews had been arrested in Vichy, France, more than had been arrested in the north under the Germans."

Repetto looked intently at Benedetto. "What are some of the things you were able to do?"

"We procured false identification papers for Jews, printed thousands of baptismal certificates for distribution, found hiding places for them in small pensions and hotels and cultivated some Vichy officials we thought might be sympathetic. Other Jews, we smuggled out to Spain or Switzerland with the help of friendly or bribed border guards."

Repetto nodded. "Yes, these are precisely the kinds of activities I have to learn about."

The friar chuckled. "Have you seen our peaceful friary now? It's become a madhouse. That is why I retreat to this small chapel. The whole place is teeming with people, day and night, seeking to escape from the Vichy and German governments. But it will get worse before it gets better. The Germans will occupy southern France very soon—of that I have no doubt. Eventually, I'll have to leave, or more likely, escape France and return to Rome. The Germans are as unmerciful to clergy that they suspect are helping the Jews, as they are to the Jews themselves. You must be careful, Don Francesco."

"The Italians aren't like the Germans; they wouldn't dare to arrest the clergy," the priest replied.

"You are probably right," Father Benedetto agreed, "but I was thinking more of the Germans. Eventually, they'll be in Rome unless they are stopped by the Western democracies—and I doubt that Britain is strong enough to do that."

August 1941, Karlovac, Croatia

When the Divis family, fleeing Prague in 1939, arrived in Karlovac, it was a Yugoslav city. Though lacking a license to practice medicine in Yugoslavia, Divis treated patients in his neighborhood. The closest licensed doctor was several miles away, so people were only too glad to avail themselves of the Czech doctor's services, license or no license. The Yugoslav authorities looked the other way, so Divis was able to make a modest living.

But in April 1941, Germany and Italy attacked the Yugoslavs. At the same time, Croatia proclaimed itself an independent state. The new Croatian government had Hitler's support and blessing—and with good reason. The Croats were staunchly anti-Serbian and anti-Semitic—indeed they hated the Jews more than the Germans did, if that was possible. And the City of Karlovac became part of the new Croatia. The new Croatian government terrified Divis. Ante Pavelic, the head of the government, and his henchmen in the Ustaše Party were a violent and brutal lot. It did not take them long to start slaughtering Serbs living in Croatia. Divis heard that in one village, the Ustaše had forced hundreds of Serbs to dig long ditches and then had buried them alive; in other villages the Ustaše had cut the Serb's throats or killed them with axes. Terrible, terrible people, Divis thought.

Divis knew his days as a Jew in Croatia were numbered. Only the fact that Karlovac was occupied by Italian troops, he felt, offered them some measure of protection. But the Ustaše were growing bolder each day and had begun to attack the Jews in the city. The

Italian commander, General Mario Roatta, had assured the Jews they would be safe. Nevertheless, Divis thought about leaving with his family. That would be difficult with the Croats in power. He berated himself for not anticipating this development and leaving while there was still a Yugoslavia.

December 8, 1941, Rome, Palazzo Venezia, Mussolini's Office

Ciano arrived promptly for his daily ten o'clock morning briefing for the Duce. As usual, there were few papers on the desk. Mussolini's office was a tribute to neatness and order. Mussolini wasted no time with greetings. "Minister, the Japanese have attacked the Americans at Hawaii, as they had promised last week.'

Ciano nodded. "I heard," he said without much enthusiasm.

"I spoke to Hitler and he is not quite sure what to do—but I told him Italy will declare war on the United States today. I will show the führer who's the one with balls!"

Ciano's stared in surprise. "Is that wise, Duce?"

"Ah, the Americans are basically a stupid people," declared Mussolini, waving away Ciano's concern. "This is a wonderful opportunity for us to become a major player at any peace settlement. America's supposed industrial potential is all their own journalistic daydreaming. I have called for a rally this afternoon. I will announce the declaration of war from the balcony."

"Excuse me, Duce, but wouldn't it be wise first to consult with your military advisers?"

"I don't need their advice. I am the best judge of what is good for this country! We shall fight the Americans and teach that paralytic Roosevelt a good lesson!"

CHAPTER EIGHT

January 24, 1942, Mid-Afternoon, Rome, Vatican Gardens
Every afternoon, after lunch and a brief nap, Pope Pius XII strolled through the Vatican gardens alone, either deep in contemplation or reading documents. During this period, the gardens were cleared of all personnel, including gardeners, security guards and any others who had reason to work there. The only other person present, Mario Stoppa, the pope's chauffeur, followed behind him carrying a briefcase in the event the pontiff wished to retrieve information. Midway through the walk, a surprised Stoppa found Cardinal Secretary of State Maglione beside him, matching his steps, stride for stride. The pontiff, deep in concentration, appeared unaware of the cardinal's presence.

"Your Holiness," Maglione said softly.

The pope stiffened as if hit with a jolt of electricity. He turned, his sharp, thin features even more severely accentuated by the expression of annoyance. Stoppa, extending his arms and shrugging, silently signaling his innocence at this unheard-of interruption.

The cardinal bowed slightly. "Please forgive the intrusion, Holiness, but there is late-breaking news that may be important to your contemplations."

The pope nodded, but his facial expression did not soften. "Go ahead, Eminence."

"BBC reports that Roosevelt and Churchill, at the conclusion of the Casablanca conference, announced that the Allies will accept nothing short of an 'unconditional surrender' from Germany, Italy and Japan."

The pontiff shook his head; his expression changed now—from annoyance to disgust. "Here I am, trying to arrange a peace settlement between the Soviet Union and Germany and they come up with this mindless formula. No one will ever convince Hitler to surrender unconditionally." The pope held up one of the papers he'd been reading. "The Russians are pushing back the Wehrmacht on all fronts. Germany must remain viable to hold the frontiers against those from the East. We must encourage peace for the survival of our Christian culture in Europe. Somehow, there must eventually be a German-American alliance against the Soviet Union."

"Perhaps it's simply Allied propaganda," Maglione offered.

"Of course this Casablanca nonsense is stupid propaganda, but in wartime, such propaganda often takes on a life of its own. All these primitive demands will do is to force Germans to identify even more intensely with Hitler; they will encourage his fanaticism, and prolong this hideous war. You must contact Roosevelt's representative in Rome and explain what we are trying to do. Get them to modify that ridiculous ultimatum. That will be all."

The pope turned his back on the cardinal and continued his walk. Stoppa followed his master.

□□□

Work and prayer took up the pope's evenings. After dining alone for supper and then saying the Rosary with the sisters in his private chapel, Pius would often work into the early morning hours, until he cleared his desk. Sometimes he met with his cardinal secretary of state if something urgent arose. This, it turned out, was just such an evening. The pope waved Cardinal Maglione to a chair next to his desk. "Have you spoken to the Americans, Eminence?" Maglione nodded. "I met with Roosevelt's personal representative, Myron Taylor. I told him about the possibility of German peace feelers and the importance of containing the Bolsheviks. He was very unsympathetic, to put it mildly. 'The Americans,' he said, 'will continue to demand an unconditional surrender.' Taylor told me the Holy See must cease to entertain any idea of a negotiated settlement."

The pontiff frowned. "I am not surprised. Roosevelt keeps the passions of the Americans stoked to the boiling point. This is but one way to do it. We shall have to pray more fervently for the Lord to show the Allies—and us—the way to peace."

June 10, 1942, Genoa, Offices of Attorney Lelio Valobra

Valobra looked over his guests, Don Francesco Repetto and a group of DELASEM leaders from various cities in northern Italy and Rome. He especially wanted Repetto kept updated when the time came that he had to run DELASEM. The stout lawyer paced around the room. "Gentlemen, if you thought things couldn't possibly get worse, you were wrong. Signore Grosser, please tell us what you found out in Switzerland."

Bernard Grosser, a large but not obese businessman, opened his briefcase and pulled out a sheaf of notes. "Our contact in Berne, Richard Lichtheim, the head of the Jewish Agency office there, told me that the Swiss authorities in Berne have now decided to stop the influx of refugees . . ."

"That's the euphemism for Jews, isn't it?" Rome's representative, Settimio Sorani, interjected.

Grosser turned his head to glance at Sorani. "Exactly. Now, as I was saying, the Swiss have decided to stop the Jews from coming into their country. Worse, they've started to send back those who have arrived in the last few weeks. You can imagine what it means to those poor Jews, especially the German ones who are forced back into the Third Reich."

Raffaele Cantoni, from Florence, cradled his head in his two hands. "My God, Grosser, that's tantamount to a death sentence. Don't the Swiss know that?"

"Of course they do," Grosser replied. "But they don't care. After all, they're only dealing with Jews. The Jews were led to the frontier and forced to cross over the border into Germany. While they were not literally handed over to the Gestapo, they may as well have been. Nobody knows what happened to them."

"They're in Auschwitz, that's what," Cantoni retorted.

Improbable Heroes

Valobra nodded. "It will also mean we'll have to change the way we operate in Italy. They'll also turn back the Jews we send over."

Repetto spoke up. "Then we'll have to do it clandestinely, with false passports and manufactured baptism certificates. We can learn from Father Benedetto, in Marseilles."

Several DELASEM members looked up in surprise. The priest smiled. "After our meeting last year, your Angelo Donati introduced me to the friar in Marseilles who has an efficient operation to smuggle Jews out of southern France. Cardinal Boetto had suggested I see him. Father Benedetto showed me his operation, dealing with false papers, hiding places, bribed local officials and border guards—quite an elaborate setup."

"We may be calling on your new expertise sooner than we thought," said Sorani, shaking his head. "This Swiss action couldn't have come at a worse time. The Germans have increased the rate of deportations to the concentration camps, the Croats have begun to round up Jews and hand them over to the Germans—or simply take it upon themselves to slaughter them. The Ustaše are a nasty bunch. Lord knows how many tens of thousands of Serbs they've butchered already. Now, it's the Jews' turn. There's been a tremendous increase in the number of refugees fleeing to Italy."

"We have a printing press in the basement of the Archbishop's Palace," Repetto offered. "I'll start running off false baptismal certificates."

"Thanks, Father, that's far more than we ever expected," Valobra said.

"No thanks are necessary. I'm duty-bound. God has shown me my sacred mission—I intend to do everything in my power to carry it out."

"Amen, Father, amen," someone from the group volunteered.

June 13, 1942, Rome, Office of the Foreign Minister

Foreign Minister Ciano read the brief diplomatic note handed to him by his visitor, Prince Otto von Bismarck, second in command at the German Embassy. The German government was requesting the Italian Army to turn over all Jews in its zone of occupation in Croatia. Bismarck sat there waiting for the Italian foreign minister to finish reading the note. From previous conversations with the German prince, the slim, smartly dressed grandson of the famous Bismarck, Ciano knew that he secretly opposed Hitler's policy toward the Jews. Ciano and Bismarck had been scheming for months to get Berlin to swallow one postponement after another on action against the Italian Jews. Fortunately, the prince seemed to have a talent for putting things to Berlin in a convincing way. Ciano put down the diplomatic note. "What will happen to the Jews if we turn them over?"

Bismarck shrugged and offered the official German line. "They will be sent to labor camps?"

Ciano noted that the reply came out as a question instead of an affirmative statement. "We know better than that, Prince."

Bismarck sighed, "They will be liquidated—but you didn't hear it from me," he said, barely above a whisper.

An Hour Later, Rome, Palazzo Venezia, Mussolini's Office

Mussolini read the German diplomatic note and handed it back to his foreign minister. Before coming over to Palazzo Venezia, Ciano had checked again with the head of Italian Intelligence in Croatia, General Giuseppe Pièche. Pièche had reported that the Germans had stepped up their campaign to liquidate the Jews, and at a top-level meeting in Berlin, the Nazis had given a secret name to the program—the Final Solution. Ciano's eyes met those of the dictator. "You are not going to honor this request, are you, Duce? You know what they'll do to the Jews."

Mussolini spread out his hands. "What can I do? They are our allies and we are at war. I cannot openly defy Hitler. When Himmler visited me earlier this year, he was ranting about how the Italians were not requiring Jews to wear yellow stars and how we were not putting them in concentration camps. I reminded Herr Himmler that Hitler had agreed to leave Italian Jews alone; that they were our internal concern. I was not about to let Italians be murdered. But this is different—these are Croatian, not Italian Jews."

"Duce, they will be killed. You can't order our troops to turn them over to the Croatians."

Mussolini rubbed his chin, staying quiet for over a minute. He took the note and scribbled on it, handing it back to Ciano. The foreign minister read the annotation, *"nulla osta,"* ("I have nothing against this").

Mussolini waved at the document in Ciano's hand. "Send it on just like that to the commanders of the Second Army in Croatia. I have not put this in the form of an order. That will permit them to use their own discretion."

June 22, 1942, Croatia, Headquarters of the Italian Second Army

General Mario Roatta, commander of Italian forces in Yugoslavia and Croatia, waving a paper in the air, sputtered. One of his field commanders, General Vittorio Ambrosio, had never seen his boss so angry. "I have never received such a. . . .a . . ." Roatta finally handed Ambrosio the paper he had such difficulty characterizing.

Ambrosio scanned the diplomatic note from the German Foreign Ministry asking that all Jews in the Italian zone be turned over to the Croats. He saw the hand-written *"nulla osta."* "Mussolini's writing?"

Roatta nodded.

Ambrosio threw the paper on the table. "I'll be damned if I will order my men to become Germany's executioners—because that's what we'll be if we turn them over to the Ustaše; they'll be killed within a day's time or turned over to the Germans for 'deportation' where, General Pièche reports, they'll suffer the same fate. Did you know that the Germans are paying the Croats for each Jew they deliver—dead or alive?"

Roatta frowned. "Yes, I've seen Pièche's intelligence reports.'

"When we came into Croatia and Yugoslavia," Ambrosio grumbled, "we guaranteed the people—and that included the Jews—their safety, their liberty and their property. As far as I am concerned, that promise became the sacred oath of the Second Army. Handing over the Jews would be a violation of our word of honor with damaging repercussions to those who have put their trust in us. I, for one, won't be a party to it."

"Nor would I expect you to be," grunted his superior. It is I who guaranteed the Jews protection and Pièche's reports amply demonstrate what will happen to them if we turn them over to the Croats." He paused, rubbing his forehead. "As far as this diplomatic note is concerned, I don't consider Il Duce's written statement an order so I don't have to confront disobeying him."

"What do you suggest we do?" Ambrosio asked. "I have already had complaints from the German ambassador in Zagreb and his demands that we round up and turn over our Jews. I told him that until we knew something of the nationality of the Jews under our control, we could do nothing, because it is possible that many of those Jews may be Italian citizens. As the ambassador knows, Hitler has agreed with Mussolini to leave the Italian Jews alone, even those in Germany."

Ambrosio frowned. "How will that help? Are there any Italian citizens living in Croatia?"

Roatta smiled. "I engaged in a little bit of historical re-engineering—I asked Professor Tommaso Perassi, Italy's great expert on international law, to come up with reasons why Croatians may be Italian citizens. After all, this territory at various times has been under our control. He provided five or six reasons."

"For example?" Ambrosio challenged.

"Well, any Serb or Croat who has performed beneficial actions for the Italian State, such as giving any sort of assistance to our soldiers in battle, could be deemed an Italian citizen; those born when Croatia was under our control are clearly Italian citizens. "Unless and until we can sort this all out," Roatta continued, "we cannot begin to consider turning over Jews who may be Italian citizens. Anyway, that's what I told the German ambassador." The slightest grin formed in the corners of his mouth.

"The reasoning seems a bit thin."

Now Roatta laughed. "Perhaps. And perhaps it's my way of telling the German ambassador to go to hell—politely, of course. In any event, our orders to the troops to help the Jews still stand. To the extent we can help the Jews get out of Croatia, for those Jews at least, our problem is solved. Don't you agree?"

Without waiting for a response to his rhetorical question, Roatta stood up and moved to the large wall map of the Balkans. "Let's start by seeing if we can move all the Jews on the Adriatic coast out of Croatia and into Italy." He tapped with his finger on the Gulf of Kvarner. "The closest spot is here, the island of Arbe, just off the northern coast on the Adriatic. It is the closest island to the mainland and we alone control it. I wouldn't put anything past those Germans, so moving them out should obviate any danger of a surprise attack on the Jews."

Ambrosio nodded. "Very good, Sir. Then we are singing from the same page. What about the Ustaše order for all Jews to turn themselves in for deportation?"

"I have countermanded it in our zone of occupation."

July 8, 1942, Karlovac, Croatia

Lev Divis recognized trouble when he heard it. The sharp banging on his door one evening portended only one thing—the Ustaše. Last week, they'd begun rounding up Jews in Karlovac for deportation, notwithstanding the presence of Italian troops. He opened the door. A Ustaše officer and several soldiers pushed their way into the apartment. "According to our records, you have a wife, Zophie, and a daughter, Bela." The officer did not wait for confirmation. "You will pack one suitcase each, ready to be picked up in a few hours. There had better be three of you. Anyone attempting to leave this building will be shot. You have been warned." He turned on his heel and stomped out, followed by the soldiers.

Divis looked out of the window. There were two Ustaše guards with weapons stationed outside. He was sure they'd also be guarding the rear entrance. "After getting this far, to be caught . . ." He shook his head.

Zophie put her hand gently on his arm. "It's not your fault, Lev."

Angrily, he threw off her hand. "Of course it is. I was stupid. I thought the Italian soldiers would protect us. We could have left before this happened." He let out a long sigh. "Now, there is no escape—none at all."

☐☐☐

After midnight, the Ustaše showed up. Without asking the Divis family to leave, they started to drag them out of their apartment. Luigi Supino, an Italian colonel who lived next door, came out of his apartment to check on the noise. "What is going on here, Captain?"

"None of your concern, Colonel. We are only taking Jews away—and assisting your ally, Germany."

The colonel stepped up to the Ustaše officer, their faces a few inches apart. "Get your men out of here. No one in this family is going away with you! These are my friends."

The captain backed up a few steps, but Colonel Supino simply matched his movements and remained face-to-face with him. "But Colonel," the Croat protested, "I have my orders."

"Perhaps I haven't made myself clear," Supino said in a low threatening voice. "I don't give a damn about your orders, and I don't give a damn about the Ustaše. Just get the hell out of here and leave these people alone."

The Croat captain backed out of the apartment. "We will return," he sputtered.

The colonel's steely stare didn't waver. "It won't matter," he said.

□□□

An hour later, a short, uniformed Croat policeman with a large, waxed handlebar moustache marched into the building, followed by the Croat captain and several soldiers. Colonel Supino, now fully dressed in his army uniform, confronted them in the entrance hall before they could reach the Divis apartment.

The policeman rolled one end of his waxed moustache with his thumb and index finger. He cleared his throat. 'I am the local commandant of police, here to take that family—and I will take that family."

Supino stood there, legs spread, hands on his hips. "No, Commandant. As the Italian commander in this city, I give the orders."

The frustrated policeman stamped his foot. "You have no authority in such internal matters. Now I insist you step aside and permit me to do my duty." He tried to push past, but Supino moved to block him.

"This is not your jurisdiction," the policeman shouted. "I warn you . . ."

"No, I am warning you, I am quickly losing my patience."

Again the policeman tried to push past. "You have no right ..."

"I tire of this argument." Colonel Supino slowly and deliberately unbuttoned the flap on his holster. Wide eyed, the policeman followed every movement of the colonel's hands.

Supino unholstered his pistol and pressed it to the middle of the policeman's moustache. "Let me make this as simple as I can so you will understand it on the first try. If you don't go away, I will shoot you. If any of these soldiers makes a move, I will shoot you. Either way, you will be dead." He pressed the muzzle harder against the policeman's upper lip. "You will take no one from this building—not the Divis family, not any other family. Now, have I made myself absolutely clear?"

The frustrated policeman stormed out of the building followed by the Ustaše men.

Colonel Supino stomped into his apartment, picked up the telephone and dialed. "Colonel Supino here. Send two men over to the building where I live. Make sure they're well armed. They will permit *no one* to enter this building until morning."

Lev Divis, who, from his apartment, had overheard the confrontation, came out into the hall and approached Supino, just leaving his apartment. Shaking his hand vigorously, he said, "Thank you for saving me and my family. It you hadn't . . ."

Colonel Supino put his hand on the grateful Czech's shoulder. "You thank me, Doctor, when I get you out of here. Besides, I'm just following orders. The Germans have been demanding that we turn over all the Jews in the Italian area of occupation, and General Mario Roatta, our commander, has flatly refused to do so. Instead, he issued orders to all Italian army commanders to assist the Jews in every way they can. So, that is what I'm doing." The colonel looked intently into his neighbor's eyes. "You know, don't you, that you must leave Croatia. It is impossible to protect you twenty-four hours a day."

Divis nodded.

"Good," the colonel said. "Now get some sleep. You and your family have a busy day ahead of you."

Divis asked hesitantly, "Colonel?"

"Yes?"

"I hate to impose on you, but I have a cousin who recently arrived here and lives a block from here. Could you take him, as well?"

The colonel ran his fingers through his thinning hair, thinking. "Your cousin can't use the streets to get here. The Ustaše will pick him up. How big is he?"

Puzzled by the strange question, Divis replied, "About your size, Colonel."

"Very good, give me his address."

Twenty minutes later, Divis looked out of the front window of his apartment. He saw an Italian military sedan pull up to the curb. He watched as the colonel and another man in an Italian officer's uniform got out of the car and entered the building, saluted by the two Italian soldiers Supino had ordered to guard the entrance.

"Zophie," Divis shouted, "Colonel Supino has just brought us my cousin. And guess what? He's dressed in an Italian uniform!"

□□□

Early the next morning, everyone in the Divis apartment was awake. The air was thick with the hope and anticipation of making a successful escape from the Ustaše. Under Italian guard, the Divis family and their cousin piled into the large official car of the Italian Army; Colonel Supino sat in the driver's seat, a big smile on his face. "Are you ready to face the rest of your life?" He did not expect an answer from the beaming family.

When they reached the Italian border, the car slowed, but the border guards on both sides, without hesitation, waved the Italian Army vehicle through the barriers and the colonel sped up as he entered Italy, heading for Trieste, a few kilometers up the Adriatic coast.

The Same Day, Croatia, near the Border with Italy

Paolo Jozsa, fearing that the Hungarian Jews were next on Hitler's list, fled to Yugoslavia, now Croatia. After six months, he was on the run again, this time from his home in Croatia. He'd left just before an Ustaše raid on his apartment house. Heading down the road on foot, he approached the border and stopped short. Stupid, stupid, he thought, of course there would be the Ustaše guards at the border post and there was no way around them. He was trapped in Croatia.

As Jozsa was contemplating his dilemma, a squad of Italian soldiers marching on the road waved to him. In desperation, Jozsa uttered two of the few Italian words he knew, "*Ebrei paura,*" "Jews fear."

The Italian sergeant leading the group turned to face the man who had uttered "Jews fear." The sergeant smiled and replied '*Niente paura.*'

That Jozsa understood—'Fear nothing.' He didn't exactly understand what the sergeant meant by it but he definitely sounded friendly, so Jozsa fell in behind the soldiers and followed.

The sergeant slowed his walk until Jozsa was alongside of him. "*Parlez vous Francais?*" The sergeant could speak limited French and so could Jozsa.

The sergeant barked some orders to his men in Italian. Then he motioned Jozsa to follow the squad. As they marched down the road, the squad surrounded him.

They were protecting him, he thought in amazement, from the roving Ustaše bands looking for Jews and Serbs. Where they were taking him? He did not wonder for long. The squad halted at the railway station.

The sergeant pointed to the train loading on the station platform. "We are bound for Italy," he said in halting French, "going home for reassignment. You will stay close to me and board the train. I will do all the talking."

The authoritative sergeant found Jozsa a seat in a railway car crowded with troops. He sat down next to him.

"I have a little money," Jozsa said. "You can have it."

The sergeant waved his hand at Jozsa. "No money," he barked. "I just want you to reach the safety of Italian soil."

Jozsa stood out as the only one in the car in civilian clothes. The soldiers stared at him in obvious curiosity until the sergeant spoke to them. Then, the soldiers offered him snacks and some wine. One soldier said something in Italian and they all laughed uproariously. Jozsa didn't understand, but smiled anyway. He was among friends.

The sergeant took Jozsa's arm and debarked the train in the Trieste railway station. "Come with me," he ordered. Jozsa felt in step behind him. "We are going to see the city authorities," the sergeant explained. "It's only a few blocks away. Let me do the talking."

Not that he had a choice, thought Jozsa, since he spoke almost no Italian.

With much hand gesturing, the sergeant engaged the authorities in a spirited conversation the Jozsa wasn't able to follow. The sergeant finally turned to Jozsa, with a broad smile that revealed a missing front tooth. "I convinced them to provide you with food and shelter temporarily, until you get a job."

"Please," Jozsa pleaded, "let me give you something."

The sergeant shook his head vigorously.

"Look," Jozsa pleaded, "I'm an artist. At least permit me do a quick portrait sketch of you."

The sergeant grinned. "Yes, of course, I would like that."

July 14, 1942, Trieste

Trieste, a lovely shipbuilding and resort city on the Adriatic, was situated on the northeasternmost corner of the top of Italy's boot. Its beaches and easygoing attitude had, before the war, attracted countless German and other European summer tourists. Visitors found Trieste, like many another European metropolis, a city of contrasts: the modern section—with its wide boulevards, tall, modern buildings and expensive shops—abutted the old city—with its small houses, many of them centuries old, narrow, winding streets and modest family-owned shops that catered to the neighborhood locals.

The Divis family, wanting to lose themselves in a heavily populated area, found a small apartment in the old city. Divis sold some family jewelry to provide for living expenses. Though not a religious man by any stretch of the imagination, he uttered a prayer of thanks for having had the foresight to leave Prague with most of his valuables and money. For the moment, he and his family could enjoy, like the rich, the summer offerings of the city, particularly the restaurants, and its free beaches, castles and parks. Eventually though, Lev Divis would have to find work. His remaining assets would not sustain them indefinitely.

Soon after his arrival he made a new friend, the Hungarian, Paolo Jozsa, also a Jewish escapee from the Croatian Ustaše. He invited Jozsa to lunch at Dante's on Via Carducci, the wide boulevard running through downtown Trieste.

"Try the pasticcio. I had it the other day, it's delicious," he invited his guest.

Jozsa shook his head. "Since being on the run from the Nazis, I have learned to eat sparsely and quickly. I am not sure I can handle such a heavy dish of pasta, cheese and meat." He ordered a salad and so did Divis, and a pitcher of the local favorite brew, Birra Dreher.

While they waited to be served, Divis described how an Italian colonel saved his family.

Jozsa smiled. "A similar thing happened to me." He described how he was saved by an Italian sergeant who refused to take money from him.

Divis chewed some salad and wiped his mouth with the napkin. "In a way, I'm not surprised. The Italian colonel who helped us explained that his commanding general has refused all demands to turn over Jews to either the Ustaše or the Germans. Not only that, he ordered his troops to protect the Jews and help them leave Croatia."

"But that was not all the sergeant did for me," Jozsa exclaimed. "He helped me find shelter and work."

Divis nodded. "I've heard many stories like yours—life-saving assistance provided to Jews by the Italian military." Recalling something humorous, he smiled. "I heard about one Jewish family that managed to board a train bound for Dubrovnik with no papers whatsoever. When the Italians checked the documents of those getting off the train, each member of this family, in turn, explained that another member, farther back, had their papers. The last family member, when he reached the Italian officer, said the first member had the papers! You know what the Italian did? He just shrugged and let them all off the train."

September 7, 1942, Rome, the Vatican, Office of the Cardinal Secretary of State

Konrad von Preysing, archbishop of Berlin, settled into a chair opposite to Cardinal Maglione. For years now, Bishop Preysing had been in the forefront of the rebel faction of the German clergy urging the Vatican to confront the acts of the Nazi Party as antithetical to the beliefs of the Catholic Church. He'd pushed for a call for noncompliance with the new racial laws and mass Catholic protest. He led the rebel faction in the German clergy. Although his followers were a minority, to be sure, he would not be intimidated into silence.

"Thank you for seeing me, Your Eminence."

Maglione smiled. "It is always good to see one of my fighting bishops from the Third Reich."

With a deprecating gesture, Preysing replied. "It's too bad the fight has gone on so long with not much in the way of concrete results. I recall sitting in this office urging action by the pope when our Holy Father was cardinal secretary of state under Pius XI."

"You demean your efforts," Maglione observed. "As I recall, that visit was the catalyst for the encyclical *Mit brennender Sorge*."

"We must have a stronger position if we are to retain our moral leadership."

The cardinal glanced at the bishop over his reading glasses. "Do you have something specific in mind?"

Preysing picked up his briefcase, took out a document and glanced at it. "Yes, I do, Your Eminence. We received information from a conscience-stricken SS officer working at a concentration camp. He tried unsuccessfully to see Nuncio Orsenigo in Berlin and finally left a report, almost in the nature of a diary, with my aide. May I summarize it for you?"

"Of course."

"He describes in horrific detail what goes on in the camps: The freight trains from Poland arrive at the camp packed with people under the most atrocious conditions. Many are already dead from starvation, thirst or the cold. The live ones are forced out onto the platform, ordered to strip and marched to barbers, who cut off their hair with a few strokes of the scissors. The hair is used as packing material.

"The column—men, women, children, old people, mothers nursing babies, all naked—is herded to gas chambers by SS troops wielding leather whips and by snapping dogs. Seven or eight hundred Jews are jammed into a room so crowded that they must stand in order to fit them all in. Then canisters are dropped into the chamber and deadly gas is released. Later, the bodies are removed, and the gold pried from their teeth by other Jews. Finally, the bodies are fed into massive ovens."

The cardinal briefly covered his eyes. "The Lord have mercy. It can't be true. So many Christians could not have acted with such bestiality."

"We have been hearing other reports like this . . ."

"I know, I know," the cardinal secretary of state interrupted. "The Holy Father grieves for the poor victims, but we must be careful not to make things worse."

"How, after hearing this, Your Eminence," Preysing replied in almost a whisper, "can you imagine things that could really get worse?"

The cardinal folded his arms over his scarlet-trimmed black-robed chest. "Oh, they could, my dear Bishop. There have been none too subtle threats from the German foreign minister that direct protests from us will only speed up the 'deportations,' and perhaps visit such outrages on our Catholic brethren in Germany and the occupied territories."

Bishop Preysing stared up at the ceiling, then looked at Maglione. "Catholic clergy are already being arrested all over the occupied territories. Many have been brutally murdered. Haven't you heard?"

The cardinal sighed. "Give me the information, I will pass it on." He stood up, indicating the visit was concluded.

Bishop Preysing frowned, rose from his chair and curtly thanked the cardinal for his time. His manner left no doubt of his feelings.

The cardinal put his hand on the bishop's shoulder. "Regardless of what you think, Archbishop, we are not the enemy. I will see what I can do."

Preysing nodded grimly and left the office.

Maglione looked over the report and prayed silently for guidance.

CHAPTER NINE

September 1941, Trieste
The beauty of Trieste could not allay Divis's uneasiness. For one thing, his remaining assets would not sustain the family indefinitely; he would have to find work. For another, he felt increasingly unsafe. One mild early summer evening, he took his wife for a long walk down to the harbor. Eventually, they reached Piazza dell'Unita d'Italia, Trieste's largest square and probably one of the largest in Italy. Multistoried *palazzi*, shops and outdoor cafés surrounded it. At Café degli Specchi, they took a table facing the wide harbor. Couples strolled by the stone-cut wall along the water's edge and children ran with abandon in the traffic-free zone. Beyond lay the ships and shipbuilding facilities. The Cinzano umbrella, set at a rakish angle over their heads, swayed slightly in the warm breeze. Dozens of umbrellas, spreading their reds and whites throughout the piazza, gave the area an almost circus-like atmosphere. In the clock tower of the Palazzo de Comune, two large brass figures of Moors slowly swung their hammers against the large bells striking six o'clock, resounding throughout the piazza.

Divis watched Zophie enjoying a glass of Campari. He regretted having to destroy the moment. He put down his glass of white Chianti and gently grasped her hand.

"I hate it when you get so serious," Zophie complained.

"As nice as it is here, we cannot stay," he warned. "It's too dangerous."

She rolled her eyes. "Lev, I don't believe I heard you correctly. We've hardly been here two months, and for the first time in six months, we're enjoying a modicum of comfort, safety and lovely weather."

Divis gave a brief chuckle. "As for the weather, the winter's misery will more than make up for the mildness you're enjoying now. The Bora, freezing winds from the Austrian Alps, will come roaring down into the city through a funnel created by the mountains. They will hit with hurricane force and last for two weeks. You see those metal poles on the sidewalk, the ones with loops at the top, lining the curbs of every street?" Zophie nodded.

"During the Bora season, they string heavy rope through the loops for people to hang on so they don't get blown into the Adriatic."

As Zophie's forehead creased, Divis could see she was getting angry. "I don't think that's a good enough reason to uproot us again." There was a mixture of fury and desperation in her voice.

"No, of course not. I didn't mean to be flippant. But there's no safety here for us. We are too close to the Austrian, German and Croatian borders. It scares me. It wouldn't take much for the Germans to overrun this place—and by the time we found out it would be too late."

Zophie shook her head violently. "I don't understand you, Lev. Why should the Germans attack Trieste? Italy is their ally."

"That's what we thought in Austria," her husband sighed. "The fact is that the Germans have always had an eye on reclaiming the area the Italians call the Alto Adige; which the Germans have always insisted was the Austrian territory of South Tyrol. Hitler won't let Italy keep it, and Mussolini isn't strong enough to prevent him from taking it. Besides, there is a strong Fascist element here with some very active black-shirted gangs. The more restrictions the Duce imposes on the Jews, the bolder these gangs get. They've already killed a few Jews. Eventually, it will blossom into a pogrom."

Anger receded from Zophie's face, replaced by a look of deep sadness and tears. She cried softly. "What can I say? You've been right before and it has saved our lives. But where could we go that's any better?"

"To Rome. There, we can get lost among the crowds of people, and unlike the native Jews, the authorities will have no record of our existence."

"They have no record of us here either."

Divis rubbed his chin, feeling the day's growth rasping against his palm and fingers. "True, but it's a lot harder to disappear in a small city like this. I also think it will be easier to make a living in Rome. I plan for us to leave in a few days."

Zophie sniffed back her tears and mustered up a barely perceptible nod.

September 1942, Turin, Home of Ettore Ovazza

After a large family dinner, Ettore and Nella Ovazza withdrew, without the children, to the sitting room for their nightly chat. She usually waited for Ettore to initiate the conversation.

Like Ettore, Nella came from a rich Turinese family. Indeed, since they were first cousins, purists might say from the same family. At eighteen, she had married Ettore. Even then she had been heavy set and frumpy, but she had not had to wait vainly for a marriage made in heaven—the family council, by custom, arranged everything.

Ovazza came from a long line of Jewish Turinese bankers, and he and his brothers ran Banca Ovazza at its headquarters in Piazza Carlina. The Ovazzas considered themselves Italian patriots. Ettore, his brothers and his father had volunteered for the army and fought in World War I, receiving decorations for bravery. Ettore returned as a captain in the artillery. But neither he nor the other Italian veterans had received the hero's welcome they had expected. Ettore found Turin run—and overrun—by anti-war Socialists who despised the veterans and excluded them from public jobs. This policy, in the midst of Italy's deep economic crisis, drove Ettore Ovazza and other bitter veterans into the arms of Mussolini's Fascist militia, which had adopted violent tactics against their Socialist enemy.

For his patriotism and early Fascist loyalty, in 1929, Ovazza along with other decorated Jewish war veterans or their widows, had been rewarded by an audience with Mussolini. The Duce had astounded Ovazza by singling him out, mentioning that he had read Ovazza's book, *Diary for My Son*. An ecstatic and grateful Ovazza, in turn, had publicized his fanatic devotion to the Fascist Party and Mussolini by putting out a Jewish Fascist newspaper, *La Nostra Bandiera* ("Our Flag"). The publication bestowed profuse praise on the dictator and supported his military adventures as "great wars of liberation."

But the onset of the racial laws confused and tormented patriot Ovazza, who had never failed to recite to others the Duce's past assurances to the Jews. Nevertheless, he continued to support Mussolini, who, he was sure, only imposed these "temporary" restrictions as a necessity of war—probably foisted on him by some extremists in the government. How could it be otherwise? Ovazza thought. Even to entertain such a possibility would be tantamount to admitting a life of failure.

As he sat comfortably, smoking, digesting his dinner and holding his newspaper before him, Ovazza fondly recalled his long-ago audience with the Duce as if it had been yesterday. Ovazza had arrived, resplendent in his artillery captain's uniform decorated with war medals and the pointed addition of a Fascist black shirt and his Fascist Party pin. He'd been proud when the Duce waxed eloquent before the group on the historic connection of the Jews to the Roman Empire, telling the story of how the Jews had asked to be allowed to mourn at the funeral casket of Julius Caesar; and how they had kept watch over his tomb for many days in appreciation of the religious tolerance that marked the Caesar's reign.

Ovazza stopped reminiscing to himself and put down his newspaper. He took a long drag on his cigarette and placed it in the large ashtray beside him. He looked up at his wife, busy knitting and waiting for her husband to start the conversation. "Nella?"

Careful not to lose a stitch, she gently laid the knitting on a small lamp table next to her chair. Then she gave him her full attention.

"It's all the fault of the Zionists and DELASEM."

He often began a conversation in the middle of a thought, leaving her confused. Nella frowned in puzzlement. "Whose fault for what?"

"You know," he said in a slightly annoyed voice as if he expected her to be privy to his thought processes, "people like Bernard Grosser and Raffaele Cantoni—they encouraged Italian Jews to desert their homeland; and that group at DELASEM finances and arranges the travel. Can you blame Mussolini for questioning our loyalty?"

"But Ettore, all that happened only *after* Mussolini made the racial laws."

"That's irrelevant," he declared, shaking his head. "You don't understand. Let me explain." He stopped to take another drag on the cigarette. "Thanks to DELASEM, *foreign* Jews are flooding into Italy, many of them Bolsheviks—and that, Nella, is threatening Italian security. Is it any wonder that the government took steps to stop the threat?"

"But Ettore, these people had no choice, they had to escape German persecution."

"I don't believe it," he snorted. "It's all Bolshevik propaganda, nothing more, designed to split the two great Fascist states."

"Still," Nella persisted, "I'm concerned for our safety if Mussolini continues to copy Hitler's policies. I, for one," she sniffed, "don't think it's propaganda."

Her independent views didn't surprise him, but they always annoyed him. Although Nella was quiet, she definitely had a mind of her own, often quarreling with his statements about his Fascist beliefs. "Even if you were right," he conceded, "there is nothing to worry about. My Fascist comrades say they will protect us."

Nella sighed. "That's what they say now, but Ettore, I'm not so sure. You must think about the welfare of our children and what we should do if the authorities begin to arrest Jews. You know, just in case"

Angered, Ovazza stubbed out his cigarette with unwarranted ferocity, picked up his newspaper again and snapped it open. "You're a woman; you just don't understand—it won't happen here," he grumbled. "Have you ever heard Mussolini speak out publicly against the Jews? No! Those who attack us are mostly acting for themselves, not for Il Duce. There's nothing to worry about."

That ended the discussion. Letting Ettore have the last word was a small price to pay for a harmonious relationship, Nella had decided early in their marriage.

October 11, 1942, Rome, Palazzo Venezia, Mussolini's Office

"There's no reason why you cannot do what we are doing with the Jews," *Reichsführer* Heinrich Himmler droned on to his host. Mussolini could barely sit there and listen to such nonsense. He kept himself occupied by sliding his hand into the lower drawer of his desk and quietly withdrawing one of the many hand grenades he kept around the office, just in case. He juggled it back and forth in his lap. It gave him perverse pleasure thinking about what this mousy head of the vaunted SS and fearsome Gestapo would do if he knew—probably shit in his pants, and the SS would go crazy! The barest outline of a smile formed on his lips. He immediately suppressed it.

Himmler's close-set eyes peered through his pince-nez. Hardly a physical model of a Nazi, Mussolini thought, looking at the *Reichsführer's* thin lips, pale complexion, feminine and almost translucent hands, dark hair and short stature. Mussolini wondered how this pathetic-looking man had wormed his way into a place next to Hitler; how such a non-Nordic-looking weakling could, with a straight face, proclaim the doctrine of Aryan superiority. *Many Jews look more Aryan than he does!*

"...and so Duce, all we are aiming for is the resettlement of the Jews and their mobilization for labor service. Our program, I assure you, is quite humane and rational. The only Jews we send to the concentration camps are the politically dangerous ones—not unlike the way you treat troublesome anti-Fascists. The other Jews are drafted for road building in the East. The old Jews are accommodated in homes for the aged or sent to the town of Theresienstadt. There, they have a nice ghetto where they're given a pension and medical care, and they can do what they like. We will be pleased to assist you by taking the Jews in Italy off your hands."

Mussolini played with the pin on the grenade. Oh, how tempted he was! But the Germans were Italy's ally and he had to deal with this little lying bastard. He'd already learned the truth about what they did to the Jews from Bismarck and the Italian Intelligence Service. Did he think Mussolini didn't know about the "Final Solution?" Mussolini, of course, did not verbalize any of these thoughts. No sense in upsetting the little man who had the ear of the führer. But he inwardly vowed that he would never surrender his Jews to Germany for slaughter, ever.

Mussolini dropped the grenade back in the drawer and stood up. "Thank you for your offer, *Reichsführer*, I will certainly sleep on it."

A smile formed on Himmler's thin lips, "It would make the führer very happy."

Mussolini knew of Himmler's obsession about germs and disease. The *Reichsführer* always kept people at a distance. Prince Bismarck had related how he once saw Himmler throw a fit when an SS functionary had carelessly moved too close and actually touched him. Feeling devilish, Mussolini came around his desk, went up to Himmler and gave him a hug, sticking his square jaw right in the *Reichsführer's* face. He took perverse pleasure at feeling the SS chief stiffen and try to step back.

Mussolini finally let go. "Give my best to the führer."

The furious Himmler could only nod politely.

The Duce burst out laughing after the second or third most important man in the Third Reich left the office, out of hearing range.

Same Day, Rome, the Vatican, Office of the Cardinal Secretary of State

Cardinal Maglione dreaded these periodic meetings with the German ambassador to the Holy See, Diego Bergen. No good ever came of them. It wasn't easy walking the tightrope of neutrality between Germany and the Allies. He was sure there would be another clash today . . .

"Ambassador," Maglione began, "is it really necessary for the Third Reich to act so brutally in Poland? You have already conquered that country—surely you can have *some* compassion."

Bergen sighed. "Lies, Your Eminence, all lies."

The cardinal tented his fingers in front of his nose. "I don't think so, Ambassador. You are even mistreating many Catholics and their clergy."

"I cannot accept your comments about Poland, Your Eminence. As I told you before, the church has no authority to intercede in the territories Germany has incorporated into its borders since the war, that is, until you finally give public recognition to that fact of life."

Maglione shook his head. "Impossible, Signore Ambassador. But I warn you, that if such brutalities continue, the Vatican may have to abandon its reserve and speak out publicly against your antireligious conduct and measures in Poland."

Bergen' face turned red. "Is Your Eminence threatening us? I can barely restrain the führer now from taking serious reprisals against the church. I am advised by Foreign Minister von Ribbentrop that there will be no holding back if the Vatican carries out a propaganda attack against the Third Reich."

The meeting ended on that note.

Same Day, Late in the Evening, Vatican, Apartments of Pope Pius XII

The pope and his secretary of state sat facing each other in the sitting room just off the pontiff's bedroom. Maglione had finished summarizing his meeting with the German ambassador. The pope, his hands folded in his lap, thought for a minute. He looked up at his secretary of state. "Is it wise to suggest threats that we can't carry out?"

"But we have to do something, Holiness. The information we have been receiving—it's simply appalling. How can we remain silent and maintain our moral authority?"

"Eminence, I must consider which is the greatest threat to the church—Nazism or Bolshevism?" Pius let out a long sigh. "I had hoped that the end of Bolshevism was near, but the Germans are in full retreat in the Soviet Union and also in North Africa. The Soviets are now allied with the Western democracies. The German nation, it seems, is the sole rampart against the threat of Bolshevism. I am afraid to do anything that would weaken Germany. At least the Germans, unlike Stalin, have not specifically targeted Catholics for persecution." Cardinal Maglione leaned forward. "What about the Jews?"

The pontiff rubbed his tired eyes. "Yes, the Jews. It distresses me deeply what is happening to those poor people. But if I speak out publicly about the excesses against the Jews, the Germans will only intensify their campaign and more Jews will die, not to mention the danger to our Catholic brethren. How can I, in good conscience, do that?"

"But, Holiness, you've seen the reports from the Delegatura, the Polish underground."

"I have, and I spoke out in my Christmas message last December against the atrocities."

"That message only condemned war generally, Your Holiness, not what the Germans, in particular, were doing."

The pope dismissed that protest. "I explained to the Allies and the Polish government in exile that I was referring to the Germans. I directed Harold Tittmann to pass on to the U. S. President that I could not mention the Nazis without also mentioning the Bolsheviks. Roosevelt would not have been pleased if I had done that."

Maglione shook his head. "But surely, Holiness, what's happening in Poland . . ."

"Don't forget, Eminence, that many bishops in Poland have pleaded with me not to speak out because it will only provoke the Nazis and make matters worse. Besides, how much of that propaganda by Germany's enemies do we really believe? I have seen those reports from the Americans and the British. I take them with a grain a salt. Truth is one of the first casualties of war."

Frustrated, the cardinal tried again. "But just as many bishops in Poland have asked you to speak out, Holiness," he reminded the pope.

Pius eyed him. His face softened. "Perhaps there is another way. Perhaps our nuncio in Berlin can meet with Hitler and gently and diplomatically sound him out about showing some mercy to the Jews."

Maglione nodded. "I'll speak to Archbishop Orsenigo."

October 12, 1942, Berlin, the Foreign Minister's Office

Ribbentrop put down Bergen's report and stared at the ambassador to the Holy See, who had traveled to Berlin to deliver it personally. The foreign minister's deep-set, darkly shadowed eyes bored into Bergen. "That dung cardinal dares to threaten us?"

Sitting silently next to the ambassador was the führer himself. Bergen, thoroughly intimidated, cleared his throat. "You must understand, *Mein* Führer, that Cardinal Maglione engaged in a bluff. The pope has always been favorably disposed to Germany. He's the most pro-German cleric in the Vatican."

"You said that before," harrumphed the foreign minister, "and then the pope delivered that anti-German Christmas message last December."

Bergen threw a quick glance at Hitler. The führer just sat there, not taking his eyes off the ambassador. "But the message was couched in such vague terms—condemning in a general way all atrocities committed during war—that few recognized it as a direct criticism of the Third Reich," Bergen pleaded.

Ribbentrop snickered. "No one except the Allies, who made the most of it in their propaganda."

Bergen frowned. "I am sure the Vatican is far more afraid of the Bolsheviks than it is of us. It won't do anything to give encouragement to the Soviets."

"They'd better not. We are prepared to eliminate the church after the war. The pope's mouthing will only accelerate these plans."

The führer growled and they both turned their attention to him. "I'll soon let the priests taste the power of the state until they're really amazed," he said in a low, threatening voice. "Now I only keep an eye on them. If I thought they were becoming dangerous, I'd shoot them all down in a heap."

"Yes, *Mein* Führer," Bergen sputtered.

Hitler did not acknowledge his ambassador. "I may just march on the Vatican and get that pack out of there." He chuckled." Then I would say, 'Forgive me, it was all a mistake.' But they'd be gone for good."

October 1942, Rome, the Ghetto

Soon after their arrival in Rome, Lev Divis and his family settled into the top floor of a house in the ghetto. Although it had been abolished years before, it was still known as the ghetto and still contained many Jews. To his surprise, he had no trouble earning a modest living. Since 1939, all Jews had been stripped of their right to practice the professions, including medicine. Dr. Divis very quickly developed a clientele of desperate ghetto Jews who needed a doctor's care. They did not pay much, if anything at all. But Divis turned no one away, so he earned a small, but sustainable, living. He earned the friendship of Attilio Nathan, an Italian shopkeeper in the ghetto, whose family went back to Roman times. Divis had successfully treated a very frightened Michele, Attilio's son, for food poisoning.

Another Jew in his debt was the Austrian refugee, Joseph Schwartz. Schwartz, stricken with a ruptured hernia, had been refused admittance to the hospital, which was not permitted by law to treat Jews. His wife, Dora, came to Divis in desperation. Divis, having no facilities, did not dare try to perform major surgery outside of a hospital. He had called on Nathan, who had a Catholic friend who worked at the children's hospital. They had managed to sneak Schwartz into the hospital, where Divis, assisted by the friend, had successfully performed the surgery. Schwartz's feet stuck out over the child's bed in which he lay recuperating, but no one saw them behind the closed curtain around the bed. Fully recovered, the appreciative Schwartz later used his tailoring skills to see that Divis was the best-dressed doctor in Rome.

November 5, 1942, Rome, the Vatican, Office of the Cardinal Secretary of State

Archbishop Cesare Orsenigo, papal nuncio in Berlin, arrived in Rome to report on his meeting with Hitler. He settled into a chair facing the cardinal. "Frankly, Your Eminence, I did not relish the task you gave me. It's distasteful enough having to deal with Hitler, but to discuss Jews. . ." He shook his head.

Cardinal Maglione nodded. "I understand, thoroughly. But we have been under pressure from some of our brethren, Cardinal van Roey in Belgium and Cardinal Preysing in Berlin, not to mention scores of our Polish bishops, to intervene against the deportation of millions of people to the camps. The Holy Father did not want a public condemnation that would instigate a German reaction making matters worse, so he suggested your private meeting with the German chancellor."

Orsenigo frowned. "You will be disappointed, Your Eminence."

"I'm not surprised," the cardinal sighed.

For a brief moment, Orsenigo hesitated, reaching for the proper words. "On November 2, I was finally received by Hitler. I had to go all the way to his Alpine retreat in Berchtesgaden. After a few pleasantries, I brought up the questions of Jews and Judaism. That immediately set him off. Turning his back on me, and without answering, he paced around the room and then went to the window, strumming his fingers on the windowsill. So I continued, detailing our complaints about his treatment of the Jews. Still, he said nothing, continuing to strum his fingers. Suddenly, he whirled around like a madman, strode over to a small table, picked up a full water glass and flung it to the ground in an absolute fury. In the face of such action, I had to consider my diplomatic mission at an end."

Maglione gazed sadly at the archbishop. "You did the best you could. I realize we put you in a difficult position. Thank you for your efforts."

Bemused, Orsenigo folded his hands in his lap. "You know, Your Eminence, for a brief moment, I wondered whether I would get out of Berchtesgaden alive."

Maglione had no reply to that.

PART III

The End of Mussolini's Role and the End of German Restraint in Italy

CHAPTER TEN

January 1, 1943, Morning, Rome, Villa Savoia

The servants in the royal palace wished Vittorio Emmanuel III, king of Italy, happy New Year. The "new" applied, but certainly not the "happy." Italian military forces had suffered disastrous defeats in Greece; North Africa was almost lost; and Italian soldiers were being slaughtered in a losing battle at Stalingrad.

Mussolini had committed his troops to a war for which they were ill-prepared and ill-equipped. The Duce slavishly followed behind Hitler like a dutiful Japanese wife. In theory, at least, the king reflected, the Crown should be able to dismiss the prime minister without a national crisis. But the king was no fool. The monarchy existed at the sufferance of the ruling Fascist government. The king, technically, was the commander-in-chief of the Italian military. But the premier was also the Duce of Fascism. Would the party accept the king's decision? He feared not, for such an action would undo Mussolini's March on Rome in 1922, the event that propelled the Fascist Party to power. The king prudently decided he'd better call a secret meeting of some of Italy's military leaders to see what could be done to neutralize Fascist power.

January 4, 1943, Rome, Villa Savoia

In his office, three days later, the king greeted General Vittorio Ambrosio, chief of the general staff; Marshal Ugo Cavallero; and Generals Giacomo Carboni and Giuseppe Castellano, waving them to chairs. The short king felt more comfortable when his guests were seated and more at his level. "Gentlemen, we have a crisis on our hands. If we permit the premier to continue on this course, Italy will be destroyed—we are not far from that right now."

The king rarely referred to Mussolini as Duce, the leader, a term that he felt impinged on his own sovereignty. "The question, gentlemen, is: should we remove Mussolini and if so, how?"

Ambrosio studied his hands, then looked up at the king. "Early on, Your Majesty, I had hoped to persuade the Duce to make a rapid disengagement from the Germans. For years, I have harped on this with him, to no avail. I don't think he will change now."

"I've been in contact with Marshal Badoglio," said Cavallero, considered one of Italy's best military leaders. "We agree that Italy must be saved from the abyss toward which Fascism is driving her. If we depose Mussolini, however, the new government should do nothing drastic to upset Hitler until we can secretly negotiate an armistice with the Allies. I have been in clandestine contact with General Eisenhower's headquarters. They will deal with us but only after Mussolini is gone. Until then, they are not interested."

Carboni, a politically attuned young general who was highly regarded for his initiative in military matters, handed the king a paper. "In anticipation of this meeting, General Castellano and I drafted possible steps for his removal. We have listed the measures to be taken to avert a Fascist counter-coup, the proposed action to arrest Mussolini and the party leaders and military plans to counter German reaction."

Castellano, who, up to now, had been involved only in routine military planning, had begun working closely with Ambrosio. This led him to start thinking about Italy's desperate situation. He had also spoken to Carboni, who confirmed that something had to be done.

The king waved Carboni's paper at Castellano. "Have you considered the political means for effectuating this proposal?"

"We are military, Your Majesty," Castellano explained. "We must leave the political strategies to the politicians."

The king grunted. "That's not very helpful, General. Well, at this time, without the support of the Senate, I am not prepared to act."

Improbable Heroes

"But the Senate is much too subservient to Mussolini to do anything on their own," Ambrosio objected. "We cannot ever hope to get a hundred senators to vote for his removal."

The king sighed. "I'm afraid I have to agree. What about going through the Grand Council?"

"That's a thought, Your Majesty," the brash Carboni interjected, presuming to reply to the question directed to his superior. "I have already been in touch with Ciano. He's on our side—and he's a member of the council."

Ambrosio, frowning, turned to face the young general. "But most of the Grand Council are Fascists put there by the Duce!" There was a trace of a scorn in his voice.

"True, Sir" Carboni replied, undaunted, "but Ciano advises me that most of the Grand Council members are frustrated and dissatisfied with Mussolini's calamitous one-man rule. Ciano is trying to find out if we can turn them. He's already met with Bottai and Farinacci, two of the dissidents whose names have been suggested in some quarters in Rome as possible candidates to succeed Mussolini." Carboni smiled. "You know what Bottai said to Ciano? 'In 1911, when he was a Socialist, Mussolini said we should give up Libya. It has taken him thirty-two years to keep his word.'" No one laughed.

Castellano took up the argument. "Other names for succession are being circulated clandestinely: Marshal Badoglio, the diplomat Dino Grandi . . ." He turned to face Cavallero, ". . . and you, Marshal."

Cavallero waved aside the suggestion. "I am not looking for power. I just want to end Italy's suicidal participation in the war. I have contacts with American military headquarters. I can be more useful in that capacity."

"The time is not yet ripe, gentlemen," the king concluded. "We must garner more support, but be discreet. This could easily blow up in our faces."

July 2, 1943, Rome, Home of Ambassador Ciano

Ciano touched his wife's hand at the breakfast table. "Edda, you must convince your father to listen to the voice of reason. There is not much time left. I have begged him time and again to approach the Allies while there's still an Italy to negotiate with. He won't listen to me; he won't listen to anybody. Dino Grandi, Pietro Badoglio and many others of that stature have joined the forces seeking to oust your father."

Edda knitted her brow in confusion. "I thought Father had purged the government of dissident elements when he got wind of the conspiracy last February."

Ciano nodded. "The purge notwithstanding, there's still a majority of the Grand Council, who, I think, would support his ouster."

Ciano himself had been dismissed as foreign minister in that purge and been appointed ambassador to the Holy See. Edda, who had always had a hair-trigger temper, had thrown a fit right in her father's office on her husband's demotion, but Mussolini would not back down. As a sop to his daughter, however, he had permitted Ciano to retain his seat on the Grand Council. "He won't listen to me," Edda sighed. "He's changed. Father is old and ill, Gallo. Can you save him from himself?"

Ciano swallowed; he shrugged. "I'm only one vote. It won't matter what I do. I could help your father more effectively if I side with the dissidents. Then I can be an important voice in any succeeding government—and be in a better position to protect him afterwards."

Edda didn't respond.

Suddenly air raid sirens sounded. She walked to the window and looked out. "Another false alarm. The Allies must be bombing Naples again. I don't know why we bother going to the shelter."

Ciano took her arm. "Come, Edda, at the rate the war is going, they'll be bombing Rome soon enough. Today may be the day."

July 19, 1943, Rome, Villa Savoia

At Ciano's request, the king met with the group of dissident Grand Council members. Ciano deferred to Grandi, who was the first to speak. "Your Majesty, the Duce has lost Africa; the Allies have invaded Sicily; the Soviets are routing Axis troops on the Eastern Front; and Rome is being bombed. Last week, we met with Mussolini for one last try. At the Duce's scheduled meeting with Hitler at Treviso we persuaded him to tell Hitler that Italy just could not continue the war. General Ambrosio and Colonel Montezemolo were at the Treviso meeting." Grandi turned to the two military officers, "Tell the king what happened."

Ambrosio cleared his throat. "The Duce simply became tongue-tied in Hitler's presence, Your Majesty. It was stupid. He doesn't know German that well, but he still refused to use an interpreter. I'm sure he missed half of what Hitler said. Instead of telling Hitler what he intended to do, he just listened. Much to our chagrin, Hitler convinced Mussolini that victory was still possible. When the Duce finally suggested peace talks with the Soviets, Hitler absolutely refused and would not let us withdraw our troops. Indeed, he wanted to send more Italians to the Balkans and Russia. The führer reviled Italians as cowards, poor performers, men without fortitude, inefficient clods. It was embarrassing to see our premier sitting there, silent."

Ciano slowly shook his head. "It seems, Sir, the Axis is like a man who is trying to cover himself with a bedspread that is too small. His head is cold if he warms his feet, and his feet freeze if he keeps his head warm. We are at the end of our rope, Your Majesty. Even pro-Nazi Roberto Farinacci and the Duce's former police chief, Carmen Senise, have come over to our side."

"General Caviglia and Foreign Minister Bastianini are siding with us," Ambrosio added. "When Mussolini left for his meeting with Hitler, we should have realized he would not live up to his promise because he refused to meet beforehand with Bastianini and me to prepare our arguments or discuss procedures and policies. All he did was scream at us that his military commanders were to blame because they weren't making war with the fury of fanatics. When I told Bastianini, he threw a fit, saying Mussolini was no longer reachable."

"After the meeting with Hitler, Farinacci had asked Mussolini to cede at least some of his powers to make the regime more efficient," Grandi advised the king. "Surprisingly, Mussolini agreed, albeit curtly, to convene a meeting of the Grand Council. Then I met with the Duce and tried to convince him to eliminate one-man rule and to adopt the reforms we proposed. He called my suggestion 'inadmissible and contemptible.' He said, 'I will not hand the reins of command over to anyone.' Your Majesty, we must seize the initiative at the Grand Council meeting. We may not have such an opportunity again."

The king, head down, deep in thought, had his elbow resting on his desk, his hand cradling his chin. His visitors waited politely. At last he looked up. "Gentlemen, the time has come. The council meeting will be our constitutional means of getting rid of Mussolini." He looked at Ambrosio. Please prepare a plan to have the premier arrested, but make sure no harm comes to him."

"I understand, Your Majesty," Ambrosio acknowledged.

July 24, 1942, Late Afternoon to the Early Morning Hours, July 25, Rome, Palazzo Venezia, Grand Council Hall

The Grand Council Hall, adjoining the *Sala del Mappamondo,* Mussolini's office, was lavishly appointed, the walls paneled in rarewoods under a high, richly carved ceiling. A heavy, wrought iron chandelier, shaped like a great wheel, hung suspended above the Oriental rug covering part of the inlaid marble floor. The inscription "Anno VII" in the floor signified the date the room was completed. By the Italian calendar, the seven years began with the 1922 March on Rome and Mussolini's assumption of the head of government. Around the walls of the hall, heavy carved tables with chairs formed a large rectangle. The Duce presided from a platform two feet above the rest of the council, his throne-like chair festooned with laurel wreaths and the symbols of Fascism. A table stood before him, covered with a plush crimson cloth.

The day was stifling hot and the tall windows were flung open, their velvet curtains pulled back. When the entire Council of twenty-eight, all in their black Fascist militia uniforms, were seated, Mussolini, also in his black uniform, emerged from his office at precisely five o'clock. The Fascist Party secretary, Carlo Scorza, rapped the floor sharply with a specially designed pole, shouting, "Salute Il Duce." As one they replied *"A noi,"* giving the Roman salute.

Many of the council members did not know what to expect. Ciano's pockets bulged with two hand grenades. Several men came armed with small pistols, carefully concealed. Dino Grandi sat next to Cesare De Vecchi, a lawyer and much-decorated veteran who had taken part in the March on Rome. Reaching under the table, Grandi passed a grenade to De Vecchi, who slipped it into his own pocket. The hall became an armed camp.

After the roll call, the Duce launched into a muddled review of the war and a defense of his own actions. He characterized himself as "the most hated man in Italy." He sat leaning forward, rather than in his characteristic ramrod straight position. He raised his knees slightly, trying to ease the pains in his stomach, a recurrence of either his ulcer or gastritis, he did not know which. His frequent use of morphine had dulled his normal exuberance. He looked the way he felt—a tired old man.

As he progressed into his defense he became more animated, blaming the battle reversals on his generals. "Never," he expostulated, "did I control the technical direction of any battle, except one—and there I won a victory." He went on to argue that the loss of Libya was actually an advantage because "we no longer need a merchant fleet and can better concentrate on the defense of Italy itself." Then he attacked "the inferior class of Italians who are physically and mentally below par and who are blind, lame, toothless, feeble-minded, shirkers—people lacking in redeemable qualities—they are the ones who have not been engaged in the war and never can be, whining that the war ought never to have begun."

The Grand Council witnessed the sad spectacle of the once imposing Duce fumbling for words, presenting a thoroughly confused, false and disorganized version of the facts. With his vast ego, he still believed he was infallible. In his rambling discourse of two hours, he never mentioned his failure to confront Hitler.

In response, Dino Grandi, the most polished and aristocratic member, launched into an unsparing attack. "You, Sir, lost the war when you tied Italy to the Third Reich. You are no soldier; Italy was doomed the day you donned the marshal's uniform!" Suddenly, Grandi's tone turned from belligerent to sad. "Already, we have 100,000 dead—all their mothers are crying, 'Assassin, assassin, the Duce has murdered our sons!'"

One after the other, Grand Council members decried Italy's disasters: the Axis alliance and Mussolini's refusal to admit Italy's military unpreparedness; the Allied invasion of Sicily and its imminent loss; the inability of the Italian Army to resist an invasion of Italy; the use of Italy's territory as the outer defense of the Third Reich; and the use of Italian troops as cannon fodder to serve German, not Italian, interests.

Ciano took a low-key approach. He quietly pushed the view that change was in the best interests of Italy—and his father-in-law.

Mussolini took a ten-minute recess at midnight to sip some milk, trying to quiet his ulcer. He spoke privately with some of his supporters. When he returned to the council hall, Grandi took the responsibility to present the motion to turn over the reins of government and control of the military forces to the king. He moved further that all national institutions, the Parliament and the Crown would assume the functions they had had just prior to the Duce's assumption of power. Although phrased diplomatically, the motion was clear—it called for Mussolini's immediate ouster.

Mussolini's mood changed from minute to minute. He first attacked the motion as "traitorous." Then he reflected sadly, "I am sixty. If I wanted to, I could look over my life as a wonderful adventure that is ending." As quickly, the old Mussolini boisterousness returned. "But I will not! The king and the people—they are on my side."

Finally, at close to two in the morning, Mussolini announced, "I tire of all this debate. I stand accused of violating the Constitution ever since I became prime minister. I accept that challenge. But I must warn you I consider the council responsible for the situation, and I could take advantage of your maneuvering to liquidate you in one stroke. I demand an end to the talking. You will now take an open roll-call vote. All will know where each of you stands."

Grandi looked at Ciano. Ciano guessed what he was thinking. With those threatening words Mussolini was trying to blackmail the Grand Council. Would they get out of this hall alive? Ciano wondered. Perhaps they had underestimated the Duce and overplayed their hand. Well, this was no time to get cold feet; the die was cast. He fingered the pin of the grenade sitting heavy in the pocket of his black Fascist militia jacket.

"Before you vote," cautioned Mussolini, "I have only this to say: Hitler and I have in our hands a weapon that will turn the tide of war in our favor, but I cannot reveal what it is at the moment."

Sadly, Ciano shook his head. Grandi leaned over to him. "I was at that meeting," he whispered. "Both of them had looked like corpses. Concerned, Ambrosio had asked the Duce about his health and he replied, 'My illness has a name: convoys. The British are sinking all our merchant ships. Nothing is getting through.' At the meeting, Mussolini had sat in cowed silence. Hitler had done all the talking."

The motion to return all power to the king carried 19 to 7 with one abstention. The Grand Council held its collective breath as the meeting adjourned at 2:40 A.M. There was no violence. They quietly filed out of the hall, went home and emptied their pockets of weapons.

July 25, 1942, Morning, Rome

Mussolini spent the morning after the council meeting touring the bombed-out areas of the city. The general who accompanied him urged the Duce to arrest those "traitors" who had supported the motion against him.

"I shall do nothing against them before I see the king this afternoon," Mussolini insisted. "I am scheduled to see the Japanese ambassador later this morning. I shall persuade him to urge Hitler to stop the war with the Soviet Union. Then when Göring arrives in Rome in a few days, we will plan together to turn Hitler around on the war. I have Göring's ear. He agrees with me. If we can convince Hitler to cease hostilities on the Eastern Front, I am sure the Mediterranean theater can be stabilized and held. The king has always been solidly behind me. I have always acted with his agreement. There is no need to roil the waters by dealing with the criminal riff-raff in the council now. There is always the police and the party to deal with them in due time."

"But Duce, they seek to destroy everything we have built."

Mussolini smiled. "You are a good man, general, but leave the defectors to me. The vote of the Grand Council is merely advisory. When I meet with the king, I will relinquish command of the military to him. That should please him. Then I will update him on the military situation, as I always do. He depends on me and will support me, so stop worrying."

Same Day, Rome, Villa Savoia

The king invited into his office, General Ambrosio; General Angelo Cerica, recently appointed commander of the military police; General Carboni; and General Paolo Putoni, head of the king's military household.

"I wanted you to know," the king began, that the Duce has requested an audience with me at five this afternoon. I have granted his request."

Cerica was first to respond. "I would like, with the permission of Your Majesty, to station my military police in the gardens of the Villa Savoia."

The king eyed the commander. "You may station the men, but they must be kept out of sight, and no arrest shall be made within the gardens. As Mussolini departs, be prepared to seize him at the entrance just inside the gates of the villa. Make sure you do it as unobtrusively and rapidly as possible. He must be given no opportunity to reach his people. We want a fait accompli before his supporters have a chance to react."

Cerica nodded. "I can use a motor ambulance to take him away before he reaches his car. I will have one waiting just inside the gate with fifty military police concealed in the bushes alongside the main staircase."

Ambrosio began issuing instructions to Cerica. "You must be sure, very quietly, to arrest his driver and get him and Mussolini's car the hell out of there. But watch out, his driver is probably armed."

"He will present no problem, I assure you."

"The radio stations at Prato Smeraldo and San Paolo, as well as the offices of Italian Radio, the Central Post Office and the telephone exchanges, must all be secured," Ambrosio continued. "Marzano from the transport section of the Ministry of Interior can supply you with the ambulance. I will call him"

Cerica jotted down some notes then looked up. "What about the Fascist M division and their thirty-six tiger tanks, just sixteen miles out of town?"

"It is not your concern," Ambrosio said sharply. "I have that well in hand. General Carboni will take over the Rome garrison after the arrest is made."

As the meeting broke up, the king ordered Putoni to remain behind. "When I am meeting with Mussolini, I want you armed and in the next room with the door slightly ajar. I don't know how the premier will react, so stand just on the other side of the door and intervene if the situation requires it."

Same Day, Five in the Evening, Rome, Villa Savoia

Mussolini's car pulled up to the gates of Villa Savoia and the Duce got out. As he climbed the steps of the main staircase, the king came down to greet him. Victor Emmanuel, always acutely aware of his less-than-five-foot height, could never shake the feeling of inferiority in the presence of Mussolini, who bore aggressively and proudly, his erect, muscular body. It didn't help that reports had reached the king of Mussolini's frequent disparagement of his king's dwarfish physical stature. Nevertheless, the king greeted his premier warmly and thanked him for coming.

After they settled into the king's office, Mussolini began to report on the latest military situation. Just behind the door to the royal living quarters, Putoni listened, pistol in hand, ready to jump in.

After a few minutes, the king put up his hand. The Duce stopped talking.

"My dear Prime Minister, you must face it; the situation is unacceptable: Italy destroying herself. The Army's morale is gone and the soldiers don't want to fight anymore. We are losing the cream of our young men at an alarming rate. You certainly can be under no illusions of how Italians feel about you—you are the most hated man in Italy." The king deliberately mimicked the same words the Duce was reported to have used at the Grand Council meeting.

Mussolini shrugged. "It is the burden that great military leaders must bear during conflict. No one likes to loose loved ones, Your Majesty, but ordering soldiers to battle is a necessity of war."

"You don't understand, Prime Minister. The Grand Council resolution is known all over Rome; the people are expecting a change."

Mussolini blinked, clearly dumbfounded. In that rare moment, uncharacteristic for him, he did not know what to say. The king waited.

Still confused, Mussolini finally blurted out, "But if Your Majesty is correct, I should present my resignation."

"And I have to tell you—I accept your resignation unconditionally," the king quickly replied.

Mussolini nodded.

"I have arranged for Marshall Badoglio to take over as prime minister. I am truly sorry that the solution could not have been otherwise." The king stood up and Mussolini followed suit.

As they left the office and headed for the main stairway, Putoni, behind the door, holstered his pistol, breathing a sigh of relief.

A dazed Mussolini approached the gate, looking for his missing car and driver. A military police captain approached.

"Where are my car and driver?" Mussolini asked.

"His Majesty has ordered me to protect you. Please follow me." Armed troops materialized, surrounding the deposed dictator.

Mussolini turned around, his pleading eyes searching for the king, but he could only catch a fleeting glimpse of the squat little monarch's back as he disappeared into the villa—the same monarch he'd disparaged for years as an ineffectual and powerless freak, the same one who had successfully deposed him, the great Duce.

Just inside the gate, the officer motioned the befuddled Mussolini into a waiting ambulance. As Mussolini hesitated, the military policeman firmly took hold of his arm and pushed the barely resisting man inside. The former Italian dictator was at a loss for words. The vehicle sped away at a high speed to a secret location, one of the military barracks in the city.

CHAPTER ELEVEN

July 25, 1943, Late Evening, Berlin, The Chancellery
Hitler, an insomniac, was holding forth on the superiority of the Nordic race, leafing through *Mein Kampf* as he expounded his views. He read passages from it to a captive—and clearly bored—audience gathered around him in the chancellery. It was midnight and the führer was good for another two hours, at least. General Alfred Jodl, chief of the Operations Staff of the armed forces, who hadn't been able to figure a graceful way out of Hitler's last-minute invitation, had already nodded off. Himmler, Goebbels and armaments minister, Albert Speer, fought to stay awake. "The Jew," Hitler droned on, "lacks those qualities that distinguish the races that are creative and hence, culturally blessed. The Jew has never possessed a state or a culture of his own. He is, and remains, a typical parasite, a sponger who . . ."

A sharp rap on the door caught Hitler in mid-sentence. Clearly annoyed at this distraction and the violation of his standing orders not to be disturbed at these late-night sessions with his friends, he shouted, "What is it?"

The door opened slowly. Foreign Minister Ribbentrop stuck his head in. "A thousand pardons, *Mein* Führer, but I have just received news from our embassy in Rome that you should hear."

Frowning, Hitler let out a long sigh of exasperation. "Come in, come in. Minister. Tell me your important news."

Ribbentrop took two steps into the room. All eyes were riveted on him, including those of the now fully awake Jodl.

"Mussolini has been deposed by the king. Victor Emmanuel has appointed Marshal Badoglio to take the Duce's place and form a new, non-Fascist government. It happened about six hours ago. I heard from Ambassador Mackensen. Badoglio advised him that Italy would continue fighting the war alongside the Third Reich."

"Traitors!" Hitler screamed, spittle flying. Himmler, phobic enough about others' germs, leaned as away from the führer as far as he dared without being obvious. "I knew that Mussolini should not have agreed to meet with the Grand Council. He hadn't convened one in three years. So why now? I would have arrested and executed all those traitors after the vote! It's all the machinations of that cretinous king."

Hitler leaned back looking down at his boots, both hands gripping tightly the padded arms of his chair, trying to catch his breath.

Goebbels had never seen his leader in such a state. Undoubtedly he was shocked that a revolutionary movement that had been in power for twenty-one years could be toppled just like that. The führer must be thinking that if the Duce could be removed so easily, then why not he?

"Führer?" Goebbels ventured.

Hitler looked up, his angry eyes blazing.

"I don't think it was the work of the king. He's too stupid and short-sighted to arrange such a maneuver," Goebbels offered.

Ribbentrop insinuated himself into an empty chair. "I believe Dr. Goebbels is correct, *Mein* Führer. Ambassador Mackensen says it is the work of Dino Grandi and Mussolini's son-in-law, Galeazzo Ciano."

Hitler ignored the comments. "That Badoglio's a liar. At the first chance, he'll surrender to the Allies." Hitler began shouting again. "His assurances don't mean a thing. He has to say the war will be continued. That's what treachery is. But we can play the treachery game also and then take over that riffraff in one stroke." He looked at Jodl. "Have the Third Pansergrenadieren and the Second Parachute Division take Rome and arrest all the Italian leaders."

Jodl frowned. "If you say so, Führer, but shouldn't we wait for more complete reports on what is going on, the disposition of Italian troops, and the like?"

"You can do that, but just make sure Rome is occupied as soon as possible," Hitler barked. "We have to start thinking and moving quickly. I don't want dozens of reports and groups of generals agonizing over strategy. I will direct the operation"

"Of course, *Mein* Führer," Jodl said softly.

"And get our men out of Sicily immediately and deploy them in the south of Italy," Hitler ordered. "I don't want them trapped on that island. Just leave the heavy equipment."

Jodl shrugged. "It will take a while, Führer. We can ferry no more than seventeen thousand a day."

Hitler threw up his hands in annoyance. "Well, crowd them in and do it. I want Rome occupied immediately."

"Should we occupy the Vatican?" Himmler asked.

"At this point it doesn't matter. We can do that at any time. We'll take over the whole bunch—the church leaders, the diplomatic corps—all those swine."

Goebbels shook his head. "Let's go slow. We have the support of Germany's Catholics now. I don't want to jeopardize that. Occupation of the Vatican per se is not that important to our war effort in Italy."

Ribbentrop nodded. "I agree with Dr. Goebbels, *Mein* Führer."

Hitler sat quietly for a minute, fingering his moustache. "Very well, I shall postpone action on the Vatican—for now. But I insist that the Wehrmacht and the SS move into Italy. Southern Italy will be under the command of General Kesselring. Northern Italy will be occupied territory; Rommel will take over there. And, oh yes, I want our troops to take possession of and annex Alto Adige, including Trieste and Fiume. The province will once again become our South Tyrol."

Jodl rose, bowed and clicked his heels. "May I take my leave, Führer, to get things going?"

Hitler nodded. Jodl backed out and closed the door behind him.

Hitler looked at Ribbentrop. "Do we know what happened to the Duce?"

The foreign minister shook his head. "No. He was spirited away by the military police after his meeting with the king. His whereabouts have been kept a secret."

Hitler turned to Himmler. "I want Mussolini located. Put as many SS and Gestapo on it as you need."

Himmler ran his hand through his short-cropped hair, thinking. "If the Duce is still in Italy, I know just the man to find him—Major Herbert Kappler, head of the Gestapo and German security in Rome. He's well acquainted with Italy."

"You will find Mussolini and then we shall rescue him," Hitler ordered. "The man for the job is SS Colonel Otto Skorzeny, a commando officer trained in kidnapping techniques. It's time to put his skills to use. I want both Skorzeny and Kappler here by tomorrow. I will talk to them personally."

Hitler's visitors turned to leave. *"Reichsführer,"* Hitler called out. Himmler swiveled around to face him. "I want those traitors, Grandi and Ciano, brought here."

July 26, 1943, Berlin, the Chancellery

Colonel Otto Skorzeny and Major Herbert Kappler stood at rigid attention before the führer. The two officers could not have been more different. At 6 feet 4 inches, the powerfully built colonel, a commando and paratrooper, dwarfed the major, a man of average height. Skorzeny sported a nasty-looking dueling scar that ran from his left ear to his chin. His comrades called him Scarface, an appellation he bore proudly. Kappler had a taut bony face and dark eyes, small but piercing. Though a Gestapo desk officer in Rome, he'd been trained in espionage and security and was an expert on Italy and Italian history. Skorzeny, a ladies' man, had impregnated several Nordic-looking German women under Himmler's *Lebensborn*—a program in which selected SS officers, with unquestionable Nordic qualities, were ordered to father children out-of-wedlock by women of pure German stock selected by the State, the children to be brought up by the State in an effort to create a pure Aryan race. By contrast, Kappler, no Romeo, was unhappily married and had been trying for years to divorce his wife.

Hitler, having reviewed their files, looked at the two men. They would make a good team. With Kappler's knowledge of Italy and Skorzeny derring-do, if any team could rescue the Duce, they could.

"You two have been selected for a mission crucial to me and to the Third Reich," he announced.

Skorzeny stiffened slightly. Hitler supposed the colonel's adrenaline was flowing at the prospect of going into action after all that training. Kappler just stood there with no reaction; the highly trained Gestapo officer must be a cool operative, he thought. *These two have just what I need.*

"Mussolini has been deposed and arrested," Hitler went on. "We must locate where he is being held and mount a rescue operation. Mussolini is vital to our efforts to keep the Italians in our camp. I intend to re-install the Duce in power. Obviously, I must find him first. That will be your responsibility."

"*Ja, Mein* Führer," shouted Skorzeny, executing a smart Nazi salute.

Kappler's reaction was much more subdued. "It may be difficult, Führer, with the anti-Fascists in control. Our ability to act freely will be restricted."

Hitler nodded. "A perceptive observation, Major, but one soon to be irrelevant. German military forces are, at this time, preparing to enter and occupy northern Italy and Rome. Our forces are already in southern Italy. Orders have been issued to Generals Kesselring and Rommel to give you every assistance."

"That will be most helpful. We should be able to locate the Duce," Kappler said in a firm voice.

Hitler stood. "Good, I am depending on you."

Kappler, forewarned about the mission by Himmler, had already told the Reichsführer that rescuing Mussolini was a waste of time and the Duce can be kept in power only at the point of a German bayonet. But Kappler, also a good soldier, would carry out his orders faithfully, regardless of what he thought.

Both officers took this as their cue. They saluted and turned to leave.

Hitler called after them. "And Gentleman . . ."

The two stopped and turned to face the führer.

Hitler's eyes bored into them. "Failure is not an option."

July 28, 1943, Rome, Offices of DELASEM

Sorani, at his desk, waited for Valobra, the executive director of DELASEM in Genoa, to come to the telephone. Meanwhile, he looked out the window. Everything looked peaceful on the street below, but he'd heard small arms being fired—just the thing he dreaded.

"Valobra," he shouted, "is that you?" Using the Italian long-distance service required strong lungs and a loud voice.

"*Ciao*, Sorani. What's happening down there?"

"I'm not sure, but there is fighting going on."

"There's no fighting in Genoa, but my sources tell me the Germans are moving substantial forces through the Brenner Pass. I expect they'll be here at any time now."

Sorani sighed. "The Jews in Rome are cheering in the streets at the downfall of the Duce and the Fascist government. They think all the racial laws will be repealed. But they're wrong. What I feared would happen is starting. The Germans will occupy Italy. Once that happens, deportation of all Jews here will not be far behind."

"Perhaps the new government will surrender to the Allies."

Sorani shook his head. "Think, Valobra. That would only make matters worse. The Allies will not be able to protect us for a long time. A surrender would only speed up the occupation and deportations by the vindictive Germans."

"Uh huh," Valobra grunted. "What's the word from France?"

"Not good. Angelo Donati is working feverishly with the Italian government to organize a massive rescue operation before the Germans march in. He fears that once the Italians surrender to the Allies—and he thinks that will happen soon—the Germans will move into Nice and other areas of France and round up the Jews. The Italian authorities have agreed to provide four ships to take the Jews from southern France to Allied-occupied North Africa. We are arranging the funds to pay for them. Benedetto is spreading the word to Jews throughout southern France to be prepared to come the Nice. The question remains whether we have the time."

"Amazing, what Donati can accomplish," Valobra muttered.

Donati, a Jew and former liaison officer between the French and Italian armies in World War I, had been an officer and director of the Nice bank, Crédit Franco-Italein, and had lived many years in France. In the course of his career, he'd developed friends in high places in the Italian government and the Vatican. Working with Father Benedetto, he had assisted thousands of Jews under German occupation to escape to the area under Italian occupation.

After a short silence, Valobra asked, "What's our next move?"

Sorani got up and began pacing around, tethered to the telephone. "We've got to speed up our preparations to transfer responsibilities for DELASEM to our friends in the church. Things can only get worse. We'll soon be on the run."

"What about Benedetto?"

Sorani heard more firing and looked toward the window to check. The street below was still quiet. "I saw Father Benedetto when he was in Rome briefly to meet with church officials. When the Germans move into Nice, he expects the Gestapo to come looking for him. He's on their list for deportation—or worse. He'll stay in southern France until the last possible minute. If he gets out, he'll be working out of the Capuchin friary here."

Valobra paused. "I'll have to contact Don Francesco Repetto and Cardinal Boetto. I think they're ready to step in."

"Good luck—and be careful," Sorani offered.

"You, too." Valobra hung up.

CHAPTER TWELVE

September 3, 1943, Rome, Gestapo Headquarters, SS Major Kappler's Office

"I have exciting news," Major Kappler told his visitor. Colonel Skorzeny leaned forward in his chair. "You found Mussolini?"

Kappler nodded. "From an intercepted Italian police radio communication checking on heightened security at Gran Sasso. There's nothing up there to justify such security preparations, so I looked into it. He's there, I'm sure of it."

"Gran Sasso, what's that?"

"It's a ski resort in the Apennines. But the news is not all good." Skorzeny's light blue eyes narrowed, the frown advanced slowly down his face, causing the long scar across his cheek to dance disconcertingly. "What do you mean?"

"They have Mussolini at Campo Imperatore, a hotel on a six-thousand-foot-high plateau."

"So?" Skorzeny said impatiently.

Kappler leaned back in his chair. "So, colonel, the plateau is reachable only by funicular railroad. We'd never make it up by that route if they cut off the power. Even if we could, we'd be easy targets ascending that way."

Skorzeny rubbed his chin. "You're right; the funicular is not the best route to mount an assault."

"What about paratroopers?' Kappler asked.

Skorzeny shook his head. "We don't have the equipment here to put together such an attack. Besides, trying to land paratroops on a high, windy plateau is too risky, and the troops floating down will be too exposed to ground fire."

"Then what?"

The colonel smiled. "I can put my hands on gliders that were shipped in with our military. It can be a quiet, fast assault. We'll be on the ground before they know it. You will have to secure the funicular station below; to keep reinforcements from ascending."

Kappler nodded. "I can do that."

As Skorzeny rose to his feet, Kappler looked in awe at the size of the commando. He would not want to be this man's target. The colonel looked all killer.

"I'll clear this with the Wehrmacht," Skorzeny said. "We'll probably mount it as a joint operation of army airborne forces and my SS commandos."

September 8, 1943, Rome, Trastevere, Home of Davide Nathan

Jews populated both the ghetto and Trastevere, separated only by the Tiber River. Davide Nathan looked out across the Tiber to the ghetto. A few minutes ago a statement on the radio had reported that Italy had signed an armistice with the Allies. "For Italy, the war is over!" the announcer breathlessly intoned. People, mostly Jews he guessed, flooded onto the street shouting, dancing and drinking in celebration.

His wife, Elena, and their seventeen-year-old daughter, Olga, joined him at the window. "Papa, aren't you going to join in the festivities?"

Nathan shook his head. "There's nothing to celebrate."

"My God, you're such a pessimist, Davide," his wife scolded. "It's wonderful news!"

Nathan looked grave. "Use your head, Elena. German soldiers have already entered northern Italy; they've occupied the outskirts of Rome, and are entrenched in the south, fighting the Allied invasion. What do you think the Germans will do? Step aside and say it's fine for Italy to join with the Reich's mortal enemies? The Germans will occupy Rome and make the Italian racial laws look like child's play. You'll see."

"But surely the Italian army in Rome will defend us against the Germans," Elena insisted.

"With what? They have old weapons, low ammunition stocks, no tanks—and they'll be up against the battle-hardened Wehrmacht." Nathan shook his head. "My dear Elena, it's no contest."

"But Davide, if the Italian troops can hold out for one week, the Allies will be here to free Rome."

"And how will the American and the British get here in just one week?" her husband snorted.

"I heard people say the Americans are going to parachute in."

Nathan laughed. "You heard people say? The people are the last to know! I hope you're right, Elena, but I don't think so. It's a pipe dream. We should start making preparations."

Elena frowned. "For what?"

Nathan grabbed both his wife's shoulders and looked directly into her eyes. "To go into hiding. I have no intention of letting the Germans ship you and Olga to a concentration camp."

But Elena was not easily intimidated. "We will do nothing so drastic until you speak to the president of the Rome Jewish community—see what he thinks."

Nathan sighed. "Very well, I'll try to see Ugo Foà as soon as possible."

Later the Same Day, Berlin, the Chancellery

Ribbentrop himself brought the news to Hitler. "I have just heard from Rudolph von Rahn, our new Ambassador to Rome, *Mein Führer*, that Italian radio reports an armistice between Italy and the Allies. General Giuseppe Castellano negotiated it and signed on behalf of Badoglio."

"Vile treachery," Hitler growled. "We will teach those Italians a lesson. Order our troops to kill, as traitors, all Italian soldiers fighting against us in Italy, Greece, Albania and the Aegean. Shoot any that surrender. Prepare to occupy Rome and arrest and execute Badoglio and the rest of that crowd, particularly that General Castellano. The Italian people will feel the wrath of the Third Reich."

Ribbentrop nodded. "Do you wish to broadcast a message to the Italians at this time, Führer?"

"Yes. Call my secretary." The secretary entered and sat down with a pad and pencil. Hitler rose from his chair and paced up and down as he dictated.

"To the Italian people: For many years the heroic German troops have won victory after victory with no help from our supposed Italian allies. In Russia the cowardly Italian troops often exposed the German flanks by refusing to fight, surrendering or fleeing. But the most vile and traitorous acts her friends, the Germans, had yet to see. It is the conspiracy to surrender to the Allies by the cowardly and lying Badoglio, who had promised to fight by our side. For this, punishment will be swift and severe. The treachery of the Italian people will not go unpunished.

"The loss of Italy has no real importance to us. For years the weight of the struggle there has been borne by us. The attempt of international plutocracy to weaken German resistance is childish. Their hopes of bringing about a collapse in Germany like that of July 25th in Italy spring from their fundamental error concerning my own personal position. The fact is that the German government is more than ever fanatically united and I am infinitely proud of being the leader of the German people; I thank God for every hour He grants me so that I may, by means of my own work, bring the greatest struggle in history to a victorious conclusion. The measures taken to safeguard German interests in Italy will be very severe. They are being put into effect as I speak and reprisals will be carried out methodically and without mercy. The fate I have decreed for Italy should remind all countries that they should stand by their obligations to their allies. To the German people now bearing this trial, Almighty God will, in the end, give them the laurels of victory as a reward, and with these laurels the preservation of their own lives."

Hitler turned to the secretary. "Type that up, let me read it, and then make a final copy for Foreign Minister Ribbentrop." He looked at Ribbentrop. "When we take over Rome, I will see that this is broadcast over the air and published in all the newspapers. It is a very strong statement. It should put the fear of God into those damn Italians. Call the secretary back in here."

When the woman reappeared at the door, he ordered, "Call *Reichsführer* Himmler and tell him I want to see him right away." She nodded and left.

"One more thing, *Mein* Führer," Ribbentrop advised. "I received a telegram from our ambassador to the Holy See."

Hitler looked up. "Weizsäcker?"

Ribbentrop nodded. "The pope is requesting more police protection from us. He fears that partisan activity will force us to withdraw, leaving the clergy at the mercy of the partisans."

Hitler smiled. "I'm sure we can accommodate the pope. I will tell the *Reichsführer* to send in more SS to seal off the Vatican."

"Weizsäcker also reports," Ribbentrop added, "that the Curia detests the Anglo-American alliance with the Soviet Union. Holding up the telegram, he read from it. " 'The Vatican has hopes that the Western powers will wake up and recognize their true interests before it is too late and act in common with the Germans to save European civilization from Bolshevism.' "

Hitler snorted. "I've tried to tell that to the British, but they and the Americans will never come around to that view while Churchill and Roosevelt are in power."

Ribbentrop got up to leave.

Hitler put up his hand. "Stay. Wait for Himmler. What I say to him will have an impact on the Foreign Ministry. I want the SS to capture the new Italian leaders and their generals, and Himmler should begin planning now the roundup of the Jews. I want your ambassadors well prepared to handle protests, particularly from the Catholic Church." Hitler laughed harshly, snorting, "We'll be collecting Jews right under the pope's windows."

September 10, 1943, Mid-Morning, the Vatican, Audience Room of the Pope

Pope Pius XII expelled a long breath. He gazed at his two visitors in the third-floor Library of Audiences where he granted private audiences. Harold Tittmann, President Roosevelt's personal representative, was there at the pope's request. The cardinal secretary of state accompanied him.

Improbable Heroes

"You must realize," the pope began, addressing the American, "that the greatest danger to the world is not Nazi Germany but the Bolshevism represented by the Soviet Union. I profoundly regret your alliance with that rogue state."

"With all due respect, Your Holiness," Tittmann replied, "President Roosevelt is totally committed to wiping out Nazism. He feels that if Germany ever won the war, it would treat the Catholics the same way it is treating the Jews. Even now, the Germans persecute Catholics and other Christians in Poland and other countries."

The pope stared at the ceiling for a minute. "I believe the Germans would be willing to discuss peace with America and Britain and join in opposing the Soviet Union. But you must withdraw that ill-conceived Casablanca demand of an 'unconditional surrender.' It may be fine for propaganda purposes, but it will only result in total intransigence on all sides."

"Any accommodation with the likes of Hitler on our part is quite impossible, Your Holiness. I am sure you are quite aware of the German slaughter of Jews, Gypsies, political dissidents and even some Christian clergy. I know I have called it to the attention of Cardinal Maglione on many occasions and supported it by documentation."

Maglione gave a slight confirmatory nod.

"Sadly, it is necessary for us to sort out the wartime propaganda from all sides to find the truth," Pius observed.

"Holiness, do you really doubt what's happening to the Jews?"

The pope shook his head slowly. "Not at all, Signore Tittmann. Just the extent to which you claim the Germans are doing it. My heart and prayers go out to those poor innocent people."

"Then why doesn't the Vatican say so in no uncertain terms?"

The pope compressed his already thin lips. "There is nothing I would like better, but if I did, the Germans would only make things worse for the Jews, and subject Catholics in the Third Reich to great danger. I know the German mind, Signor Tittmann. I was the papal nuncio in Berlin for many years. You must trust that what I say is true."

"I understand your position, Holiness, but we strongly disagree with it. It would be hard to imagine how things could get any worse for the Jews. As far as the partisans are concerned, I can assure Your Holiness that the Vatican is in far more danger from the Nazis than from the Bolsheviks. As we speak, the danger is right outside your doorstep. My government fails to understand why the Vatican asked the Germans for more SS troops in Rome. They are the ones responsible for all the atrocities, for heaven's sake."

The pontiff stared at Tittmann. "Heaven has nothing to do with it, Signor Tittmann. Rome is crawling with irresponsible elements who would take over if the Germans should withdraw from Rome."

"Irresponsible elements, Your Holiness?"

"The partisans," Cardinal Maglione explained, "who are mostly Bolsheviks."

"Exactly," the pope cut in. "Without the Germans, we face mortal danger with the Communists and anti-Fascists in power."

"I respectfully protest," Tittmann proffered in a low voice, "that the Holy See is overreacting. Many of those partisans include American and British agents, escaped POWs and anti-Fascists who are no more Bolsheviks than I am."

Cardinal Maglione smiled politely. "Then we will have to agree to disagree, Signore Tittmann."

Later the Same Day, Rome
Joseph Schwartz, Davide Nathan, Lev Divis, and for that matter, most of Rome, watched as the Wehrmacht completed its occupation of the city. Hitler's angry voice blared from all radios and loudspeakers, warning that he would severely punish Italian treachery. The streets filled with German soldiers under the command of Field Marshal Albert Kesselring, who, that evening, proclaimed martial law for all German-occupied Italy. Premier Badoglio, his cabinet and military commanders all left Rome and fled behind Allied lines in Brindisi, leaving the Romans to fend for themselves and at the mercy of the Germans. The Badoglio government left no orders for the Italian army, which did not know if it was to fight the Germans, the Allies or both. The confused soldiers did nothing and were rapidly disarmed and incarcerated by German troops.

Same Day, Rome, the Ghetto, Home of Joseph Schwartz

Dora Schwartz had just set the table for the Sabbath dinner. She placed the candlestick holder on a smaller table, in preparation for welcoming *Shabbos* with the lighting of the candles. Next to the candlestick holder she placed a plate with a *challa,* the Sabbath bread, and covered it with a napkin.

She heard the door shut. "Is that you, Joseph? Where have you been?"

"Never mind the Sabbath dinner, Dora. The Germans have arrived in force. Hitler is threatening our lives. We are in danger and have to leave at once."

Dora picked the napkin off the *challa* and covered her eyes. "Again, Joseph? Is there no place in Europe that we won't be driven out of by those monsters?" she sobbed.

Schwartz hugged his wife and sighed. "I know, darling, I feel the same way. But we don't have any choice if we want to remain alive. As foreigners, it is harder for us to blend in with the Italian Gentile population."

Dora removed the napkin from her face. "Where will we go, what will we do?"

"We'll just have to see. The one thing I am sure of—we must leave the ghetto now. The Germans could conduct a *razzia* at any time."

Her eyes widened. "A roundup of Jews here in Rome, right under the nose of the pope?"

Joseph shrugged. "If we lived inside the Vatican, perhaps it would help us, but we don't, so we must go into hiding."

A dark look clouded her face. "Joseph, we are already in hiding."

"Yes, my dear, but hiding in the ghetto with the Nazis on our doorstep puts us in harm's way again. Get ready to leave. Don't take much of anything. It will slow us down."

Schwartz knocked on his neighbor's door. "Rafanelli, we are leaving before the Germans come for us. You and your family should leave, too."

Enrico Rafanelli, a Jewish Fascist, reacted angrily. "You foreigners always panic. Right away, you run like cowards."

Schwartz, surprised at his neighbor's vitriol, backed up a few steps. "I saw what happened in Vienna when the Nazis marched in," he explained. "People who reacted just like you are in concentration camps today—or worse."

Unmollified, Rafanelli only became angrier. "It's people like you that will cause the Germans to react against us! They have been here for years and never bothered us. Just leave quietly, if you must and don't make a damn fuss!" He slammed the door in his neighbor's face.

□□□

A few hours later Joseph Schwartz and his family, each taking what could fit in a suitcase, walked to the nearest train station. Every time they passed a German soldier, Dora grabbed Joseph's hand and squeezed. He could feel the terror in her grip and struggled to keep his own inner calm. But the Germans ignored them; these Germans were simply enjoying the sights on their first visit to the Eternal City.

Chaos ruled the railway station. Crowds moved in every direction, many of them Italian soldiers fleeing from pursuing German troops. "I'm not sure this was such a good idea." Joseph whispered to Dora, out of the hearing of the two children.

"Where are we going?" Dora whispered back, her eyes glistening with tears she had unsuccessfully tried to stem.

Schwartz said nothing; panic started to set in.

"Joseph, Joseph Schwartz," a high-pitched voice rang out.

He blanched at being singled out. The young woman walked up to them.

"Adriana!"

She smiled. "*Ciao*, Dora. What are you all doing here on your Sabbath? You look lost."

Adriana Faggini, a practicing Catholic, had discovered the tailoring genius of Joseph Schwartz. She had become a steady customer for tailor-made clothes. A happy woman in her late twenties, she and Dora had hit it off immediately.

Dora hugged her friend. "Oh, Adriana, we are in trouble. With the German crawling all over Rome we're trying to leave. But where to go? We just don't know."

Adriana patted her cheek. "Stop worrying, we'll figure it out."

Schwartz gave her an uncomprehending look.

Adriana ran her fingers through her black hair, careful not to knock off the sunglasses perched on the top of her head. Suddenly, her olive-toned Mediterranean face lit up brightly. "I know! You will come with me to Ancona, to my parent's house—until you think what to do. I am on my way there now."

"We couldn't impose like that," Dora protested.

"Nonsense. They are wonderful people and I assure you, will, welcome you with open arms. Now come, you must not stand on ceremony with your lives at stake. It is a very pleasant two-hour train ride."

September 14, 1943, Airport near Hitler's Headquarters at Rastenburg, East Prussia

The two-engine Fokker circled the field once and came in for a smooth landing. Hitler watched as the exit door swung down to form stairs to the tarmac. Goebbels had been against restoring Mussolini to power, arguing that Fascism was dead in Italy and the Duce would serve no useful function for the Third Reich. The army generals were against it, favoring an outright military occupation of Italy without the complication of a Mussolini government. But Hitler was convinced that the collapse of a Fascist system would set an unfortunate example for his own citizens. Once Mussolini was re-installed, Hitler was sure the Badoglio government would collapse. Besides, although there were not many people he felt indebted to, Mussolini was one of them, having led the way, while Hitler still languished in jail, to the first successful Fascist takeover of a government. Hitler couldn't exactly explain it, but he had a lingering fondness for the ineffectual Italian dictator.

Mussolini appeared on the steps of the airplane in a rumpled suit, half bent over in pain. No longer vigorous and proud, the man was an emaciated wreck. His skin had a yellow cast. It seemed to Hitler that the Duce had shrunk physically.

Hitler stepped forward; with his left hand he grabbed Mussolini's shoulder and with the right, he enthusiastically shook his hand. It was a show of warmth the führer rarely bestowed on another human being. "Welcome back, Duce."

Mussolini, still looking confused, nodded. "Thank you for rescuing me, Führer."

Back in the Wolf's Lair, Hitler's Rastenburg headquarters in East Prussia, there were no air raid alerts, so the Duce and the führer emerged from Hitler's bunker to stroll through the adjoining gardens. Mussolini described to Hitler the daring rescue attempt. "I couldn't believe it. First I heard airplanes in the distance. No one thought anything of it. Then I looked out of the window and saw many gliders being released from their towlines and begin approaching the plateau. The gliders made no noise. They swooped down in an eerie silence—never saw anything like it."

Hitler smiled. "The operation was planned by my top commando, Colonel Skorzeny. I knew that if anyone could rescue you, he could."

Determined to complete his story, Mussolini continued. "Anyway, all the gliders landed safely, except one, which crashed. My guards were so surprised they put up no resistance. Heavily armed German troops piled out of the gliders and spread out. They came in so quickly, the troops in the barracks never knew they were under attack until the German soldiers entered the buildings and disarmed them. It was amazing—not a shot was fired!"

"How did they take you off?" Hitler asked.

Mussolini shook his head. "Even more unbelievable! Somehow, they produced a tiny Fieseler-Storch reconnaissance plane. I don't know where it came from. Your huge Colonel Skorzeny bundled me into the plane despite my protests. I'm a pilot and I knew so small a plane could not, at that altitude, take off with so much weight. Undaunted, the colonel strapped me in and then squeezed himself beside me, powered up and took off. Well, as I feared, the plane had trouble gaining altitude and the landing gear actually hit some rocks at the end of the strip. I thought for sure we would crash but the plane cleared the precipice and had several thousand feet of drop permitting it to recover as we sailed off the plateau."

Hitler, his hands behind his back as he walked, turned his head to look at his guest. "I shall have to reward the entire team, an incredible performance, simply incredible."

"Tell me," Mussolini said softly, "is my family safe?"

"I feared that Badoglio would try to eliminate them," Hitler said, reassuringly, "so I had them all brought to Germany—safe and sound. We even have your daughter, Edda, and your son-in-law, Count Ciano here."

Mussolini nodded. "Thank you again, Führer."

Hitler waved away the gratitude. "No need for thanks, Duce, just return to power immediately in northern Italy. Reconstitute the Fascist government, depose the monarchy and restore the full validity of the Axis alliance. That will be thanks enough."

Mussolini sighed. "Führer, I am tired, I am ill and I'm getting old. I'd rather just retire to my summer home in Italy. I have no desire to rule again or revitalize the Fascist Party. Surely someone else would be better suited . . ."

"No," Hitler interrupted. "Only you are Il Duce. The Italian betrayal could have caused the collapse of Germany, if the Allies had known how to take advantage of it. So it is important to reverse that situation immediately by returning you to power in Italy and severely punishing the traitors. That should intimidate any of our allies tempted to imitate Italy's cowardly actions."

Mussolini looked down at his shoes. "I just don't know . . ."

"I have to tell you quite honestly, my generals wanted to treat Italy like a conquered enemy, suggestions that I have so far resisted. But I warn you, only you can save your country from that fate. If you don't return to power, I will have do to Italy the same things I did to Poland, and you do not want that, I assure you."

"I'm not sure my health will permit me to rule."

Hitler struggled to keep his voice pleasant. "When you stopped in Vienna on your way here, my best doctors examined you, and they have assured me that with the proper diet and medications you will be just fine. They have been ordered to take over your treatment."

Mussolini sighed. "Very well, Führer."

"Good. A condition of the resurgence of the Fascist Party will be for you to deal with the traitors who deposed you, particularly members of the Grand Council who voted against you. All of them, especially Grandi, must be found and executed. We have a few of them in custody and Count Ciano is under guard in Munich. We will return him to your reconstituted government. He must be executed, as well."

Mussolini rubbed his forehead. "I can't do that, Führer. He's my son-in-law!"

Hitler turned away from Mussolini, and bent over to examine some fall marigolds in full golden color. Disappointed, he wondered if his generals weren't right. Would restoring Mussolini to power be a mistake? This man was such a weak imitation of the old Duce—with such a defeatist attitude. Had he always overestimated Mussolini out of affection for him? Nevertheless, he could not abandon him now. But he would impose his will on the Italian—and supply the backbone he would need to serve German purposes.

Hitler broke off a marigold and straightened up, handing it to Mussolini. "My dear Duce," he said placatingly, "your son-in-law was one of the leaders of the coup. If you do not call him to account, how can you expect to deal with the other Fascist traitors?"

Mussolini looked at the golden flower and inhaled its pungent scent. Hitler broke off another flower, stripping off some of its pale green leaves. "You should try this in a salad. I highly recommend its excellent healing properties."

Mussolini handed the blossom back to Hitler. "I have to figure out how to handle this in my own way."

Hitler decided not to push today. "I understand. Your familial feelings make it difficult. But the SS will deal with that traitorous general Cavallero, who negotiated that despicable armistice with the Allies. You do not have to worry about him."

Mussolini shrugged.

"In the meantime," Hitler continued, "you must prepare to assume power immediately."

"How?"

"We have prepared a secure place at Lake Garda, between Salò and Gargnano. A force of SS troops is already in place there and will be responsible for your security. I know I can trust them."

"Why can't you just release the Italian soldiers you have under detention? From them I can constitute the core of my security force."

Hitler shook his head. "There are too many traitors among them. It would be too dangerous. Form your government and then we will talk about it—and don't forget, you must have your Fascist militia reconstituted to help us deal with the Jews in Italy."

Mussolini's eyes narrowed. "Am I to have no say in these matters? Will I be a prisoner in my own country?"

Hitler sighed. "Of course not, Duce, but I am taking it on myself to provide for your security. Certain restrictions and procedures are necessary to assure your safety. The Jews, of course, are a menace to all of us. For too long, they have been neglected in your country. You—and I—will remedy that."

Mussolini frowned; he didn't look too convinced. Hitler didn't care, as long as a Fascist government could be set up again as a showpiece for his other wavering allies.

CHAPTER THIRTEEN

September 15, 1943, Rome. Home of General Giuseppe Castellano; Later, Gestapo Headquarters
His wife poured the general another cup of *caffè latte*. Giuseppe Castellano smiled appreciatively. He admired this brave woman.

To escape the German occupation, Premier Badoglio and his colleagues had fled to Brindisi, under the protection of the Allies. But not General Castellano. The general knew the Germans would be out to get him for his involvement in the armistice with the Allies and that remaining in Rome would be dangerous. But would be damned if he'd scamper away with his tail between his legs on account of the Huns. He tried to convince his wife to go live with relatives in the south for the time being, but she refused, saying her place was at his side.

Earlier, Castellano had been asked to negotiate, on behalf of Badoglio, an armistice with the Allies. He had traveled to Lisbon to meet with the Americans and the British but the task had turned out be a far more difficult task than any command responsibility he'd had in World War I or the Ethiopian war. The Allies wanted surrender first, then talks. In vain, Castellano had tried to explain that without Fascism, the Italians were not an aggressive people. He made his arguments to British General Kenneth Strong and a very suspicious American General Walter Bedell Smith. Castellano urged Allied landings at specified areas, but Strong and Smith were very closed-mouthed, frustrating the Italian general. Castellano really had nothing to bargain with, and in the end, he had accepted unconditionally, the entire package of terms imposed by the Allies.

☐☐☐

Herbert Kappler, now a colonel, thanks to his part in the rescue of Mussolini, decided to carry out personally the arrest of General Castellano. Followed by a squad of SS, Kappler climbed the steps to the general's imposing home and rang the doorbell. Castellano, holding a steaming cup of coffee, answered the door.

"General Castellano, I'm Colonel Kappler of the Gestapo and you are under arrest. You will accompany me to Gestapo headquarters."

The general's eyes locked onto Kappler and never wavered. "By whose authority?"

"Under my own authority as a Gestapo officer and head of German security in Rome."

Castellano broke eye contact and grabbed his hat off the rack. He turned to his wife. "I don't think I shall come back from there."

The old general was perceptive, thought Kappler. He admired Castellano's calm. The Gestapo colonel grudgingly admitted that the general, who had refused to flee with Badoglio to the safety of Allied territory, seemed to have ice water in his veins. Since the general refused to go into hiding with Badoglio and his cronies, his arrest became simply a matter of ringing his doorbell and taking him, unresisting, into custody.

☐☐☐

At Gestapo headquarters at 145 Via Tasso, Kappler closed the door to his office and offered Castellano a chair, moving his own chair to sit opposite the general. There were no guards in the office. Kappler wanted to talk to the general alone. He offered the prisoner a cigarette. Castellano declined. Kappler shrugged and lit one for himself.

Kappler inhaled deeply on the cigarette and exhaled a long stream of smoke. "General, I am prepared to spare your life if you are able to convince all Italian troops in Rome to lay down their arms. That would convince us that you are not the traitor."

Castellano looked at Kappler. "Doing what you suggest, Colonel," the general said calmly, but firmly, "would make me the traitor you accuse me of being. I cannot and will not communicate such a message to the Italian soldiers."

Kappler had hoped to convince Berlin to spare the general, but Castellano's refusal made that impossible. His orders from Berlin were to execute this fearless Italian—and he didn't like it—not one bit. It was one thing to shoot Jews, but an entirely different thing to shoot brave generals like this.

Kappler sighed and stubbed out his cigarette in the ashtray. He stood up and walked over to his desk, picking up the telephone receiver and dialing. "He's all yours."

Berlin had insisted he witness the execution but was very glad he did not have to do it. He waited uneasily while Castellano watched him.

A Gestapo agent from Himmler's staff entered the office, walked over to behind the seated Castellano, unholstered his pistol and dispatched Castellano with one shot to the right temple. The agent bent over the body and placed the pistol in the murdered general's right hand.

Kappler immediately telephoned the general's wife to inform her of her husband's "suicide" and invited her to see the body. A few minutes later, as she entered the Via Tasso headquarters, he greeted the grieving widow with his "heartfelt sympathy" for the loss of her "greatly respected" husband.

Signora Castellano's obvious disbelief made Kappler uncomfortable. Calmly, she stated, "I am absolutely certain my husband did not have a gun when he left the house with you. How do you suppose he obtained one while he was in your custody? I understand the Gestapo is quite efficient when it comes to restraining their prisoners."

Kappler shrugged. "We are not perfect, Signora Castellano. It happens sometimes, and I do apologize. Your husband probably had the gun secreted on his person. Would you care to look for yourself?"

She nodded and the colonel led her into the room where Castellano's body lay sprawled out, pistol still gripped in his right hand.

"We have issued a press release," Kappler said softly as the widow looked at the body, "praising your husband as one of the finest officers in the Italian military, who, unable to bear his country's dishonor, put an end to his life."

She stood there quietly, taking in the scene. Then, turning an unrelenting gaze on Kappler, she said, "Very good of you, Colonel, but there is one thing you seemed to have forgotten."

As she continued to stare at him, he looked away and focused instead on the swastika banner hanging on the wall just over her right shoulder. "And what's that, Signora?"

"My husband was left-handed."

Same Day, Berlin, SS Headquarters, Office of Colonel Adolph Eichmann

SS Colonel Adolph Eichmann looked at his subordinate, Captain Theodor Dannecker, the veteran of many roundups and deportations of Jews throughout German-occupied Europe. While Eichmann appreciated his work, he didn't like to be in Dannecker's company because the captain had a bad tic, often forcing his head to one side, almost like snapping a whip—it was that pronounced. It made the Eichmann feel uncomfortable, like he had to fight developing a tic himself. But the tall, gangly, and somewhat uncoordinated Dannecker was good at his job and therefore someone to be tolerated—for now.

"It's a crime what those cowardly and traitorous Italians did—stabbing us in the back like that," Dannecker growled.

Eichmann took off his glasses and wiped them clean, then looked through them to make sure. He leaned back, waving his glasses in his left hand. "Oh . . . I don't feel that way, Captain, I think it's a good thing."

Dannecker frowned. Some anger, at least as much as he dared, crept into his voice. "How can you say that? They betrayed us!" His head snapped violently from the tic.

Eichmann smiled, putting his glasses back on. "Oh, I agree—they shamelessly double-crossed us; but calm down and think about it, Captain," his smile broadening, "now we have a free hand to deal with the Jews. At the Final Solution conference at Wannsee, I promised to deliver 58,000 Jews from Italy and Sardinia. It was Mussolini who kept forestalling my efforts at every turn, and our Foreign Ministry helped him by forbidding me to interfere in Italian affairs. Now the restraints have been lifted."

"I see what you mean, Sir."

Eichmann waved a paper in front of the captain. "I have issued top secret orders to all Gestapo officers in Italy that the Italian Jews are now subject to the same measures we used in other occupied territories. The eight thousand Jews in Rome will be taken first, but we will not use local police. They are too unreliable."

Dannecker leaned forward. "And you have something in mind for me, Sir?"

Eichmann looked down at his fingers, falling into a speculative silence. Then he looked up. "That damn Kappler in Rome continues to resist liquidating the Jews. He says they are too well assimilated into the Italian population and culture, that the Italian citizens would consider our efforts an attack on Italians generally. Kappler thinks they could give us trouble."

"What do you suggest, Colonel?"

"Me, I don't give a damn what the Italians think or how they may react. I want you to go to Rome and personally oversee the roundup of the Jews. You will neutralize Colonel Kappler's opposition."

"But Colonel . . ."

"Don't worry, Captain. You will have specific orders from *Reichsführer* Himmler that will supersede anything Kappler tries to order you to do."

"I understand, Colonel."

"That will be all, Captain."

Dannecker nodded, stood up and headed for the door.

"And Captain . . ."

Dannecker stopped and turned around.

"Keep it low-key until we are ready to move. I don't want the Jews to be frightened and go into hiding. For now, let's make it appear that we are fine, reasonable Germans with no hostile intent toward them."

September 17, 1943, a Villa on Lake Garda on the Outskirts of Gargnano

Mussolini wasn't finished with breakfast yet, but Rachele had already started clearing the dishes, throwing them into the sink with such force that some shattered. He hadn't seen his wife so worked up since the time in Milan when she found out he'd taken up with Clara Petacci shortly after dumping Margherita Sarfatti. Clara didn't have much of an intellect and her subservience was a welcome change from the challenging, quarrelsome Sarfatti. Now, at Garda, he was thinking, just wait until Rachele finds out I have had Petacci sneaked into Gargnano, in a small house nearby!

"It's outrageous," Rachele shouted at her husband, whipping in the air, the dishtowel she was carrying. "There are German guards all over the place. Bene, they won't even let you go into town unescorted. You are not a leader, you are a prisoner. You can't go anywhere without getting their permission. You have sunk to a level lower than that of a puppet. I just can't believe the Duce has submitted to such indignities."

"I know, Rachele, but what choice do I have? The Germans call us allies, but they are enslaving our people. Italian soldiers are being shipped to Germany to work as slave laborers under the most abysmal conditions; here, the German military and the SS act brutally to our citizens. At the same time that Hitler showers me with platitudes, the Germans act like an occupying power. They have annexed our sacred land, Alto Adige and Venezia Giulia. We have lost the great cities of Trieste, Fiume and Venice."

"I have never known you to be shy, Bene. Why don't you object?"

Mussolini shrugged. "I did, vigorously, not only to the annexation of Italian territory but to the enslavement of our soldiers and military abuse of our people. Hitler just ignores me. I haven't even received the courtesy of a response from him, Ribbentrop or anyone else in the German government."

"You should resign, Bene."

"And then what?" he blustered. "Hitler would treat Italy like Poland and slaughter or enslave even more Italians. He told me as much when I met with him at Rastenburg. That's why I agreed to return. No, Rachele, I have to do his bidding. I have re-instituted OVRA, my secret police, and given my blessing to the Fascist gangs who will arrest the anti-Fascists. I will round up the Jews as the führer has demanded. My lot in life, my dear Rachele, has been reduced to that."

"What about Gallo?"

"Gallo, I fear, is a *dead* man."

"My God, Bene, how could you? He's our son-in-law! You will have to deal with your daughter. You know how headstrong and outspoken she can be."

"Yes, I know—and you'd be wrong if you thought it doesn't worry me terribly."

Same Day, Rome, Gestapo Headquarters

Colonel Kappler headed for the south wing of the yellow-marbled front of Gestapo headquarters, the heavily guarded entrance at 155 Via Tasso. He usually did not use the entrance at number 145 because he found the walk through the ugly prison extremely distasteful. He didn't relish hearing the screams coming from the interrogation rooms. Kappler climbed the steps to number 155, was admitted and passed in, ignoring a life-size portrait of the führer in the hall. His aide intercepted him before he reached his office, handing him a sealed envelope. "An 'urgent' message from the *Reichsführer* for 'your eyes only,' Colonel."

Kappler took the envelope and closed his office door behind him. He had a bad feeling about this as yet unread message. He wandered over to the window looking out on the enclosed garden with its pond, fountain, and cypress trees. The peaceful scene belied the interrogation and torture going on a few feet away behind a brick and concrete wall so thick that no sound escaped into the garden or the street.

The Reichsführer was going to order him to deport the Jews, he was sure of it. Stupid, stupid, stupid! For the small number of Jews in Italy, Himmler would roil the whole Italian population, who seemed to love their Jews, and rouse the Vatican, which had been, up to now, remarkably subdued about the Final Solution. I have barely enough SS to provide security in a calm Rome, he thought. How the hell am I going to round up Jews, as well? It wasn't that Kappler harbored any sympathy for the Jews or for what the führer was doing to them; he had no remorse whatsoever. But here in Rome, deportations simply didn't make sense.

He ripped open the envelope. Signed personally by the *Reichsführer*, it was addressed to all German security units in Italy. Quickly he scanned the usual bureaucratic preamble and found the operative paragraph:

> All Jews, regardless of nationality, age, sex, and personal conditions, must be transferred to Germany and liquidated. The success of this undertaking will have to be ensured by a surprise action and for that reason it is strictly necessary to suspend the application of any anti-Jewish measures of an individual nature, likely to stir up among the population suspicion of an imminent action.

Kappler stroked his cheek, surprised at the complete change of tactics from other occupied areas where the first action taken was either the immediate roundup, or liquidation, of the Jews. It seemed that providing the Jews with a false sense of security had become the order of the day.

September 19, 1943, Rome, Offices of the Union of Italian Jewish Communities and the Home of Rabbi Zolli

Rabbi Israel Zolli sat patiently in the outer office of the Union of Italian Jewish Communities, an umbrella organization overseeing all Jewish groups and synagogues in Italy. He was waiting to see its president, Dante Almansi, and Ugo Foà, president of the Jewish Community of Rome.

Zolli knew that with the Germans tightening their control in Rome more with every passing day, Jews had to go into hiding before it was too late. He and his family would not wait around to be deported. In an unsettling conversation with a friendly police commissioner, Zolli had been warned to disappear; that in Prague, the first thing the Germans did was to arrest and deport the chief rabbi. The people can't believe they are in any danger, he thought. If I can convince influential men like Almansi and Foà, the people will listen and take steps to protect themselves. He knew it would be an uphill battle. The two leaders had been reluctant to meet with him, but at his insistence they had finally agreed. He was, after all, the chief rabbi of Rome.

A secretary ushered Zolli into Almansi's office. Foà was already there. Zolli felt a creeping sense of rejection. Both of them, in earlier telephone calls, had dismissed his warnings out of hand, and now, they had probably just discussed it and already made up their minds.

Almansi's tone was not particularly friendly. "Now what's so important, Rabbi, that you had to have this meeting today? You know it's a very busy time with the holidays coming up shortly."

"There *is* no time, gentlemen," Zolli urged. "As we speak, the Germans are tightening their grip on the city. The Jews of Rome must go into hiding. You must close down the Union and the synagogues—destroy all your member lists—we must make it difficult for the Nazis to find us."

Foà sighed unhappily. "Rabbi, you must stop this; you're spreading panic among our people. Now you want to interrupt the functioning of all Jewish offices and the traditional conduct of Hebrew life? Ridiculous! We will do no such thing."

"Listen, Rabbi Zolli," Almansi said, trying to be reassuring, "I spoke to a high Italian minister just yesterday and he said the Jews were in no danger. It makes sense. Have you heard of a single Jew in Rome being hurt by the Germans? There are so few of us compared to countries like France, Poland and Russia, that it's not worth their trouble to deport us all the way to the East. I have it on good authority that the German Army is opposed to any persecution on political grounds . . ."

"Of course it is," Foà broke in, "because any persecution by the Germans in the Vatican's backyard would produce the greatest outcry from the pope. The Germans don't want to endanger the pontiff's neutrality. Colonel Kappler from the SS stopped by my office. He would like to arrange a meeting with Jewish leaders concerning our security. He assured me that the SS plans no actions against the Jews in the city that's the home of the Catholic Church."

Zolli mournfully shook his head. "With all due respect, gentlemen, that is not the case. A friend of mine, an employee at the German Embassy, warned me that Jews will be rounded up and sent to Poland that the SS is flooding into Rome to prepare for the roundup. The Nazis are trying to lull us into a false sense of security to make it easier to pick us up when they're ready."

"Who is telling you such garbage?" Foà asked angrily.

"I can't say because it would put my friend in great danger."

Foà snorted. "That's what I thought. As chief rabbi, you should be instilling confidence in your congregation in these difficult times instead of discouragement and panic. Go, Zolli, buy a lire's worth of courage in the store. That should help." Foà laughed harshly.

"Please, gentlemen, we must take some measures to protect our people. We must see that they are dispersed. The citizens of Rome hate the Nazis and would willingly help us to hide Jews with Christian families, in remote villages and in churches . . . and we could use the considerable funds of your organizations to support such an operation. But you must start by destroying all your lists of Jews."

"Up to now, the German soldiers have acted with absolute correctness," Almansi noted, trying to keep the discussion on a reasonable, friendly plane. "They even buy cameras, watches and souvenirs at Jewish shops, paying full price. I'm sorry, Rabbi, but I simply do not share your concern."

Foà slapped the table with force. "And I'm certainly not going to destroy our membership lists and close down our organization," the anger spilling out of his voice. "Closing the synagogues and going into hiding are just the things that will *provoke* the Germans. It's a terrible idea and I, for one, will not encourage such conduct. As far as I am concerned, your suggestions are crazy and this meeting is over."

Rabbi Zolli shook his head sadly. "Then I will have to do what I can to warn my congregation, with or without your help. I assure you, gentlemen, that I will take steps to go into hiding and protect *my* family."

"How did the meeting go?" Adele asked later when her husband had returned home.

Zolli shucked off his coat and threw it on a chair. He'd always been meticulous about hanging it up. He met his wife's eyes. She frowned—he had the look of a defeated man.

The rabbi sighed. "Terrible, they will do nothing, not even destroy the lists through which the SS can locate the Jews. Can you imagine anything so stupid?"

"What are you going to do, Israel?"

"We don't have time. I saw two Gestapo agents follow me home. You know, as chief rabbi, I will be the first one they grab. We must go into hiding."

"What about the High Holy Days—they're nearly here?"

Zolli sighed. "They will have to be held without me. It's too dangerous for me to conduct services anymore. Who knows what the Nazis will do when they have so many Jews assembled in one place during the holiday? I will warn my staff at the synagogue and hope that they will spread the word. Then we will disappear."

Same Day, Assisi, Seminary of San Damiano

Assisi, tucked into the foothills of the Apennines 120 kilometers north of Rome, was the birthplace the gentle ascetic, Saint Francis, the patron saint of Italy. Of a population of five thousand in 1943, more than one thousand were priests or other members of religious orders. There was not a single Jew. As far as anyone knew, no Jew had lived there since the Middle Ages. It was not surprising, therefore, that Father Rufino Niccacci, a Franciscan friar and priest attached to the Seminary of San Damiano and guardian of the Franciscan friary, had never met Jews, much less pondered their fate.

Born a peasant who had felt the calling for a religious vocation, he was a gentle man who loved prayer, a good smoke, some red wine and tasty food; he wanted only to serve God and Saint Francis quietly in this lovely place.

The town of Assisi, with its medieval churches, monasteries, friaries, and convents, made it easy to devote one's self to the Saint. The clergy and religious orders of Assisi took loving care of the shrines of Saint Francis and his disciple Saint Clare, created long ago by the orders of Franciscans and Poor Clares. It was to these sites that Christians from all over the world flocked to pray and contemplate. Tourism was the principal source of income for Assisi.

"The bishop wants to see you right away," the sacristan of the Church of Santa Maria Maggiore informed Father Niccacci in his office in the seminary. Niccacci, his brown habit flowing behind him and his sandals flapping, rushed to the Bishop's Palace adjoining the church. Bishop Giuseppe Placido Nicolini, dressed in a black cassock piped in reddish purple, a matching zucchetto on his head, received the Franciscan right away.

The bishop extended his arm and Niccacci kissed his ring. "You must keep this absolutely secret, Father" the bishop warned.

Niccacci raised his eyebrows but nodded assent. "I have some Jewish refugees who fled Rome hiding here in my palace. I want you to take them by train to Florence, where Cardinal Dalla Costa will take them off your hands and send them on to Genoa. There, Cardinal Boetto will try to get them out of the country on a neutral ship."

Niccacci frowned. "But Your Excellency, what if they are stopped by the Germans? How can I protect them?"

The bishop handed him a paper. "This is a letter I prepared vouchsafing your charges as Christian pilgrims returning to their homes from Assisi. That should be sufficient. Now come with me."

In a room deep inside the palace, the bishop introduced Niccacci to his new charges—the first Jews he'd ever seen. They looked like ordinary Italians. He knew, on an intellectual level, he shouldn't have been surprised, but this was no intellectual exercise. After all, this sedentary and unassuming friar, heretofore leading a simple friar's life, had suddenly been thrust into a role like that of a partisan on a perilous mission. Strong feelings—excitement, danger, and fear of failure—swept over him.

September 21, 1943, Florence, Office of Elia Cardinal Dalla Costa

Father Niccacci arrived at the cardinal's office in Florence with his Jews, an absolute nervous wreck. He explained to Dalla Costa that nine of the Jews had posed as pilgrims, while the tenth, a rabbi, had been dressed in a friar's habit. He had taught the rabbi a quick Latin prayer. During a check on the train by OVRA, the Italian Secret Police, the rabbi had intoned the prayer continuously and been waved on. The cardinal smiled as Father Niccacci described the scene.

Later, a Gestapo check had really scared the life out of Niccacci when the German officer demanded the rabbi's identification papers. In response, the rabbi had kept on repeating the Latin prayer while Niccacci said a few of his own. Just then, a British fighter had swooped down over the train and fired on it. The Gestapo officer had jumped off the train and commanded the engineer to get it out of there.

The Good Lord, Dalla Costa decided, had bestowed his own special brand of protection on the simple priest.

□□□

The cardinal succeeded in sending the ten Jews on to Genoa, but he feared that not many more Jews could be spirited out of the country that way. As the German occupation become more complete, the danger became too great. Even in Florence, he was running out of hiding places for Jews. He'd insisted that all religious houses receive Jews, even monasteries of enclosed nuns, despite the horrified protests of their mother abbesses.

Dalla Costa himself had had a close call when three of his nuns were arrested and accused of harboring Jewish women in their convent. He had interceded in person with the German high command. Dressed impressively in his official black cassock with scarlet piping and sash, he took full blame and told the Germans that he expected them, as soldiers, not to make subordinates responsible for the orders of their superiors. "It was my Christian duty to assist and defend these poor persecuted people" he'd explained, "as one day, perhaps soon, you will be persecuted and then I will defend you." The commanding officer must have been a good Catholic, because he had ordered the nuns freed and permitted the cardinal to leave, as well. The incident had convinced Cardinal Dalla Costa that Florence was becoming too dangerous a place to hide many Jews.

He turned his thoughts to the pleasant little town of Saint Francis's birthplace, Assisi.

PART IV

Gestapo Preparations

CHAPTER FOURTEEN

September 24, 1943, Rome, Gestapo Headquarters, Office of Colonel Kappler

Kappler had never seen the usually unflappable Eitel Möllhausen, German consul to the Holy See, in such a state. "I saw Himmler's order," Möllhausen cried. "I won't be a party to such gross stupidity."

Kappler was not surprised at the outburst. He knew Möllhausen refused to join the Nazi Party and, having been brought up outside of Germany, did not have the anti-Semitic and Aryan superiority ethic of a good Nazi. Kappler pretended ignorance. "What do you mean, Consul?"

A look of disgust came over the consul's face. "Don't play games with me, Colonel. I saw the order to transfer and 'liquidate' the Jews. Liquidate! Can you imagine?"

Kappler's eyes narrowed. "You weren't supposed to see that message; that's a gross breach of security."

Möllhausen jumped up and leaned against Kappler's desk. "But I did see it!"

Kappler leaned his chin on his hand. "And . . .?"

"And I proposed to General Kesselring that the Jews could be put to better use building fortifications instead of being deported. He agreed he could use such labor, but he refused to become involved with the bureaucracy by making such a request."

Kappler nodded. "I'm not surprised. It's a political minefield to oppose deportation of Jews. You should know that. I've been slapped down several times for suggesting a go-slow approach. So be careful."

"I've already made suggestions to the foreign minister and was told to mind my own business and leave it to the SS to round up the Jews for the concentration camps where they belong." Möllhausen stormed out.

Kappler pondered his next step. The thought struck him: Perhaps I can kill two birds with one stone—both fool the Jews and do it in a way that could be highly profitable to the Third Reich. He smiled for the first time that day.

September 26, 1943, Rome, Gestapo Headquarters, Office of Colonel Kappler

"Please, gentlemen, have a seat, be comfortable." Kappler motioned the two Jewish leaders, Ugo Foà and Dante Almansi, to the chairs in front of his desk. The colonel smiled affably. "I appreciate your prompt response to my invitation. I apologize for any inconvenience."

"No trouble, Colonel. What can we do for you?"

Kappler could detect the apprehension in Foà's voice. "It's more a question of what I can do for you, Signore. Tell me, how many Jews of Italian nationality are there in Rome?"

"We don't know exactly, Colonel, probably over eight thousand, I would guess," Almansi offered.

Kappler smiled. "It's more like twelve thousand. Tell me, do either of you have any complaints about the treatment of Italian Jews by the Germans in Rome?"

"No, Colonel, your people have been absolutely correct," Foà assured him.

"And you would like to keep it that way?" Both men nodded vigorously and then exchanged quick glances.

The colonel's face suddenly turned hard, his tone threatening. "Well, I have difficulty with that. You see, my government considers all Jews, whether Italian nationals or not, enemies of the Third Reich and, I might add, among the worst enemies that we are fighting. Therefore, I am bound to treat you as such."

"But, Colonel," Almansi protested reasonably, "we Jews in Italy have done nothing against the Germans."

"Oh, come now, Signore, we know you are all part of international Jewry's conspiracy to take over the world and in particular, destroy Germany; you Italian Jews are no different."

"How can we possibly be a danger to you?" Foà pleaded.

"Perhaps not with firearms but with the weapons of gold and money." Kappler examined his fingernails for a few moments before continuing. The visitors waited silently.

"As part of my duty as a soldier of the Third Reich, I will relieve you of those weapons. If you fulfill our demands, we will not take your lives or the lives of your families. We want your gold in order to buy new arms."

Foà and Almansi exchanged glances, each hoping the other had an appropriate response. Kappler, however, did not wait.

"I expect fifty kilograms of gold deposited in this office. If that is done, you will not be harmed. If not . . ." Kappler shrugged.

"If not, Colonel?" Almansi asked, his voice cracking. Foà shot him an angry glance.

"Then you Jews will be deported to the Russian frontier and neutralized."

Almansi nodded. "And when do you expect us to deliver this fifty kilograms of gold?"

"You have thirty-six hours."

"But, Colonel," Foà protested plaintively. "It's impossible to raise such a sum in so short a time."

Kappler slammed his open palm on the desk. "If you had the impression I am negotiating, gentlemen, I am not. Those are my *demands*." He looked at his watch. "But never let it be said I am unreasonable. It is now Sunday, nine o'clock in the evening. I will expect the gold on Tuesday, at *one o'clock* in the afternoon. So you see, that will give you *forty* hours instead of thirty-six."

"Will you accept lire?" Almansi asked.

Kappler issued a short, harsh laugh. "Why should I? I can print as much of it as I want. But I tell you what: I will accept British pounds or American dollars in lieu of gold." He rose from his chair.

"Gentlemen, there is nothing more to be said. I expect to see you in three days."

As soon as the visitors had departed, Kappler's SS aide shut the door behind them and turned to face the colonel. "Will the ordered roundup be cancelled if the Jews come up with the gold, Sir?"

Kappler sighed. "No, I'm afraid it will make no difference. In the end, I'll have to carry out the deportations. But at least we'll have fifty kilograms of gold that the Jews will not be able to hide from us."

□□□

Outside in the street, Almansi and Foà headed back to the Main Synagogue. "It's pure extortion," Almansi said furiously.

Foà smiled. "Actually, I was relieved. If we pay the ransom, our people will not be subjected to the horrors that Jews in other parts of Europe have experienced. They did not have such a choice. So we had better make the most of it."

"And how do you expect to raise that amount of gold in three days?" Almansi groused. "Thanks to Rabbi Zolli and a few others, many of the richest Jews have already fled or gone into hiding."

Foà shrugged. "Then we will have to make do with what we have; and what we don't have is time, so let's get started right away. We gathered gold for Mussolini to fight the Ethiopian war and we will do it again."

October 2, 1943, Rome, the Main Synagogue, First Day of Rosh Hashanah

As each man wrapped himself in the fringed *tallis*, the prayer shawl, while murmuring the ritual brief prayer, the congregation settled in for the Rosh Hashanah morning service, the first day of the ten-day holiday, the Days of Awe—the renewal of faith, the atonement for sins. Foà, the president of the synagogue, stepped up to the *bema*. All eyes focused on him. The congregants buzzed in puzzlement. Always, the service began with the lighting of the candles. Foà knew they were confused because Rabbi Zolli was not up on the *bema* this morning and hadn't been there at the service last evening.

Foà cleared his throat. "I am very proud of our Jewish community, which, in a feat without precedent, raised the fifty kilograms of gold in so short a time. It was not even necessary to borrow from the Vatican, which offered to lend us any shortfall. Your donations, and those from many of our Christian friends, of rings, jewelry, candlestick holders and art objects have saved this community, its children and its children's children. It is a mitzvah of life-giving unparalleled in modern times. How appropriate that it should occur on the eve of our sacred High Holy Days. The leaders of the Jewish community thank you."

Foà felt that he had to say something about Zolli's absence. As the rabbi had promised, he and his family had disappeared; presumably, they were in hiding. Foà wasn't surprised, but he hadn't expected the chief rabbi of Rome to do it so soon, especially just before the holidays. Now that the gold was paid, Foà decided he must prevent wholesale panic among the congregants, which he had no doubt would overtake them if they knew that their chief rabbi had left his post. He had agonized all night about what to say. Now he reassured them.

"One more thing. I regret to announce that Rabbi Zolli has fallen ill and will be unable to lead the services during the High Holy Days. Let us pray for his rapid recovery and his speedy return to this *bema*."

Surely the Lord would forgive me this little lie, he thought, even if it is Rosh Hashanah. After all, I do it with the best of intentions—and for their own good. Besides, that cowardly rabbi was wrong. The fifty kilograms of gold we gathered by the deadline has saved the Italian Jewish community. He and his followers went into hiding for nothing.

□□□

At the conclusion of the services, Davide Nathan waited by the main entrance. He spotted Foà leaving and hurried alongside him.

Foà smiled and offered wishes for a healthy New Year.

Nathan reciprocated and then asked. "Can I speak to you for a moment, Signore Foà?"

Foà nodded.

"Quite honestly, I'm worried about remaining in Rome, now that the Germans have taken over. Shouldn't we be disappearing from view?"

"A lot of people have been asking me that. My advice to them—and to you—is to stay put. The Germans have already extorted fifty kilograms of gold from us in return for our safety. They're happy. I am confident they will keep their word."

Nathan shook his head. "I just don't know . . ."

Foà stopped walking. "Look, Signore, if you go into hiding and your neighbors go into hiding, and others follow suit, it will only provoke the Germans, making it difficult for the rest of us. Please—go about your normal life. If things change, we will certainly let you know. I, for one, plan to stay where I am, doing what I have always done." He patted Nathan on the shoulder and took his leave.

Somehow the Jewish leader's assurances did not relieve Nathan's feelings of apprehension. The absence of Rabbi Zolli was particularly disturbing. He had meant to ask Foà about it but had forgotten. He wondered if the rabbi was really ill. He had no reason to doubt Foà, but he kept wondering anyway.

October 3, 1943, Rome, Main Synagogue

Foà looked out the window of his office in the Main Synagogue, disturbed by the commotion in the street. A convoy of German army trucks had pulled up in front of the entrance. German soldiers were banging on the front.

In some perplexity Foà climbed down the stairs and slid back the locking bolt. Before he could pull the doors open, the impatient Germans shoved against them so hard, they almost knocked Foà over.

Colonel Kappler pushed in front of the soldiers and entered the synagogue. "We are here to collect all your files and membership lists," he barked. "No one will be permitted into the synagogue offices until we are finished."

Foà spread his hands. "But why? We gave you the gold."

"We believe your files will show a conspiracy against the German people, not that I feel the slightest obligation to give you an explanation. Where are they kept?"

Foà pointed to the stairs.

"Now, out of the way before I have you forcibly removed," the colonel threatened.

"But why the membership lists?" Foà cried out as the colonel disappeared up the stairs toward the office. Kappler did not respond. A German soldier prodded Foà outside with the butt of his rifle and did not permit him to re-enter until Kappler and his troops had finished their search and left the building.

Same Day, Genoa, Offices of DELASEM

Lelio Valobra and Raffaele Cantoni greeted Don Francesco Repetto warmly when he entered the DELASEM office.

"Thank you for coming, Father," Valobra said. "I think it's time for us to go underground."

Repetto nodded. "I thought as much. I've been busy enlisting the aid of priests, nuns and monks across northern Italy who are willing to hide Jews or find Italians willing to take them in."

"We'll have to destroy our lists of Jews, and that, unfortunately will make it harder to find and warn them," Cantoni said sadly.

"There's no need to destroy the lists," Repetto remonstrated. "I can hide them inside the pipes of the organ at the cathedral. The Nazis will never find them and they'll be available any time we need them."

Valobra nodded, handing the priest a paper. "Here's a description of the structure of DELASEM and a list of our contacts around northern Italy. Also, we channel money into Italy from Switzerland." He handed Repetto another list. "These are the banks in Italy where the funds are deposited. We've arranged with the banks to authorize you to draw out money as needed."

Gently placing his hand on Repetto's shoulder, Cantoni said, "Father, we owe you a debt of gratitude we can never hope to repay."

The priest grinned slightly. "Saving these poor souls is repayment enough. It is I who am indebted to you. Through you, the Good Lord has revealed to me my sacred mission in life—and it's such an important one."

Same Day, Assisi, the Basilica of Saint Francis

Bishop Nicolini was celebrating Sunday mass for the Feast of Saint Francis, the anniversary of the saint's death 717 years earlier. Father Niccacci, standing near the main doors of the upper church of the two-level basilica at the western end of the town, heard a racket just outside. He stuck his head out the doors to see that a long convoy of German military transports had entered Assisi and climbed the hill to the basilica. A German officer hopped out of the first vehicle, and approached Niccacci, standing in the doorway. He saluted and announced, "Captain Ernst Stolmann, Luftwaffe. This town is now occupied and under military law. I am the commandant. I demand to see the bishop and the mayor."

Niccacci hurried back into the church, walked quickly down a side aisle toward the altar and at an appropriate moment, whispered into the bishop's ear. The bishop turned around and glared at the German officer standing in the back of the basilica. "You tell that German," he whispered back, "that I have no intention of interrupting the mass. You will deal with the German and find out what he wants."

"Me, Your Excellency?"

The bishop only nodded, returning to the altar to continue the liturgy.

Niccacci spotted the mayor, Arnaldo Fortini, sitting in a back pew and motioned to him. Together they approached the German.

"The bishop cannot be disturbed now, Captain," whispered the mayor. "What is it you want? Perhaps we can help you."

Stolmann scowled. "The German Army has taken over this town. You are now under martial law. Posters signed by *Reichsführer* Himmler are going up announcing a nighttime curfew. All weapons must be surrendered and anyone engaging in sabotage will be summarily executed."

The mayor's eyes met those of Niccacci. Both had a look of disbelief.

"Are there any Jews living in Assisi?" the German captain barked.

The mayor shook his head. "None, Sir, and there haven't been any here since I've been mayor."

Stolmann nodded. "Very well. As mayor, you will select twelve anti-Fascists, to be held by us as hostages."

"Hostages?" the mayor asked in astonishment.

The captain smiled thinly. "Yes, in case of any attack on German soldiers, three will be shot."

The mayor turned his back on the German officer and stomped away. The officer returned to his vehicle and sped away down the hill.

Niccacci hurried to catch up with the mayor. "Signore, what will you do?" the priest asked, slightly out of breath.

"I'm enraged, Father. There is no way I, as mayor, will turn over any of my townspeople as hostages to those animals. I have been mayor for two decades. It is time to resign. Let them get someone else to do their dirty work."

Same Day, Rome, Main Synagogue

Foà's visitors, Renzo Levi and Settimio Sorani argued in vain. Foà simply had no intention of going into hiding himself or urging any the synagogue's congregants to do so. "We must encourage the Jews to remain calm and not flee," he insisted. "We should not give the Germans any reason to attack us."

Sorani sighed. "Look, Foà, why do you think the Germans took your membership lists and files? So they will know where most of the Jews live when the SS rounds them up."

Foà shook his head violently. "No, no. We paid the gold as agreed and the Germans will keep their word."

"Foà, Foà," Levi pleaded, "you're living in a dream world. The Germans don't give a damn about their word. They just want to kill us all."

Foà folded his arms across his chest. "As I have said many times, there are too few Jews in Rome for them to worry about, especially with the pope's presence here, unless we give them an excuse. I, for one, won't give them any reason to act against us."

"Look what's happening in the concentration camps," warned Sorani, wagging his finger. "They are killing our people. What will happen to the Jews of Rome will be on your conscience, if you're *unlucky* enough to survive."

"You are falling for the Allied propaganda on the BBC about the gassings, aren't you? Well, it's unthinkable and I don't believe it for one minute." But Foà's tone had a distinct edge of desperation.

Levi shrugged. "I surely hope you're correct, Foà, but we're not taking any chances. We're leaving and urging as many as we can to go into hiding."

"You mustn't do that," Foà shouted, "you will endanger . . ."

But Levi and Sorani had already risen and left the office, slamming the door behind them.

Later that Day, Rome, Offices of DELASEM

"I'm glad you made it out of Nice safely, Father Benedetto," Sorani said with obvious affection for the French friar.

Benedetto sighed heavily. "I'm just thinking of all the Jews who were not so lucky to get out before the Germans occupied the Riviera. Donati and I came so close—just a few more days and we'd have them on ships for North Africa."

Levi shook his head. "You shouldn't feel guilty, Father. Think of all the people you did get out over the Italian border."

"Look at it this way," encouraged Sorani kindly. "Providence sent you to Rome at the time of our greatest need."

The friar glanced at Sorani questioningly.

"It's becoming too dangerous for DELASEM to continue to function openly," Sorani explained. "The other day, at the offices of the Yugoslav consul, I tried to get a message to the pope, but unfortunately, it was the precise moment the Gestapo arrived to take the consul into custody. They arrested me, too, despite my false ID. Bad timing! They gave me a pretty good beating trying to find out why I was there, but eventually they released me without finding out I was Jewish. That narrow escape convinced me that if the Nazis strike before we can hide, there will be no DELASEM, no rescue effort and no help for the people who will need it the most. Father Benedetto, we're closing our offices and going underground. We have already destroyed our membership list."

Benedetto looked at the two DELASEM leaders. "I'm ready to take over the operations of the organization. It will be moved to the Capuchin convent on Via Sicilia. It's an excellent location. We have a well-hidden backdoor exit onto Via Boncompagni, good for a quick escape." Benedetto smiled. "While rummaging through a storage room in the convent, I found an old printing press among the cast-off articles and old furniture. It still works! If we can find a good typesetter, I'm sure we can produce acceptable false identity cards."

Levi nodded. "Oh, I know several Jews in the ghetto who have those skills. You will have all the help you need in that area. We can also provide you with considerable funds. But the big question is, with so many Jews at risk, where are we going to hide them all?"

Father Benedetto looked reflectively at the two Jewish leaders. "Leave that to me. We were successful in Nice in arranging clandestine accommodations for Jewish refugees. I am quite sure we can do the same here."

Sorani frowned. " 'We,' Father?"

Benedetto smiled. "My assistants—other members of the clergy and lay persons—they—we—have already begun to locate rooms to rent in private homes, small hotels and boarding houses. You will find that most Italians are only too glad to help their Jewish brethren."

The Jewish leaders shook their heads in disbelief. Who would have thought that simple priests, members of religious orders and ordinary citizens would become the improbable heroes in the rescue effort?

Benedetto continued. "And with your funds, most of the Italian bureaucrats will be only too happy to accept a bribe to look the other way." Catching the look passing between Sorani and Levi, he shrugged. "Gentlemen, please, it's all in the good service of the Lord. We will be forgiven."

The two Jews laughed but more out of a sense of relief.

"Don Francesco Repetto in Genoa will give overall guidance to the clandestine DELASEM," Sorani said. "He has been provided with most of our funds and will dispense them to you as needed. If communications become too dangerous, we've made arrangements with the American and British ambassadors in the Vatican to provide you with funds."

Benedetto nodded, "I know Don Francesco quite well. He came to see me in Nice and we did some advance planning in anticipation of this day."

"And Father Cipriano Ricotti, a Dominican friar, will assume DELASEM duties in Florence, under the direction of Cardinal Dalla Costa," Sorani added.

"Are you warning the Jews in Rome?" Benedetto asked.

Levi sighed. "We have a problem there, Father. We just can't convince the leader of the Rome Jewish community to do it. He thinks such a step will incite the Germans into the very action we fear; he also thinks that the presence of the pope in Rome will automatically protect us."

Benedetto shook his head. "I know the Nazis. Such considerations will not stop them. They are single-mindedly determined to deport and destroy every Jew in Europe."

"You're right, Father," agreed Sorani. "We don't need any convincing. Unfortunately, if Ugo Foà can't be persuaded to get the word out, our own abilities to both warn and convince those in danger are substantially diminished."

Levi went to a file drawer, pulled out a large cloth sack and dumped its contents on the table in front of Benedetto. "These are ration cards we bought on the black market and accumulated to feed the Jews in hiding."

Benedetto picked up a ration card and examined it. "It's a good start. Now, if you will provide me with a typesetter, we can produce identity cards to go along with these."

Same Day, Rome, Gestapo Headquarters, Office of Colonel Kappler

Kappler had crossed paths with SS Captain Theodor Dannecker before. He hadn't liked the sadistic bastard then, and his feelings hadn't changed. The tall, unnaturally thin and seemingly uncoordinated Gestapo officer sitting in front of him certainly looked the part of one of Eichmann's henchmen. Sharp features, in a perpetual scowl, contributed to his unpleasant appearance, which was accentuated by an extremely annoying tic that jolted his head to the side. Kappler stiffened reflexively at the other man's every jerk.

Dannecker did not hide the scorn in his voice as he handed Kappler a sheaf of papers. "These are *our* orders. I am empowered by the *Reichsführer* to carry out the roundup of all Jews in Rome. Colonel Eichmann expects more cooperation and assistance from your office than you have shown in the past. As a start, we expect you to turn over the lists of Jews that, I understand, you obtained from the Main Synagogue office."

Kappler shook his head. "I don't expect a person the likes of you, Captain, to understand the subtleties of the situation here in the Eternal City, but let me say that rounding up the few Jews who live here is just plain political stupidity."

Notwithstanding the tic, Dannecker eyes bored into Kappler's, and his voice grated. "Colonel Eichmann warned me to expect such an uncooperative reaction from you. These orders are immutable and unappealable—to be carried out without delay." He held out his hand. "Now give me the list. That list and the secrecy of the planned roundup are essential to the policy's success."

Kappler shrugged, reached into a desk drawer, pulled out a file folder and handed it to Dannecker. "I don't have enough men to carry out this roundup, much less control the passive and possibly armed resistance that it may provoke."

Dannecker said with a frosty smile, "Rest assured, Colonel, we can handle it. I have come with a detachment of forty-four fully armed Death's Head Corps men, and we shall have the local SS and the Wehrmacht in Rome at our disposal. Do not worry yourself. I have handled these roundups before and this one will be no problem, so long as you do not make it one."

CHAPTER FIFTEEN

October 10, 1943, Rome, Main Synagogue, Office of Ugo Foà

An adamant Dante Almansi sat in Ugo Foà's office shaking his finger at his host. "We've got to rethink our position, Foà. Yesterday, in front of the synagogue, on Yom Kippur no less, the Gestapo arrested several of our more prominent citizens and they haven't told us why. That certainly convinced me we'd better not wait any longer. I'm closing down the Union offices and disposing of all my membership lists. As leader of the Rome Jewish community, you should seriously consider warning its members and getting the hell out of here yourself."

Foà stubbornly shook his head and grimaced. "You too, Almansi? Please, don't panic now. There's no reason to go into hiding—nothing's changed. Those arrests were exceptional situations; they were probably persons known for their anti-Fascist or partisan activities. I still have contacts within the Italian government and I am assured that so long as we don't aggravate the Germans, they will leave us alone."

Almansi slowly stoked his chin. "Can't you see what's happening? We were wrong, Foà; *you* were wrong. I beg you, send out the alarm before it is too late."

"No!" Foà shouted. "If I do that, the Germans will be provoked. The people must be kept calm. I shall tell them not to do anything rash or stupid."

Almansi sighed. "You're the only one who is acting stupidly. Sorani and Levi are right. I intend to join them in hiding, and you'll do the same if you know what's good for you."

Same Day, Rome, Capuchin Convent on Via Sicilia

"Follow me, Signore Fatucci." Father Benedetto led the Jewish typesetter back into the inner reaches of the convent. He smiled apologetically. "For obvious reasons, we must work well out of sight of prying eyes."

Renzo Fatucci nodded. They entered a back room piled high with discarded furniture. Benedetto pointed to one corner of the room. "I have cleared a space over there for the printing press."

Fatucci examined the old press. "Hmmm, this really is an ancient relic," he said as with sure and knowing hands, he checked the operating parts. He nodded. "It's old but serviceable. I can print what you need on this. It'll be slow, but you'll be satisfied with the results."

Benedetto smiled. "Excellent, that's just what I wanted to hear. Can we get to work right away?"

Same Day, Rome, Office of Ernst von Weizsäcker, German Ambassador to The Vatican

After Rudolph von Rahn, German ambassador to Italy, the two diplomats sitting in the office of Ernst von Weizsäcker, German ambassador to the Holy See, were the highest-ranking German diplomatic officials in the Rome: Eitel Möllhausen, consul to the Holy See, and his assistant, Embassy Secretary Albrecht "Teddy" von Kessel. Möllhausen ran his fingers through his receding hair. The suave Möllhausen, whose olive coloring gave him more of an Italian Mediterranean than an Aryan look, said despondently to Weizsäcker, "I've tried everything. Rahn has taken a hands-off attitude. Berlin came down hard on him for *my* written request to postpone the roundup. Quite predictably, Rahn ordered me not to interfere. Since our ambassador to Italy won't do anything, my last hope is you. As ambassador to the Holy See, can you at least let the Vatican know? Perhaps then the pope will break his silence and derail the *Judenrassia* operation."

"You must do something, Ambassador, because Rahn won't," Kessel added, his voice cracking slightly.

Weizsäcker eyed the distraught diplomats sitting before him. He was sympathetic. Both, he knew, secretly opposed the Nazi Party and its policies. Kessel had been more indiscreet; he himself had heard Kessel at more than one social function criticizing the führer specifically and the Nazis generally. Once, Rahn, in the presence of Weizsäcker, had warned Kessel that his tongue would earn him his neck stretched at the end of a rope. In fact, Weizsäcker knew far more about what was going on in the concentration camps that either Möllhausen or Kessel. They didn't know the half of it. Weizsäcker wished he'd never received from his secret source, that now heavy burden on his conscience, the minutes of the Wannsee conference, minutes that laid out the "Final Solution" in all its gruesome details. Weizsäcker came from a distinguished Prussian family with a long military history—soldiers, yes, but murderers, no. Over the years, he had tried to be prudent with low-key protests and even some secret resistance but without much success. Even when he was second only to Ribbentrop in the Foreign Ministry, his efforts had borne no fruit. Just what am I supposed to do? he had asked himself. Destroy my diplomatic career and end up in a concentration camp, or worse?

Weizsäcker sighed. "I don't have to tell you, Herr Möllhausen, Herr Kessel, this is a very dangerous situation. Both of you have acted very foolishly by taking such an open stance of opposition. What I decide to do—*if* I decide to do anything—will be done in absolute secrecy. I shall tell no one, including you gentlemen. That will be the safest way for all of us, and we have never had this conversation. Is that clear?" He stood up, indicating the meeting was over.

Möllhausen rose, nodded and left. Kessel, clearly furious, followed him out, slamming the door behind him.

□□□

In the corridor, Kessel looked at Möllhausen. "You think Weizsäcker will do anything?"

"He's of the same mind as we are, but he doesn't advertise it. I am sure, in his own discreet way, he will alert the Vatican," Möllhausen answered assuringly.

"But it's not going to be enough," said Kessel gloomily. "I have one more avenue to check out, a friend of mine."

"Just be careful, Teddy."

Later that Day, Rome, the Office of Alfred Fahrener

Alfred Fahrener, a Swiss citizen connected with the Institute of International Private Law, an adjunct of the League of Nations, threw up his hands in frustration. "I passed on your message, Kessel," he told his visitor. "I went to see Ugo Foà. I told him that the Jews must leave their homes and disappear from view as soon as possible. I assure you, I left nothing out. But Foà just thanked me for my concern and said there was nothing to worry about, that the Germans were behaving 'very correctly'—those were his actual words."

"Idiot!" Kessel shouted. "That's just what the SS wants the Jews to think. They will be taken away like lambs to the slaughter."

"Did you ever think, Kessel, that maybe you're the one who is overreacting? Perhaps things will not be as bad as you anticipate."

Kessel jumped out of his chair, flinging his arms in the air. "Don't you understand, Fahrener? It is not what I 'anticipate;' it is what I *know* will happen. The Jews must go into hiding; they must vanish." Kessel sat down abruptly, putting his head in his hands. "If they don't," he moaned, "they will be killed and their blood will be on our hands."

"You've done all you can," Fahrener said soothingly.

Kessel shook his head slowly. "No, my friend. If I weren't so afraid of being arrested and tortured by the Gestapo, I would have done much more."

October 11, 1943, Rome, the Vatican, Office of the Cardinal Secretary of State

". . .so that's where things stand, Your Eminence," Weizsäcker concluded. "Some of my colleagues hope the pope can intercede and use his influence to stop the German roundup. Me? I must only represent my government and, in fairness, warn you that such an action could invoke reprisals by the Third Reich."

Maglione looked at his visitor through tented fingers, his thumbs lightly resting on both his temples. "Your ambivalent attitude is not much help, Signore Ambassador. It is you who must intervene; use *your* influence on behalf of the Jews for the sake of humanity and Christian charity."

Weizsäcker gave a quick, harsh laugh. "What influence, Your Eminence? My instructions are just the opposite. It is the pope who has the influence. I don't have to tell you what will happen if the Jews of Rome are deported. That is all I will say on that subject. I have said too much already."

The cardinal frowned but did not immediately respond.

Weizsäcker filled the silence. "What will the Vatican do if these things continue?"

"The Holy See isn't prepared to put itself in a position to have its neutrality questioned," temporized the cardinal, "and that's what would happen if we voiced disapproval of Berlin's actions. It would instigate retaliation against not only the Catholics in Germany but with even more severity against the Jews. And with the German army at our doorstep here in Rome, who knows what will happen to the Vatican? But rest assured, Ambassador, I will tell the Holy Father of our meeting."

Weizsäcker sighed. "And, please, Eminence, I was never here. I have done all I can safely do—and no more." He left the office feeling depressed. Why should he put his life on the line for the Jews? He spoke to no one as he strode back to the embassy and slammed the door of his office behind him. He reached into his liquor cabinet, pulled out a bottle of schnapps and downed two large shots. It didn't do any good.

Same Day, Genoa, the Main Synagogue

Before the war, when his father had been president of the Genoa Jewish community, Massimo Teglio had shown little interest in religion, professing to be an agnostic. Then he had committed an even greater stir within his family by marrying a Catholic. He led the life of a carefree sportsman, piloting his cherished hydroplane over the skies of Genoa and before that, flying all sorts of old single-engine planes, and that was the way he wanted his life to continue. He'd been helping Jews on and off since 1938 but the war really came crashing down on him with terrifying reality when his wife, a Red Cross worker, died in a bombing raid. His playboy days were clearly numbered.

Up to now, the Germans in Genoa had shown absolutely no interest in the Jews. But Teglio had friends in the Christian community, many of them in positions of authority. He'd heard disturbing reports about a German raid at the Main Synagogue in Rome on Yom Kippur. When he saw that the largest synagogue of Genoa was still keeping its doors wide open as if nothing were amiss, he was furious.

He strode into the office of the secretary of the synagogue, Giorgio Baquis. "Baquis, are you crazy. Why is the synagogue still open? Didn't you hear what happened in Rome?"

"But—but—the Germans have never bothered us here," stammered Baquis.

"Nor did they bother the Jews in Rome, until Yom Kippur," Teglio retorted.

Teglio had struck a chord. Baquis looked stricken. "What shall I do?"

"First, hide all your lists of the names and addresses of Jews in Genoa."

Baquis nodded. "Where?"

Teglio sighed. "Just give them to me, I'll take care of them."

"Are you going into hiding?"

Teglio nodded, leaving with the lists.

October 12, 1943, Genoa

Without warning, two SS officers entered the synagogue, the day after Teglio's visit. The only people there were the janitor, Bino Polacco, and his two children. Polacco, terrified, shrank back.

"You there!" one German shouted. "We are here to pick up the list of the names and addresses of Jews in Genoa. Produce it immediately."

"I—I am sorry, Sirs, we no longer have such a list."

"Where is it?"

"I don't know, Sirs."

The gloved fist of one officer shot out, knocking the janitor down and loosening some teeth.

"Let's not waste time," the second officer said. He swooped down and picked up the janitor's two children, one in each arm. "If you do not produce the list, we shall kill these children. You want that to happen? Then get those damn lists!"

"Please, Sirs, the lists are not here," the janitor pleaded between sobs. The other SS officer took out his pistol and held it to one of the children's heads. "Then where are they?"

"Massimo Teglio took them," he cried.

"Show us where he lives."

Polacco nodded dumbly. The SS officers followed him out of the building and through several streets until he pointed out Teglio's apartment house.

As a precaution, Teglio had moved from the third floor to an abandoned apartment on the fourth floor. He happened to look out of the window at the moment that the janitor, his children and the two SS men were approaching the building. When he spotted Polacco pointing out the building, he understood immediately.

He decided it would be foolhardy to stay in the abandoned apartment because when they did not find him in his own apartment, they would surely search the entire building. As the SS entered the front door, Teglio grabbed the lists and stuffed them inside his shirt. He raced up to the roof, taking the steps two at a time.

As he reached the top floor, he could hear the banging on his third-floor apartment door. He stepped onto the roof and ran to the edge. He hesitated. He was an aviator, not a climber or an acrobat. He looked at the nine-foot jump down to the next roof. *I could break a leg!* he thought. He took a deep breath. *That's better than being dead, I suppose.*

Cautiously he peered over the edge of the roof. By hanging by his hands, he could cut the drop by over five feet. He climbed over, hung there momentarily and then let go. He still hit the tarred roof below with sufficient force to give him a stiff jolt but nothing worse. Hastily, he checked inside his shirt. The lists were still there.

He climbed in a back window, raced down the stairs and slipped out the front door and down the street. Now the war became personal; his own immediate safety was at stake. He would have to react accordingly.

Composing himself, Teglio walked into a neighborhood trattoria. He telephoned warnings to as many Jews as he could and asked several Catholic friends to do the same. He had already begun saving fellow Jews. Now he'd devote himself to it full time. He'd go into hiding, but he'd not run away.

□□□

Several blocks away, Bernard Grosser, who should have been in hiding, confidently walked the streets carrying on his business. He had a close relationship with the Genoa chief of police, who, the last time they met, had even offered him a loaf of bread, knowing that Jewish rations had been cut drastically. Despite Grosser's repeated refusals, the chief had forced the gift on him.

"Grosser!" a voice boomed out, interrupting his musings.

Grosser turned around. He didn't know the man's name, but he recognized, despite his civilian dress, him as being with the Genoa police.

"Grosser, I'm a police agent", the man explained, "and I have orders to pick up you and the other Jewish leaders. Do me a favor; don't be seen on the streets so much. Disappear so we can forget about you."

Before Grosser could react, the police agent turned the corner and disappeared. Grosser hurried home and made a few telephone calls.

October 13, 1943, Genoa, Cathedral of San Lorenzo

Massimo's Teglio hurried down Via San Luca and reached the corner of Via San Lorenzo. He looked around—no people in sight in front of San Lorenzo Cathedral. He resisted the temptation to run, not wanting to call attention to himself. Instead, he walked rapidly toward the church and slipped inside.

Luck was with him today, Don Francesco Repetto was there, busy in the sanctuary. Teglio hurried up to him.

"Don Francesco?"

"Yes, Signore?" The priest couldn't quite place him. Now that the Germans were looking for him, Teglio had shaved his moustache, trimmed back his heavy eyebrows and began wearing eyeglasses.

""It's Massimo Teglio, Father."

"Teglio, I didn't recognize you. What have you done? The Germans have put a price of one million lire on your head."

Teglio nodded. "I know. I hid the synagogue's lists of Jews, before they could snatch them. I barely got away. Where's Valobra? I need to speak to him."

"He and the others have gone into hiding because the police warned Bernard Grosser yesterday that the Jewish leaders would be arrested."

"I want to be part of the rescue effort to save the Jews in Genoa. I did some work in the past with COMASEBIT, and now want to be part of the DELASEM team.'

Repetto smiled. "Well, fortune is smiling upon you, my son. It just so happens I have taken over the leadership of DELASEM. With all the Jewish leaders in hiding, DELASEM has gone underground. Do you need a place to hide?"

"No thank you, Father," said Teglio shaking his head. "I have lots of friends in Genoa. I plan to move from apartment to apartment, and only to those with clear escape routes."

Repetto raised an eyebrow.

Teglio shrugged. "Tonight, for example, the place I'm staying in has no back door, so I will hang a rope out of the bathroom window facing the alley and climb down that if I have to. Tomorrow, I have a bed in the leper hospital—the Germans would never even enter such a place."

"But you must stay off the streets, Teglio. That's where most of the danger is."

Teglio laughed. "I only move around the city during the lunch and dinner hours. The Germans have to eat, and you know how punctual they are about their habits. I will be in touch with you in a few days, Father." He disappeared out a side entrance of the cathedral.

Same Day, Turin, the Home of Ettore Ovazza

Ettore Ovazza never thought it would come to this. An early Fascist leader, a fanatic follower of Mussolini who participated in the March on Rome that brought the Duce to power, he was certain that his loyalty, his war record and his Fascist comrades would protect him, even after the Duce had been deposed.

Today, a friend in the Fascist militia had just warned him that the Fascist police and the Germans were going to start arresting prominent Jews and their families, beginning with the young men of military age. This would be a prelude to a roundup of all Jews all over Italy, and Ettore and his family were targets.

Ovazza called his son into his study. A roughly dressed man sat next to the desk, someone the son had not seen before.

"Riccardo," Ovazza began, "you are of military age and the one in the most immediate danger, so you will have to leave Turin immediately. After I have made the necessary arrangements, the rest of the family will follow."

Riccardo blinked. "To where, Papa?"

Ovazza pointed to the stranger. "This is Rudy Lercoz. He's the guide who will escort you across the border into Switzerland. There, you will wait for us."

"Please, Papa, I'd rather leave with the family."

Ovazza raised his voice. "And I am telling you to go, *now!*" Then his tone softened. He tore a page from his prayer book and then ripped it in half. "Here, take this half. I will keep the other half. When you are safely over the Swiss border, give Signore Lercoz your half of the prayer, which he will deliver to me. If the two pieces match, he will get the balance of his fee." Ovazza held out a thick envelope to Riccardo, who took it. "Sufficient funds are there for one half Signore Lercoz's fee and your own needs until we are reunited. Be brave, Riccardo. Show them you are an Ovazza."

October 14, 1943, Mountains Near the Swiss Border

Riccardo Ovazza, young and in excellent physical shape, had no trouble keeping up with Rudy Lercoz. The two made their way up the steep mountain trails, heading for the Swiss border. They stopped for the night after the sun went down. Lercoz lit a small fire and put on a mess tin of soup.

"Isn't that dangerous?" his charge asked. "Won't the German patrols spot the fire?"

Lercoz settled back, lighting a cigarette. "Sonny, you leave the guiding to me. That's what I get paid for."

Riccardo shrugged.

"And speaking of pay, I want to be paid now."

Riccardo shook his head. "Not until you get me safely across the border."

Lercoz rose to his feet, looking down on Riccardo. "Pay me now or I won't take you. Oh, and the price is doubled."

"Go to hell, you crook!"

Lercoz bent over and reached in his backpack. He fired two quick shots into Riccardo's chest. The boy died instantly. Quickly, Lercoz rifled through the dead youth's pockets, took his fee, the rest of the money and the half page of the prayer book. He paused, thought about it and then put some of the money back in Riccardo's pocket.

A few minutes later, a flashlight illuminated Lercoz's face.

"We saw the signal fire," a disembodied voice said.

"What took you so long to get here?"

The leader of the German SS patrol stepped close to the fire, shining the light into the guide's eyes. Lercoz blinked.

"The Jew tried escape. I had to shoot him."

The SS officer looked at the body. "You're a liar. This boy's been shot in the chest. He couldn't have been running away. But it doesn't matter. You actually saved us the cost of bullets." The SS officer went through the boy's pockets and found some Swiss francs. "How much did you take for yourself?"

Lercoz shrugged. "Just my fee."

The SS officer turned to his men. "Ever meet an Italian who wasn't a thief?" he snorted.

Lercoz ignored the jibe. "Are you still paying for information on Jews in hiding?"

"Five thousand a head. You get paid when we find them."

Lercoz nodded. "There's a family of three Jews," pointing to the dead boy, "his kin, the Ovazzas. They'll be at the Hotel Lyskamm in Gressoney, waiting to hear from me. They are planning to sneak across the border to Switzerland soon."

October 15, 1943, Gressoney, Italy, Hotel Lyskamm

Lercoz showed up at the hotel early in the morning and asked for the guest from Turin. Ettore Ovazza came out of the hotel dining room to meet the guide, interrupting his breakfast.

The guide handed him Riccardo's half of the prayer book page. "He's safely across the border, waiting for you."

Ovazza smiled. "Excellent, my wife will be delighted to hear that." He pulled out an envelope packed with Swiss francs and handed it to the guide.

Lercoz nodded and left.

□□□

Lunch had been finished and the dining room cleared. The owner of the hotel, Arnaldo Cochis, sat relaxed behind the reception desk. Two men approached him in leather long coats. By their dress, he didn't need to see their identity cards to know that they were Gestapo agents.

The taller of the agents flashed a photo. "Have you seen this man?"

Cochis went through the motions of carefully examining the black and white snapshot. He looked up. "Is there a reward?"

The taller agent nodded. "He's a Jew. If we catch him here there's five thousand lire in it for you."

"And if there are three of them?"

"You do the math," the agent growled.

Cochis nodded. "Room 302."

"Under what name are they registered?"

"Ovazza."

The tall one looked at the other agent. "They used their real names, Kurt—Jews with a lot of balls."

"Or very stupid," Kurt muttered.

The one called Hans stuck out his hand. "I want their key—right now."

"I think they're out for a walk."

Hans grabbed the key. "That's all right, we'll wait for them in the room. If you warn them, you will be in serious trouble."

"No chance, gentlemen," Cochis reassured him. "I want that reward."

◻◻◻

When the three guests from Turin returned some time later, Cochis handed Ettore Ovazza the key to the room. "Did you have a nice walk, Signore Ovazza?" Ovazza took the key without responding. He didn't like to chat with this obsequious little bastard. From the first moment when they checked in he had a bad feeling about the proprietor. He had even considered moving on but had to await word from Lercoz, finally deciding it was just a case of nerves. Now he herded his wife and daughter up the stairs to their room. Unlocking the door of 302, he found the two Gestapo agents comfortably relaxed in armchairs. "Welcome back, Herr Ovazza," said the taller one. "We've been waiting patiently for you, your lovely wife, Nella, and your sweet young Elena. Are you enjoying your vacation? The Swiss mountains in the background offer a beautiful vista for your walks, don't you agree?"

"What do you want with us? We have done nothing wrong," demanded Ovazza with more confidence than he felt

Hans conjured up a skeptical look. "Nothing wrong? You are Jews. That is enough. But you also left Turin in violation of our very clear regulations, and you are trying to hide from us." He looked to Kurt. "Does that about sum it up?"

Kurt nodded.

"But we are just taking a short vacation. I have been working very hard and . . ."

"Enough of these fairy tales," Hans shouted. He stood up.

"Look," Ovazza pleaded, "I was a high official in the Fascist Party; I was with the Duce on the March on Rome . . ."

"And you are a Jew," Hans snickered. "I rest my case."

Kurt chuckled.

"Please, Gentlemen, I can pay you well."

Hans waved away the statement. "Your money won't help you out of this, Jew. Save it for the hotel bill." He laughed with gusto. "Besides, we will take the rest of it from you later."

◻◻◻

Having locked the Ovazzas in their room and posted a guard under their window, the two Gestapo agents strolled through the hotel gardens enjoying the fall weather and the riot of colors dominating the forest—the oranges, yellows and golds of the turning leaves. Then they treated themselves to a fine dinner and delighted in discovering some fine French wine in the hotel wine cellar. They finished off three bottles and went to sleep it off in a room provided, under pressure, by Cochis.

□□□

An hour later, Cochis, still at the desk, recognized his next visitor immediately, that damn partisan, Mario Rossi, here to stir up trouble. He watched Rossi look around, making sure the lobby was empty this late at night. Rossi went up to Cochis at the reception desk. "Give me the key to the room of the Jews," he whispered urgently.

"Are you crazy? Get the hell out of here!"

"You must give me the key. Otherwise they'll kill him, his wife and his daughter."

"HELP, HELP," Cochis screamed. "The partisans are attacking."

"You Nazi bastard," Rossi cursed. He pushed through the double doors leading to the hotel kitchen as the German guard entered the front door to the lobby. Rossi raced through the kitchen, jumped off the back porch and disappeared into the forest.

October 16, 1943, Gressoney, Italy, Hotel Lyskamm

The Gestapo agents were finishing a large breakfast. As the waiter began clearing the dishes from the table, Cochis approached, handing them a bill for the wine, meals and room. Hans looked over the bill and smiled. "It looks in perfect order. Herr Ovazza will be happy to pay the bill."

A few minutes later, accompanied by the Gestapo agents, a German military truck drove up to the Hotel. It carried the Ovazzas to Intra on Lake Maggiore. There they were herded into the Gestapo office. While Nella Ovazza tried to calm the almost hysterical Elena, Ovazza approached the taller agent.

"Are we to be deported? Look at my daughter. How young and innocent! Can't you let her go with my wife? Just take me."

Hans sighed. "Why do you Jews think we Germans are so heartless? We have children too, you know. We are going to spare you and your lovely family the agony of deportation and separation."

He pressed on Ovazza's shoulder, forcing him onto a straight wooden chair.

"You will let us go?" Ovazza asked softly, unbelievingly.

Hans stood behind him. "Not quite, Herr Ovazza." He withdrew his short Walther PPK pistol from its underarm holster.

Nella screamed and Ovazza had barely started to turn in the chair when the retort of the pistol reverberated throughout the small room, blowing off the back of the Jew's head. Two quick shots followed in succession, dispatching the remaining Ovazzas.

Kurt shook his head. "I just wish you wouldn't do that in such a confined space. I'll be deaf before my thirtieth birthday," he complained.

Hans shrugged. "It's just a small pistol. You should be thankful. You're a lot better off than those Jews."

Kurt jiggled his finger in his ear, trying unsuccessfully to relieve the pressure. "What will we do with the bodies?"

Hans smiled. "We'll cut them up." He went to the window and pointed. "See that kindergarten school down the street? We can easily fit the pieces into its large furnace. It's Friday. By this evening, the school should be empty for the entire weekend." He uncorked the bottle of wine he'd taken from Cochis's stock and poured two glasses, handing one to Kurt. He raised his glass. *"L'chayim."*

Kurt frowned. "What?"

Hans smiled. "It's a Jewish toast, meaning 'To life.'" He laughed raucously.

Kurt failed to see what was so funny.

Same Day, Rome, a Borrowed Apartment

Rosina Sorani confronted her brother in the sitting room of a Catholic friend. "Settimio, how long must we remain in hiding? If I don't get back to my own apartment, someone will steal everything I have."

Settimio shook his head and laid his hand on her shoulder. "Your possessions aren't important when your life is in danger."

"How do you know they're looking for us?" she said petulantly, shaking off his hand.

"I heard from the police chief. He found out that the Germans were compiling a list of Jews to be rounded up along with their entire families."

Rosina put her hand to her mouth. "Oh, my God, all my friends . . ." She seized her coat.

Settimio reached for her but she was already at the door. "Where are you going?"

"To the ghetto. I must warn people."

"No, Rosina, it's too dangerous."

"I must, otherwise I could never live with myself." She was out the door.

□□□

"Please, Gisela, you and your family must go into hiding," Rosina implored a short time later.

Her friend shook her head adamantly. "I'm not giving up my home and possessions on some rumor."

"It's not rumor. Settimio got it directly from the police chief," Rosina cried in frustration.

"Leave us alone," Gisela shouted. "You and your brother are nothing but panic-mongers. Ugo Foà has assured us that if we remain calm and do not upset the Germans, nothing will happen to us."

"He's wrong, Gisela, terribly wrong. Settimio should know, he's with DELASEM and . . ."

"Shut up and get out of here," the woman screamed, covering her ears. "I don't want to hear any more of this." Gisela pushed Rosina through the door and slammed it shut.

□□□

Hours later Rosina returned to the borrowed apartment, throwing her coat on the floor. She burst into tears.

Settimio grabbed her by the shoulders. "Rosina, I am so glad you're safe. That was a foolish thing to do."

"I shouldn't have even bothered," she sobbed.

"What happened?"

"No one believed me! Even my friends called me a crazy woman. They threw me out of their homes. Some people in the streets threw stones at me." She sat down, her head in her hands. "I only wanted to help," she wailed.

"Rosina, it's not your fault. They didn't believe me or Renzo Levi either." He lit a cigarette and blew the first puff up to the ceiling. "That son of a bitch Foà will have the blood of thousands of Jews on his hands, if he survives."

October 1943, Florence

Nathan Cassutto had looked forward to a career in medicine. After graduating from rabbinical school, he had decided he'd rather be a doctor. He had graduated at the top of his medical class, winning a scholarship to the Rockefeller Institute in New York City. While his academic qualifications couldn't have been better, his timing could not have been worse. It was then 1938 and under the racial laws, he could not obtain a passport to leave Italy. These same laws had also prevented him from practicing medicine in Italy. But at least a portion of his training did not go to waste; he had become a rabbi in Milan, a decision to which many Florentine Jews owed their lives.

In 1943, despite the dangers of the position, he accepted the post of chief rabbi of Florence. Almost immediately after the Italy's armistice with the Allies, Rabbi Cassutto began urging his congregants to disperse and hide. Working with Cardinal Dalla Costa, archbishop of Florence, he had hidden Jews in churches, convents and homes in small villages, many under false names. He didn't merely preach disappearance; he went from house to house to warn people and then guide them in what to do. Unlike Jews in Rome, therefore, Jews in Florence took heed of the danger, and the German roundup, when it came, netted very few Florentine Jews.

Rabbi Cassutto, however, did not follow his own advice. He disappeared from public life but refused to leave Florence, trudging the streets to provide Jews with hiding places, money, food and false documents. That he knew it was just a matter of time before his luck ran out did not deter him in the least, but he did provide for the safety of his wife and two sons. She took refuge in a convent, and the two boys were placed with two non-Jewish families in Florence.

PART V

The Horror Begins

CHAPTER SIXTEEN

October 15, 1943, Vatican, the Study of Pope Pius XII

"I must say I found Ambassador Weizsäcker's position bizarre," Cardinal Maglione reported to the pontiff. "On the one hand he seemed quite reluctant to say it but left a clear impression of what would happen to the Jews deported to Germany. On the other hand, he sternly warned of reprisals if we intervene in any way. I explained that if we maintain our silence, it is not out of approval of such atrocities but solely out of concern for not making matters worse. I made no commitment one or the other on what the Holy See would do."

The pope stared out the window, giving the cardinal secretary of state a clear, profile view of his sharp, austere face. "I take it Herr Weizsäcker wasn't satisfied," Pius said without turning around.

"No, Your Holiness. He said some of his colleagues in the German Embassy to Italy were urging you to protest as the only way to stop the roundup or at least delay it, but he himself did not take their position. He added, as an afterthought, that there were two thousand SS troops and Gestapo lodged at Pensione Sta. Caterina, ready to move out."

The pontiff nodded slowly. "A strange man. He sounds frightened. Ambassador Rahn, anticipating your meeting with Weizsäcker, has tried to preempt his colleague by warning me directly that a formal protest would make the deportations more severe. Two German ambassadors in the same city—it makes for a confusing diplomatic situation. What do you think?"

"With all due respect, Holy Father, I think Weizsäcker was trying to warn us that unless you protest, these people will be deported and liquidated. I suggest we do protest to forestall German action."

The pope sighed. "And you'd be wrong, Eminence. I know Hitler and his colleagues. I lived in Germany during their rise to power, and Rahn is absolutely correct. Any protest by me would almost certainly instigate greater atrocities here, in Germany and in the Eastern Territories. Believe me, I would not do those poor Jews a favor by speaking out."

Cardinal Maglione shrugged, "I don't know, Your Holiness . . ."

The pope stood up and paced around the study. "Do you recall that after Mussolini was deposed, our sources informed us that Hitler was so enraged that he planned to send SS troops to occupy the Vatican? That his generals only at the last minute had dissuaded him? Do you believe that?"

Cardinal Maglione nodded.

"Then I must assume that it would not take much for Hitler to change his mind again. My own safety is of no concern to me, but an occupied Vatican would not be much assistance to our fellow Catholics, much less to the Jews. Hitler, I am sure, would also take severe reprisals against our German Catholics."

"I understand, Holy Father. Nevertheless, may I suggest that it is incumbent upon us to lend some helping hand to the Jews."

The pope looked at Maglione. "I'll leave that up to you. Help the Jews, but be discreet about it."

The cardinal's eyes followed the pope pacing around the room, his white robes flowing behind him. "We will have to issue some sort of statement, even if it's not a protest," Maglione noted.

The pope frowned. "I suppose you're right. But do it after the deportations are carried out—and show it to me first. We cannot condemn the Germans directly. As much as it pains me to say this, we need the Germans in Rome. Without them, Bolsheviks would overrun the city. That is a far greater danger to our civilization than the Nazis."

A Few Minutes Later, Vatican, Office of the Cardinal Secretary of State

Monsignor Giovanni Battista Montini opened the door slowly. "You wanted to see me, Your Eminence?"

Cardinal Maglione nodded. "Come in, Monsignor. We have work to do and I need your advice. The Holy Father has given us permission to help the Jews. How can we do it quietly but effectively?"

Montini looked at Maglione. "By 'quietly,' I assume you mean that issuing a strong statement of condemnation is out of the question?"

The cardinal sighed. "You have assumed correctly, Monsignor."

"Why? The Holy See should seize the moral high ground, shouldn't it?"

Maglione leaned back in his chair and closed his eyes. "I am not at liberty to discuss that question. Let's just leave it at that."

"Very well. Then I suggest you order all our extra-territorial monasteries and convents in Rome to open their doors to the Jews."

"The convents for women, Monsignor?" Maglione asked in astonishment. The mothers superior and abbesses will be up in arms against such an invasion of their sanctuaries by lay people, especially men."

"No doubt, but these are trying times, Your Eminence. The church requires their flexibility and dedication in order to save lives—that should take precedence. And that should include the Vatican itself."

"Of course we will provide shelter here, but it will be a lot harder for Jews to seek haven within our walls since we are surrounded by German troops. Sheltering them at the extra-territorial properties makes a lot more sense."

"If we did open religious houses for women would it be pursuant to the orders of the Holy Father?"

Cardinal Maglione sighed. "Let's just say it is pursuant to *my* interpretation of the wishes of the Holy Father."

"We will probably require your personal intervention with the mothers superior."

"You will have it."

"Thank you, Your Eminence. I will set to work immediately on getting the word out to the clergy."

Montini turned to leave. Halfway out the door, he turned back. "Oh, as for getting Jews into the Vatican, Your Eminence, there are many ways. We've been doing it for Allied airmen and escaped POWs for years. Just ask Monsignor O'Flaherty."

The cardinal shook his head ruefully. "I should have known better. Now go. I must come up with something that will address the deportations without offending anyone."

"Excuse me, Your Eminence?"

Maglione smiled. "Nothing concerning you, Monsignor. Just ignore the mumblings of an overworked old man."

Montini closed the door behind him.

Maglione wandered over to the window, his hands locked together behind his back. His thoughts went back to the prior pope, the feisty Pope Pius XI; now there was a fighter. The cardinal smiled on recalling how *that* Pius had refused to give an inch to Hitler. During Hitler's visit to Rome in 1938, the crusty pontiff had closed the Vatican museum and decreed that the pagan Nazi cross should not be allowed to hang from any church properties—and then left town. Who knows what would have happened had Pius XI lived? Maglione sighed; the "what-ifs" won't help a thing. He walked back to his desk, picked up his pen and started drafting a statement.

October 16, 1943, 4:30 A.M., Rome, Staging Area Near Gestapo Headquarters

SS Captain Dannecker stood on the hastily erected platform near headquarters, looking over the hundreds of assembled SS troops. It was Dannecker's show, so Colonel Kappler stood off to the side, observing. Dannecker raised his voice so the assemblage could hear him. "This is an auspicious day in Third Reich history. This is your opportunity to rid the Fatherland of one of the last pockets in Europe of our most dangerous and implacable enemies, the Jews. We must act resolutely and without mercy. The young Jew of today, if permitted, will grow into the fanatic fighter against the Fatherland." His pronounced tic, unsuccessfully suppressed, made him appear even more ominous than his murderous message.

Kappler watched the performance. It never failed to amaze him how many otherwise intelligent Germans fell for this "dangerous enemy" line. Kappler certainly had no love for the Jews and carried out his assignments as ordered, but he could not force his thinking self to accept such claptrap.

"In one half hour," Dannecker continued, "you will head to the ghetto and to Trastevere and pull in every last Jew there. Take them out of their homes and stores, off the streets or wherever you find them.

"They will be shipped immediately to the camps in the East and we will be rid of them. However, to make your task easier and avoid any resistance, the Jews must be told they are going to serve in labor camps. I do not want to hear any bravado talk about concentration camps and liquidation centers. That is not, however, to say that you should not act sternly and, if necessary, brutally. Any Jew who resists or attempts to hide you will shoot on the spot—it will serve as a good example to the rest. No exceptions can be made for age, gender or health. Half-Jews, baptized Jews and those married to Christians are not exempt, nor are those Jews formerly influential in the Fascist government. In other words, your selection will be easy—ALL JEWS! The Italian Fascist police are supposed to help you, but I would not count on it. They are very unreliable and highly unsympathetic to our program.

"By the end of the *razzia* I intend to report to the führer of our success here in Rome. And you will make it happen. *Heil* Hitler!"

The military trucks roared to life and the SS troops scrambled in over the tailgates. One by one, the trucks pulled out of the assembly area, their headlights searching the dark road ahead to find the ghetto, to find Trastevere just across the Tiber, and to find the Jews asleep in their beds.

Dannecker turned to a group of men who had not yet moved out, the special force that he personally had selected. "Your assignment will be to seize the influential and rich Jews living outside the ghetto and Trastevere. Each of you has a list with the names and addresses of the Jews you will arrest. This information came directly from their synagogue records, so I expect it is accurate and up-to-date. The instructions are the same for you. No one, I repeat, no one, is exempt. If anyone refuses to go, don't waste your time, shoot the entire family."

Same Day, Same Time, Rome, the Streets of the Ghetto

Incorrigible—that was the only way eight-year-old Mino Moscati's parents would describe him. Despite their repeated warnings, he was out of the house again while they slept peacefully and unaware. Mino had a little business going—selling cigarette papers on the street to the early risers off to work. Sitting on the curb under a streetlight, engrossed in counting his inventory, he failed to hear the approach of the Italian police officer until he was tapped on the shoulder by the officer's baton.

Mino jumped up to run, but the officer was too quick, grabbing his arm.

"I didn't do anything!"

"No, then why are you trying to run away?"

"You scared me, coming up behind me like that. Let go of me!"

The policeman only held on tighter. "Are you Christian or Jewish?"

Mino looked down at his feet. "Catholic."

"In the ghetto? I don't think so. You're coming with me." Mino's resistance could not match the strength of the adult officer. He found himself being dragged to the police station.

The officer pushed Mino into the police commissioner's office. "Another Jew, Commissioner."

The commissioner nodded. "Leave him here and return to your post."

The policeman left. The commissioner watched as the young boy was tensed to flee. "Calm down, young man, I'm not your enemy. What's your name?"

Mino sat silently, arms folded defiantly across his chest.

"Look at you! Such a big shot! Do you have any idea how much danger your mother and father are in?"

That got Mino's attention. He unfolded his arms and shook his head.

"If you want me to help you, I need your name. It's up to you."

"Mino Moscati."

The commissioner ran his finger down the list on his desk. "You and your family are on the list to be detained by the Germans."

"Detained?"

"Sent to a concentration camp. Do you understand what that means?"

Mino nodded.

"Good, then get out of here, fast, run home and warn your family. The Germans will be in the ghetto any time now to start the roundup." The commissioner pointed to the back door out of his office.

Mino took off. The commissioner shouted to his back, "Don't let me catch you in here again." Then he smiled.

□□□

Five minutes later Mino was explaining, "But Papa, the policeman told me that the Germans were coming to take us all away to concentration camps."

Mino's father, however, still seethed about his son's persistent disobedience. "What were you doing out at that time of night?' he roared.

The mother shushed him. "Didn't you just hear what Mino said? Let's leave now, just in case it's true. We can always come back later."

The father reluctantly turned back to his bedroom and began to put on his clothes. As soon as he and his wife were ready, the three of them walked out the apartment door. The mother gave a small shriek. A German soldier stood at the far end of the hall. He pointed his rifle at them. "You, Jews! Wait there and don't move. I have to get the truck."

The father, picking up Mino and holding him away from the barrel of the rifle, nodded. "We will wait."

The German soldier took off down the street. As soon as he disappeared around the corner, the father put Mino down, pushed everyone out the back door of the building and headed in opposite direction from the soldier.

Avoiding all the major streets, they took the narrow winding lanes of Portico d'Ottavia along the banks of the Tiber and reached the outskirts of the ghetto without encountering Germans. Mino's father pointed. "That building there—I have a Catholic friend." He knocked on the door and they all waited.

"I am looking for Luigi Barzelli," he told the sleepy man who finally appeared. "I'm a friend of his and I need his help. Would you tell him, please?"

The man shook his head. "I'm just the janitor. Signore and Signora Barzelli left for the country last week because of the bombardments. I don't expect them back for quite a while."

"What are we going to do?" Moscati asked plaintively. "The Germans are arresting all Jews, including children like my son, Mino, here." He patted Mino's head.

The janitor looked at them for a few moments. To Mino, it seemed like an eternity. Then the janitor nodded and waved them into the building. "Come in, I have a key to their apartment. I'm sure they would not mind housing their friends."

The family stepped inside and the janitor closed the door and bolted it shut against the mean streets.

Same Day, 5:00 A.M., Rome, Trastevere, Apartment of Davide Nathan

Sixteen-year-old Olga Nathan had never been a late sleeper. She was usually up before the break of dawn, staring out the window, waiting for Trastevere, and the ghetto across the Tiber, to wake up and come alive. This morning started out no different until she saw her friend Flora racing down the street.

She leaned out of the window. "Flora, what's the matter? Who's chasing you?"

Flora slowed down and looked up. "Olga," she cried, "run, run—and take your family. Get out of here!" She resumed running.

"Wait," Olga shouted. "What's wrong?"

Flora shouted back without slackening her pace, "It's the Germans, they are marching on the ghetto and taking all the Jews they can find, pulling them out of their homes. They are only two blocks from here, you don't have . . ." Flora's voice trailed off as she rounded the corner and disappeared from sight.

Olga went into her parents' bedroom and shook her father. "Wake up, Papa!" Both her mother and father sat up in bed. "The Germans are almost here. We have to leave," Olga explained, half crying.

Davide Nathan jumped out of bed and started dressing while his wife, Elena, pulled the blanket over her shoulders as if to protect herself. "Maybe Olga and I should stay here," she suggested. "The Germans are probably only looking for men for a work detail."

"Get out of bed, Elena. Both of you, put on coats immediately," Nathan said loudly, his tone insistent. "If what you think is true, you can always come back later. But right now we will not take chances."

Sticking his head out the front door of the apartment house, he looked both ways up and down the street. His store was a block and a half down the street. He could see it from where he was standing. "I'll go first and open the store so you won't be waiting in the street. When I signal, you'll come, one at a time." With that, Davide Nathan was gone.

On his signal, Elena disappeared out of the door, walking at a rapid pace. Olga peeked out into the street. She watched her mother enter the store. Wrapping her raincoat tightly around her nightgown, Olga started running towards the store. Suddenly, she froze. An Austrian soldier had rounded the corner, directly in her path, his rifle pointed at her.

The soldier was just as startled. He stared at her, then lowered his rifle.

Schnell, schnell! he whispered, waving her away from him.

She nodded and broke into a run, arriving at the store several seconds later.

Her mother pulled her inside. "Oh, Olga, I thought for a moment that . . ."

"I'm all right, Mama," she gasped, trying to catch her breath. "But I was very lucky. Where's Papa?"

"He's in the back calling Uncle Attilio."

Davide Nathan returned, shaking his head. "No answer at their apartment at this early hour." Tears welled up. "The Germans have taken my brother and his family."

Elena reached for his hand. "Or more likely, he fled his apartment the way we did ours and is hiding out somewhere."

Her husband sighed. "I certainly hope so."

Same Day, Same time, Rome, the Ghetto, Apartment of Attilio Nathan

He was having a bad dream—at least that's what Attilio Nathan thought until the screams wafting though the open window from the street below brought him to consciousness. He leaped out of bed. and ran to the window. In the predawn darkness he saw a man running down the street—he didn't know him. The man shouted, "Jews, run, run, the Germans are here!" Nathan heard the crack of a weapon being fired—the man crumpled in the middle of the street.

Nathan stuck his head out. Down the street, Germans were lining up men, women and children against a wall. People were being pushed roughly out of the buildings, the German soldiers seemingly impervious to the heartbreaking pleas and screams. If anything, the noise seemed to make them more violent. A convoy of military trucks pulled up. The soldiers started prodding the people with their rifle butts to make them climb into the trucks. Children and infants were thrown in bodily if their parents did not move fast enough.

Momentarily transfixed by the brutal scene under his window, he suddenly sprang into action. "Get up, all of you," he shouted at his family. "The roundup has started. We've got to get out of here!"

Rosa was already up and dressing. Nathan shook his fourteen-year-old son Michele, roughly. "Get up, this is no time for sleep. Our lives are in great danger!"

The three raced down the stairs. The Germans were already pounding on the front door. "It's too late," Rosa cried.

"No," he whispered urgently. "Follow me." Nathan pushed them into the storage room in the back of the building. He found a wooden crate and shoved it against the wall under a small window three feet above them. He could hear the front door crash in. The Germans were in the building.

"Hurry, out the window. I'll give you a boost." He cupped his hands around his wife's foot and propelled her out of the window. He did the same for Michele. He heard the Germans approaching the storage room. With a burst of adrenaline he grabbed the windowsill and pulled himself up and through the window.

Improbable Heroes

Fearfully, they crept to the end of the alley. Nathan looked around the corner. This side street seemed quiet. Without talking, he waved his family to follow him.

"Where are we?" Rosa whispered, many blocks later.

"On Via Filipine," he replied. "See that church? That's our destination."

She looked puzzled. "How will that help?"

"For years, I've done business with the priest in that church. We're good friends. He'll help us."

The three of them entered the church. They found the priest lighting some candles in preparation for the first mass of the day. He motioned Nathan to approach. "I have been expecting you. I know all about what's happening."

"What can you do?"

The priest laid a reassuring hand on Nathan's shoulder. "Do not worry, Signore. The church is prepared to hide you. You wife will be taken to the convent of the Religious Teachers Filippini to live there with the sisters. You and your son can hide in the church in the Lateran Palace." He smiled. "You aren't the first. We've been hiding Italian soldiers and anti-Fascists there for some time now."

Nathan suddenly slapped his head. In all the excitement, he'd not thought about his brother, Davide. If they hadn't escaped by now, it would be too late to warn them. *Damn me for forgetting!*

The priest watched him stomp around but left him alone to deal with his private devils.

□□□

Back in the ghetto, twenty-nine-year-old Arminio Wachsberger was not so lucky. He awoke to the banging on his door. He knew right away. Only *they* knocked like that. He threw on a robe and opened the door. An armed SS trooper stood there yelling *"Schnell."* The German shoved a white card into his hand that told him in Italian that he must go into the street immediately with only one small bag. Those violating instructions, the card said, would be shot on the spot.

In the street, clutching his bag, Wachsberger was prodded by the rifles of other SS men even though it was not necessary. He wasn't resisting. The scene bordered on the surreal: a crippled woman, thrown on a truck wheelchair and all; children screaming looking for their parents; young people helping the elderly climb into the trucks to avoid the impatient batons of the SS.

Then on the curb, a figure caught his eye. A two-year-old boy sat there, crying softly. My God, it's my nephew! he realized. With one sweep of his arm, he grabbed the boy up and hugged him close.

"Where's your mama?"

The child only cried louder.

A German soldier prodded Wachsberger to climb on the truck. Wachsberger handed the little boy up to those in the truck and scrambled over the tailgate. He held his nephew close as the truck roared to life. The last one on the truck, he sat looking out over the tailgate. Then he saw his janitor, a Catholic, who was watching the roundup from the doorway of the building where Wachsberger lived.

"Enrico," Wachsberger screamed above the din of the truck engine. The janitor looked up. Wachsberger lifted the young boy high in the air motioning the child toward the janitor.

The janitor nodded. He ran to the truck screaming, "Stop! Stop! That's my son, he's a Catholic!"

A German soldier immediately sprang into action. Banging on the tailgate he yelled at Wachsberger, "Give that boy back, you dirty Jew—you want his blood for one of your disgusting rituals?" He pointed his rifle. Wachsberger gently handed the boy down to the German, who passed him on to the janitor. Wachsberger settled back as the truck picked up speed.

Same Day, Same Time, Rome, Home of Ugo Foà

Foà lived in a fine home several blocks outside the ghetto. He'd have been unaware of what was occurring in the ghetto had he not received several frantic calls about the roundup.

"It's a mistake, I'm sure," he told his wife. "This must be their campaign to arrest people in the resistance."

His wife looked frightened. "Maybe we should leave, just in case?"

Foà sighed. "I suppose so. We can visit our friends in the country and see what happens." The next moment he heard a vehicle pull up. He walked over to the window and pulled aside the curtains. A large truck, a German cross on its hood and swastika flags on its fenders, screeched to a halt at the curb. He looked at his wife. "I'm afraid we're too late." He opened the door in response to the pounding.

A German SS captain slapped his riding crop into his gloved hand. "Ugo Foà? I have orders to take you in," he announced in heavily accented Italian.

"This must be a mistake, Captain. Colonel Kappler has . . ."

"No mistake, these are Colonel Kappler's orders. You will stop talking. Both of you pack one small suitcase each and come outside immediately. I will wait here for you." He withdrew his pistol from its holster. "If you delay, you will be shot."

"Where are we to be taken?"

"To a labor camp. Now, no more questions. You must move. We are out of time."

Later that Afternoon, Rome, Just Outside the Ghetto

Father Libero Raganella spotted them from the doorway of his boys' school. It didn't take much perception to realize that this family, the parents and two boys, was in trouble.

He stepped outside. "Are you Jews?" he asked politely.

The man reacted as if a bee had stung him.

"Do not be afraid," Father Raganella said soothingly. "I'd like to help you. Please, step in here, off the streets." He motioned them inside the doorway.

The man looked at his wife. She inclined her head toward the church, so they stepped inside.

"I know about the roundup," the priest assured them. "I expect you need a place to hide."

The man nodded.

"You can't stay here. It's too dangerous for the young boys, but I will try to take you to safety." The priest looked at his watch. "The curfew is about to begin. We don't have any time. If we're caught out in the streets we'll all be shot. But I have an idea."

They followed Father Raganella out into the street again. "There's the Church of Santa Susanna just down the block. They have a convent and a cloister. Let's head for it—quickly."

Father Raganella led them into the church. "You wait here, I'll speak to the mother superior."

□□□

A few minutes later, Father Raganella faced an irate mother superior. "You can't be serious, Father," she protested. "This is a convent of women. I cannot receive anyone, much less men and boys, into the cloister."

"But Reverend Mother . . ."

"I won't hear of it; it's impossible. It cannot be done, simply cannot be done." She folded her arms firmly for emphasis.

"I realize the difficult position you are in, Reverend Mother, but there is something much more at stake than the sanctity of this cloister. If you send these people into the streets after curfew, their lives and those of their children will be forfeit."

The mother superior paced around the room in anguish. She crossed herself. "But this goes against everything we have established here. What am I to do?"

Father Raganella scratched his head. "You needn't do anything at all, Reverend Mother. Just leave the chain off the convent gate and let me push it open. Then it is I, not you, who has violated the rules. That is a far better solution than causing the deaths of those innocents in the middle of the street."

The mother superior nodded. "May the Lord forgive me for having been so callous."

October 18, 1943, Rome, Tiburtina Railway Station

Kappler, observing the proceedings in the railway station, took perverse pleasure in Dannecker's situation. He'd warned him repeatedly that Italy was not like Poland. The Italians would harbor and hide Jews—and that's just what they had been doing. He could have told Dannecker, but didn't, that Portico d'Ottavia, running through the ghetto along the banks of the Tiber, was a cramped, humid labyrinth of narrow, twisting alleys, many of which were impassable for large vehicles, such as German army trucks. He decided to let the smart-ass captain find out for himself.

Kappler also knew that the smart Jews had already gone into hiding. He had to smile. When he had escorted Dannecker, after his arrival in Rome, to Wehrmacht headquarters and the captain had sought the help of the German army, the unsympathetic commander in Rome, General Rainer Stahel, had declined, saying the Wehrmacht didn't fight unarmed civilians. Then the general had added for good measure, "Good luck, Captain. Half the population of Rome is already living in the homes of the other half."

After supervising the loading of the Jews into waiting cattle cars, SS Captain Dannecker was not in good humor. Of the estimated 8,000 Jews in the Rome ghetto and the adjoining area of Trastevere, his troops had been able to round up only 1,239 of them. So much for his proud report to the führer! Colonel Kappler gloated to himself.

"I will get the rest of them," he growled to Kappler.

The SS colonel fixed Dannecker with a steely gaze. "I'm afraid you underestimate the enemy, Captain. You're fighting the most improbable heroes—ordinary Italians, priests and nuns who won't give up the Jews so easily. Oh, you'll get a few of them; there are always careless ones, but face it, your *razzia* is basically *kaput*."

"We'll starve them out since they have no ration cards. Then we'll see how much the Italians like to share their meager food."

Kappler turned away. He decided to spare the unhappy captain the joke going around headquarters about the tourist guide who, in response to questions about the location of Michelangelo's Moses, said, "For some days now, he has been in the home of friends."

The doors of the freight train slid shut on its human cargo and the locking bars slammed into place. Steam escaped from under the locomotive. Slowly, the train moved forward, gradually gathering speed.

Dannecker's lack of successful roundup was no solace to the 1,259 poor souls caught in his net. They were headed, in an unheated freight car with no food or water, for God knows what.

CHAPTER SEVENTEEN

October 21, 1943, Florence, a Street and the Archbishop's Palace

He spotted a familiar figure walking close to the buildings just off Piazza di San Giovanni. He couldn't believe it. Hurrying up to him, Rabbi Nathan Cassutto asked, "Professor Frascati, what are you doing out on the street? You'll be picked up by the Fascist militia—or worse." He grabbed the professor by the arm and pulled him into a doorway. "Why are you still in Florence?"

"Ah, it's you Rabbi," the man said with a start. "I—I didn't know where to go. I have no false papers."

Cassutto sighed. Another incautious Jew, and this one was a friend. "The archbishop's place is just across Piazza San Giovanni, Professor. Follow me and be careful. It's very dangerous out in the street without a false ID."

A few minutes later, Rabbi Cassutto and Professor Dino Frascati were ushered into Cardinal Dalla Costa's office.

"Thank you, Your Eminence," said Cassutto politely, "for taking the time from your busy schedule to see us."

The prelate waved away the statement, smiling. "Rabbi, it's obvious your day has been busier than mine. I see you have found another one?"

"Yes, Your Eminence. This is an old friend of mine, Professor Frascati. He needs papers and a place to hide."

"Take him down to Father Ricotti's office. He's all set up to help."

□□□

Father Cipriano Ricotti, a Dominican friar and priest smiled when he saw Rabbi Cassutto. After introductions, Ricotti shook Frascati's hand. "You've come to the right place, Professor. Do you have any papers with your photo on them?"

"Just my Jewish identification papers," he replied, extracting them from his briefcase.

The rabbi slapped his head. "Which you are carrying around with you? What if you were searched?"

Frascati gestured futilely.

"That's all right, Professor. You'll be fixed up in a minute." Ricotti removed the photo from its page and carefully pasted it on a false ID for one Carmine Ronga. The newly created Ronga watched as the priest stamped the document.

"This, Signore Ronga, is the town stamp of Eboli," he explained.

"The one near Salerno?"

"The very same. It's one of the towns we have made stamps for because it's in Allied hands so that there is no way for the Fascists or Germans to check whether the ID papers have actually been issued there."

He handed the new false ID to Frascati. "A few more details and we'll be finished."

Ricotti left the room and returned a few minutes later with a baptismal certificate, also under the name Carmine Ronga. He smiled. "Well Signore Ronga, you are now a Catholic in good standing, congratulations."

"I don't know how to thank you, Father Ricotti."

The priest put up his hand. "Don't thank me yet, 'Mr. Ronga,' you still need a ration card."

"You have one for me? They're almost impossible to obtain."

The priest smiled. "Not if you have friends in the office of the Central Italian Municipality. He pulled out a stack of blanks, selected one and put the others back in the drawer. He inserted the name Carmine Ronga on the card and handed it to Frascati, who looked at it in surprise.

"It already has the seal of the City of Florence embossed on it!"

Father Ricotti shrugged. "Courtesy of my Sicilian friend in the municipality who has access to the seal. That should permit you to leave Florence safely. I will send someone to escort you to a small village north of here. It's one of the villages that has agreed to provide rooms to refugees. You should be safe if you are careful. Just don't tempt fate by putting your new IDs to too severe a test."

Ricotti turned to Cassutto. "Isn't it time for you yourself to leave the city? You've done all you can. Most of your Jews, unlike those in Rome, went into hiding at your urging, and the *razzia* the Germans conducted here turned out to be a total fiasco."

"I'll stay in the city a little while longer, Father. As you see, there still are people surfacing like the professor, who will need my help."

"You won't be able to help anyone if the Germans catch you."

"I'll be careful, Father," promised Cassutto as he and Frascati took their leave.

Same Day, Genoa, Rabbi Pacifici's Hiding Place, a Church-Owned Apartment

Rabbi Riccardo Pacifici, a DELASEM officer, had understood very early—at the time of the armistice—the terrible danger the Jews of Italy were facing. Having safely hidden his wife and children in two Florentine convents, he was free to confront the enormous task of convincing his congregation to go into hiding. His newfound ally in this effort was Massimo Teglio, someone whom he'd never seen in the synagogue on the Sabbath or during the High Holy Days. Teglio, having narrowly escaped the Gestapo, had not fled Genoa. Ignoring Father Repetto's advice to get himself to Switzerland, he had stayed and thrown himself into his new mission—saving Jews—with all the vigor he'd previously reserved for piloting his hydroplane and pursuing the playboy life. Now he was assisting Rabbi Pacifici, going from home to home and not leaving until he had convinced its occupants of the danger.

"I really appreciate your help," Pacifici told Teglio, during one of Teglio's rare—and dangerous—meetings with Pacifici.

Teglio nodded, absently examining some papers lying in front of him on the rabbi's desk. He picked up one of the ration cards

DELASEM had been distributing along with the false IDs. "How do you get these cards?"

Pacifici looked at Teglio, a wry smile on his face. "With great difficulty. We buy them, one at a time, from individuals."

"It must be a slow and time-consuming process. Are you able to obtain enough cards?"

Pacifici shook his head. "Far short of what we need."

Teglio frowned. "That's because you're going about it the wrong way. Let me see what I can do. I'll be back a little later." He was out the door before Pacifici could question him.

Teglio, drawn into the clandestine world of the now underground DELASEM, had become very adept at obtaining needed materials. He was determined to find a better source for ration cards.

□□□

Two hours later, Teglio stuck his head in the door. "You busy, Rabbi?"

"Please, come in." Pacifici waved him into the room. Father Repetto was sitting beside the desk.

Grinning from ear to ear, Teglio tossed a large stack of cards on the rabbi's desk. "Here, Rabbi, how's this for a start?"

Pacifici riffled through them—all ration cards. He handed them to Repetto, who waved them in the air. "But how . . .?"

"Simple. I found out the police officer who handled unclaimed ration cards and I met with him. He was only too happy to sell them to me. He pocketed the lire, of course. Now, I have a running arrangement with him. Every month I can pick them up in bulk."

Repetto, who now headed the national DELASEM organization, fished around in his leather portfolio. "Here, I have some papers for you. They should give you some protection if you're stopped."

Teglio looked at the false ID with his picture under the name "Giobatta Triberti," along with a baptismal certificate in the same name.

"Signore Triberti, you are now a lay member of the Company of St. Vincent. Congratulations!" Repetto laughed loudly. Then, turning serious, he looked at Pacifici.

"Rabbi, you are too well known, especially by the Gestapo. They've engaged in an intensive search for you. You can no longer really disregard my warnings to leave Genoa."

"I am sorry, Father Repetto, but I cannot leave yet. There is too much to do."

"You see how pig-headed your rabbi is?"

Pacifici looked narrowly up at the priest.

Repetto shrugged. "Sorry, Rabbi, it was a callous non-kosher reference. I meant bull-headed."

□□□

Repetto had joked, but he really was frustrated at the rabbi's lack of appreciation of the danger he was in. Repetto had even sought the assistance of Cardinal Boetto, who insisted that Pacifici at least move into a church-owned apartment. Pacifici relented and gratefully took up his offer.

As a result of the efforts of Repetto, Pacifici, and Teglio, the German *razzia* in Genoa, as in Florence, netted few Jews. Teglio had only one failure: his own sister. He had left his sister's apartment convinced she would go into hiding immediately. But she'd waited three days and then called for a taxi instead of getting on the train. She and her family had been arrested in the taxi. He tried to find out what happened to them, but in vain. He had enlisted Repetto, who had gone to his information sources—still with no results. He finally had to advise Teglio that it would be a miracle if he ever saw them again.

Same Day, Genoa, Office of Cardinal Boetto

Having arranged refuges in Genoa homes and apartments and nearby villages for the Italian Jews to hide in, Repetto had then thrown himself into the graver problem facing foreign Jews in Genoa—those who were unable to flee the city because they didn't speak Italian and lacked funds. Where to send them? He was particularly concerned about the Schwartz family, who escaped had from Rome just before the *razzia*. They had hidden out in Ancona until the Fascist gangs there made it too perilous. The family had finally ended up here, intending to escape to Switzerland. But the situation had changed for the worse. The border crossings had become too dangerous and even if they could get across, the Swiss authorities would force them back over the border and into the arms of the Germans. Repetto went to see Cardinal Boetto.

□□□

The cardinal, at his desk, heard out his visitor, nodding his head as he considered the problem. A solution presented itself. "Instead of sending the refugees up north to cities such as Genoa, where Mussolini holds power and the Fascist goon squads run wild, we should reverse the procedure—send our refugees south."

"How, Your Eminence?" asked Repetto, looking perplexed.

"Use the same people who brought them up here in the first place. They can take them back down. I'll speak to Cardinal Dalla Costa in Florence. He's always a source of good ideas."

□□□

Returning to the DELASEM office, Repetto pondered the problem of what to do with the Schwartzes. He'd run out of private homes and pensions in Genoa, which, even if available, were much too dangerous for the heavily accented foreigners. That left the monasteries and convents, something he considered a last resort. He'd heard that those in Rome were taking in refugees, on the orders of Cardinal Maglione and Monsignor Montini. But here? He just didn't know, so he visited the Schwartzes, hidden temporarily in a nearby church, and asked them to go with him to see Cardinal Boetto.

"Your Eminence, this is the Jewish family from Austria I was telling you about, Joseph and Dora Schwartz and their children, Sophia and Fredrick."

"You have a wonderful family, Signore Schwartz," the cardinal said kindly. Let us see if we can keep it that way."

"Thank you, Your Eminence."

Turning to Father Repetto, the cardinal ordered, "Take them over to one of the women's convents."

"We'd have to separate them, because males are not allowed..."

"No, no, Don Francesco, I don't mean separate them. My conscience won't allow me to add more to the afflictions of this family. Go to the mother superior and tell her to find a small corner in the convent to accommodate them all."

"But, Your Eminence, the convent rules!" exclaimed Repetto in surprise.

"You keep saying that," the cardinal replied with some irritation. "You tell the mother superior that the Holy Father has granted me special authority and I am applying it to the rules of the convent. If she has objections for the Holy Father and me, bring her in here and I will straighten her out! If she wishes, she can dress them like sisters and hide the men, but they will be sheltered. This is a family; what God has joined together, let no man—or the mother superior—put asunder. You tell her that!"

Same Day, Rome, Vatican, Office of the Cardinal Secretary of State

Cardinal Maglione felt besieged and somewhat resentful. The low-key response of the Vatican to the roundup in Rome was, after all, not his decision, and they knew it. Nevertheless, Sir Francis D'Arcy Osborne, the British ambassador to the Holy See, and Harold Tittmann, Roosevelt's representative, had just been in his office loudly protesting about the Vatican's position on the German *razzia,* or more accurately, its lack of position. Secretly sympathetic to the Allies' arguments, the cardinal secretary of state found it extremely difficult having to explain and justify the Holy See's stance. Earlier in the day, Maglione had seen German Ambassador Weizsäcker, who personally opposed the action against the Jews. Maglione told him that the Vatican hoped these things would not continue because the Holy See did not want to be faced with the need to express its disapproval. A weak warning, Maglione admitted to himself, but one, he thought, that would be in accordance with the pontiff's wishes.

Same Day, Rome, Vatican, Office of Monsignor Montini

The aide of Monsignor Montini, assistant secretary of state, rapped lightly on the door and stuck his head in. "Monsignor, the telephone is ringing off the hook. Jews seeking asylum are flooding into the convents. The mothers superior need instructions—some are almost hysterical."

Montini sighed heavily. "Prepare instructions for Cardinal Maglione's signature. All convents and religious houses in Rome shall open their door to Jews hiding from the Germans, be the refugees women or men."

The aide's eyes widened. "Men in the houses of sisters and nuns, Monsignor?"

Montini nodded. "We shall tell the mothers superior that for the duration of the war, they will dispense with those rules of cloister that prohibit visitors. They have to understand that the Lord, for now, has more important ways for them to express their devotion to Him—by saving lives. If any abbess or mother superior has difficulty with that, you let me know."

"Very well, Monsignor Montini." The aide bowed and backed out of the room, shaking his head—he'd be the one having to deal with the irate reverend mothers face-to-face.

Same Day, Rome, Store of Davide Nathan

Davide Nathan looked out of the window of his wholesale textile store. The street was quiet. The Germans hadn't thought to search the store. The Austrian soldier, who originally stopped Olga in the street, saw her run into the store. But he'd kept it to himself. Thank God they're all not beasts!

After the *razzia,* the family stayed in the back storeroom with no lights for a few days. But without food and only meager sanitary facilities they had to abandon this hiding place. Nathan had sneaked out for food. He brought back some bread and cheese but it was becoming too dangerous. Spotted by a German patrol, he'd barely escaped through the basement of a nearby building.

"We are going to leave now," he announced to his wife and daughter.

"I'm afraid, Papa. If the Germans see us on the streets . . ."

Nathan put his arm around his daughter. "I know, my little Olga, but if they seal off the ghetto, we may never be able to get out."

"Where will we go?" his wife asked. "We just can't wander the streets."

"I know. I know. I have a Catholic friend, Arturo Candotti, who has also been a long-time supplier to my business. His home is well away from the ghetto. If we can get there, I'm sure he'll help us."

Cautiously they entered the street and headed out of the ghetto. Ordinarily, it was an easy ten-minute walk, but not this time. Nathan led them from house to house, ready to leap into a doorway if they encountered a German patrol. It took them well over an hour before they reached a main street outside the ghetto. A bus waited at the stop—it was empty.

The bus driver eyed the bedraggled group boarding his bus. "Jews, huh?"

They didn't answer.

"That's all right, you needn't be afraid. The last ones I'd ever help are those German bastards." Then he looked at Olga and shrugged an apology for his language. "Where are you going?"

"A street just off Porta Maggiore," Nathan answered.

"This bus is supposed to go to Via Vittorio Veneto." He eased the bus doors closed. "Oh what the hell, I'll take you there." He smiled. "Nonstop!"

The driver took off and sped down Corso Vittorio Emanuele, then headed east past the Coliseum, ignoring all the angry riders trying to wave down it down.

"Which building is it?"

Nathan pointed to a four-story structure. The bus pulled up right in front of the door.

"Thank you very much."

"It's nothing. Just get inside quickly . . .and good luck."

□□□

Nathan rang the bell, and a few minutes later Arturo Candotti greeted his friend. "Davide! Come in, come in, I was so worried about you. I called you several times. When you didn't answer, I thought the Germans . . ."

"We managed to evade them. Arturo, we need a place to stay for a little while."

Candotti slapped Nathan on the back. "Well, you've come to the right place. You're welcome here, of course. You must be hungry. But first, let me say hello to your family."

Same Day, Berlin, Office of *Reichsführer* Himmler

An SS sergeant handed the *Reichsführer* a folder containing correspondence. "From Colonel Kappler in Rome, Sir."

Himmler nodded. "That will be all." The sergeant gave a smart *Heil* Hitler and left the office.

Himmler pulled the report out of the folder and began reading, skipping though the preliminaries:

> ... *Judenaktion* initiated and carried out today according to plan ... All available forces of security and police forces put to use. Participation of the Italian police, considering their unreliability in this affair, was not possible. We therefore carried out a series of arrests in rapid succession in twenty-six precincts . . . . The behavior of the Italian people was outright passive resistance, which in many individual cases amounted to active resistance . . . . As the German police were breaking into some homes, attempts to hide Jews in nearby apartments were observed, and it is believed that in many cases they were successful. The anti-Semitic part of the population was nowhere to be seen during the action, only a great mass of people who in some individual cases even tried to cut off the police from the Jews. In no case was it necessary to use firearms.

Himmler detected an I-told-you-so tone. Kappler's obstructionist attitude, as well as those of Kessel and Möllhausen, had not gone unnoticed by the *Reichsführer,* even before hearing about it from Dannecker and Eichmann. And that anti-Nazi, Weizsäcker didn't fool him either—Himmler had a thick file on him. Ordinarily, their conduct would have bought them a one-way ticket to Dachau, but times had changed—the tide of war had changed. North Africa had been lost; the Soviets were advancing all along the Eastern Front; Sicily was gone, and the Allies were advancing up the Italian peninsula. Germany was on the defensive, despite what the führer and Goebbels claimed. No secret weapon would save them. The führer would never permit it, but some day—not yet—an approach to the Allies will have to be made in secret or Germany will be destroyed. Perhaps Roosevelt and Churchill would be interested in joining forces with the Wehrmacht against the Bolsheviks. If so, they would need someone to keep order in the Third Reich—who better than me?

He leaned back in his chair mulling over Kappler's report. The failure of the *Judenrein,* getting rid of the Jews, in Rome was a minor blip—there were not that many Jews to get excited about. And then there was still Hungary to deal with—a million Jews there, still untouched. I'll just let the Rome mess go for a while, he mused, and concentrate on Hungary. Ultimately, I'll have to devise a strategy to ease Germany out of the war without getting myself strung up by piano wire. But we're about a year away before our defeat will become obvious. Then there will be time to move. At least the pope kept his mouth shut. That should make deportations in Hungary easier, when they start . . .

October 22, 1943, Rome, Office of Ambassador Weizsäcker

Weizsäcker held the telephone to his ear with one hand and ran his fingers through his thinning gray hair with the other. His superior, Ribbentrop, at the other end of the line, railed in anger against the pope.

"But Foreign Minister, I have the Vatican statement in front of me. It talks generally about the cruelties of the war without any specific reference to the Germans or the Jews. In typical Vatican style, it is meandering and totally unclear. My advice to you is to let his statement simply fade away because very few people will recognize in it a special allusion to the Jewish Question. If you issue a statement objecting to it, you will only be suggesting to people who had made no such connection, that perhaps the pontiff was, in fact, criticizing Germany."

Ribbentrop still needed convincing.

"Foreign Minister, the only threat of a papal protest will come if we continue the roundup of the Jews," repeating Maglione's empty, half-hearted threat. Weizsäcker was not being honest with the foreign minister. He knew no such threat would be carried out because the pope had no intention of undercutting his neutral relations with Germany. Weizsäcker knew this pope: the Holy Father's determination was driven more by his fear of Bolshevism than by anything the Germans could or would do to him or the church. It wouldn't be the diplomat's first untruth to keep the pot from boiling over.

Weizsäcker hung up the receiver feeling he'd dodged another bullet. The foreign minister had accepted his advice—and he knew from Kappler that Himmler had suspended the *razzia,* for now. Most of the action against Jews now, he understood, would be on the individual initiatives of special SS squads assisted by the Italian police and perhaps the Fascist gangs operating out of Milan, Genoa, and Florence.

October 24, 1943, Berlin, Office of Colonel Eichmann
"Major Krumey," demanded Eichmann, "did we get a response from Auschwitz concerning the arrival of the more than 1,200 Jews from the Rome roundup?"

Hermann Krumey, Eichmann's first assistant in the Jewish Department of the Gestapo, smirked. "It just came in, Sir, from Commandant Höss. I have it right here. It's the Auschwitz log entry for October 23."

Eichmann took the paper.

> RSHA-Transport, Jews from Rome. After the selection, 149 men registered with numbers 158451-158639, and 47 women registered with numbers 66172-66218, have been admitted to the detention camp. The rest have been gassed.

Same Day and the Day After, Poland, Auschwitz Concentration Camp
Arminio Wachsberger, newly arrived from Rome, looked at the seemingly unending rows of barracks. So this was Auschwitz. He'd heard from the clandestine BBC broadcasts to Rome that this was one of the "extermination" camps. He prayed it was just Allied propaganda, but he didn't think so.

The roundup in Rome had been terrible. Children and old people clubbed for not moving fast enough; people shot for the least provocation and left to lie in the street in pools of their own blood. He'd never forget the woman with a baby who, when the SS guards were not looking, tossed it to a very surprised total stranger looking on at the curb. The man held the baby close to him and walked away.

But as bad as the roundup had been, the train ride had been worse. With little to eat or drink for five days, many people in the packed freight cars had died—and the Germans refused to remove the bodies. As the train passed all the labor camps in Germany, the ones to which Wachsberger expected he would be sent, it became clear to him that he was headed for Poland. Able to speak fluent German, he picked up a lot of information by simply listening through the slats of the freight car when it stopped—information denied to the other prisoners. He didn't share it because none of what he heard would give them any hope.

The train had pulled into Auschwitz at night and remained sealed for several hours. Suddenly, at dawn, the doors were slid open and German guards screamed at the Jews to get off. The confused Italians understood no German and Wachsberger started shouting translations to them. The Jews were driven out of the train cars by SS guards with batons swinging and dogs on short leashes snapping at their heels. Under bright floodlights and amid much shouting and chaos, all the children, the elderly and most of the women were herded to the left. The physically fit men and women were ordered to the right. The left line was marched away. He never saw them again, nor did he expect to.

An SS officer pulled Wachsberger out of the line and took him to Commandant Höss's office. Wachsberger stood in front of the commandant's desk.

"Please, sit down, Herr Wachsberger. I have singled you out for special duty because I understand you speak fluent German. We need you to interpret at the medical facility," the commandant said in a casual manner, as if this were a normal situation of an applicant being advised he got the special job.

□□□

The next day, after the *appell* (roll call), Wachsberger reported for his first day of work at the medical center. A doctor greeted him affably in German and assured him the work would be pleasant and would have its own rewards—such as extra food and cigarettes. He waved Wachsberger to a chair in front of his desk. "And your name is . . .?"

"Arminio Wachsberger."

The white lab coat of the slim, good-looking doctor did not quite hide the black SS officer's uniform he wore underneath. He extended his hand and shook Wachsberger's. "Welcome, Herr Wachsberger, I am Mengele, Doctor Joseph Mengele, chief medical officer at Auschwitz."

CHAPTER EIGHTEEN

October 24, 1943, Genoa, a Local Convent off Via Roma

Sister Rita approached the new sister sitting in the far corner of the cloister. She smiled and extended her hand holding some cards and papers. "Your new identification papers have arrived, Signora. Here, keep them with you. You are now Sister Agnes, formerly Gretchen Dengler of Arosa, Switzerland. Because of your German accent, we had to find an appropriate hometown for you. The authorities are not likely to check there."

Almost hidden under her coif and veil, Dora Schwartz's eyes glistened, wet with tears of gratefulness. "Thank you so much, Sister Rita. We owe you our lives."

"Please, Sister. Your safe arrival here is thanks enough for us. False IDs have been delivered to your husband and children, as well."

Sister Agnes, née Dora Schwartz, biting her lip, offered a nod of appreciation. "I only hope I can return the favor some day."

Sister Rita smiled. "You may yet have the opportunity. God works in strange and wondrous ways. Now, Sister Agnes, have you learned some of our prayers so that you not only look like a one of us, but sound like one, too?"

The ersatz sister nodded.

Sister Rita sat down next to her. "Good. I am ready for your inaugural performance."

Same Day, Rome, Home of Arturo Candotti

Davide Nathan watched Arturo Candotti shuffle into the sitting room. He knew immediately that there was trouble from the expression on his host's face.

Candotti sighed. "Bad news, I'm afraid. The concierge saw you and your family enter the building and go up to our apartment. He's hysterical. He says we will all be shot for harboring Jews, that if you don't leave today he will have to inform the German authorities. I'm afraid he's serious." Candotti spread his hands helplessly. "He's really not a bad person, just a very frightened one."

Nathan stood up. "I understand. We will prepare to leave immediately. It's just as well. I was never comfortable with the danger we have created for you and for your family by our presence here."

"What will you do, Davide?"

"I've been doing a lot of thinking. I have a Catholic relative in Trastevere. Many years ago she married a Catholic and converted. They are people of modest means; she's a laundress and he's a street musician—but good people."

"How will you get there?"

"Walk, I suppose."

"Without papers? That's madness. I will not hear of it. Look, in my business, I have access to a small truck. I will drive you."

"No, no. It's too dangerous," his guest protested.

"I insist. No one bothers business trucks. You will sit behind stacks of merchandise in the back of the truck. It should take no more than a few minutes. But we must leave before the curfew."

□□□

When the Nathans arrived in Trastevere, any concern about imposing on Nathan's cousin, the laundress, evaporated when she greeted him with a hug that he could feel arose out of genuine affection. After welcoming them, she immediately prepared a meal, filling their plates with *gnocchi* and *ricotta* cheese, even before her street musician husband arrived home.

Same Day, Rome, the Vatican

Born in Killarney, Ireland, forty-five-year-old Monsignor Hugh Joseph O'Flaherty held the position in the Vatican of notary in the Congregation of the Holy Office, associated in many people's minds with the sinister sounding, Roman Inquisition. The Holy Office, of course, used none of its more infamous predecessor's methods; it consisted of a group of prelates who examined challenges to the faith, arguments on morals and all aspects of the church's teachings and then advised the cardinals of any threat to the faith. O'Flaherty, who had been a boxer in his younger days, kept himself in excellent physical shape. It was a good thing, too. On more than one occasion, he had had to move fast to avoid the Gestapo in the course of his efforts to hide both Allied pilots shot down over Italy and escaped POWs. Maglione had put Father Benedetto in touch with Monsignor O'Flaherty, who, he felt, possessed unique qualifications to assist the Capuchin friar in keeping Jews out of the clutches of the Germans.

In the middle of St. Peter's Square, the tall and athletic O'Flaherty, resplendent in his black cassock piped in purple-red, black cape, and the round, brimmed *cappello romano* on his head, presented a startling contrast to the diminutive Capuchin friar in his plain brown robes and small skullcap.

O'Flaherty sported a wide grin. "It's good to see you, me old son. It's been years since you left Rome."

"You remember?" asked Benedetto in surprise.

"Of course, Father. How could I not? Your reputation precedes you. What you did in Vichy—amazing! It's a grand man you are."

"Indeed, I might say the same for you, Monsignor. I assume you're still saving Allied escapees?"

"As I ever was. But let's not stand out here in square. Come away in and we'll talk. Maglione told me yourself would be coming, but he didn't say when."

□□□

When the two friends were settled in O'Flaherty's small office, he continued the conversation. "I've found places to hide Allied escapees in homes of reliable friends, in rented apartments, and on a temporary basis, in churches, religious houses, and monasteries.

Osborne, British Ambassador to the Holy See, is of great help, providing the funds we need. A grand fellow, he is." O'Flaherty's eyes sparkled through his small, round wire-framed glasses. "We even hide a few here in the Vatican." He winked.

The austere Capuchin had to adjust to the Irish priest's freewheeling spirit and language. But adjusting to unique situations or problems as they arose had become part his stock-in-trade—and a necessity to his own survival. "We obtain funds from the secret accounts of DELASEM," he told O'Flaherty, "so that's no problem. But I do need assistance in finding hiding places for Jews."

"You can count on me, of course. Just tell me where to meet them and meself will make the necessary arrangements."

"Arrangements?"

There was that O'Flaherty grin again. "I provide the lads with a full set of monsignor's clothes: cassock, hat and cape; and the lasses with sister's habits. Makes it easier and safer to escort them through German lines, it does."

Even seated, O'Flaherty towered over Benedetto. The friar looked up at the Vatican priest. "What about false identification papers? We can produce some on an old church press."

"Ah, we have John May, Ambassador Osborne's butler—at least that's what the Brits call him. Now there's a nice lad. He can find anything on the black market—printing presses, food, trucks, you name it. And not to boast too much, Friar, we even provide forged money to the refugees—made right here in the Vatican, it is!"

Benedetto, all business, betrayed no reaction. "We can produce some false papers, but not enough. Can you do anything there?"

O'Flaherty made a fist and examined his fingernails. "Not to push the sin of pride too far, if I may boast a little, we have a grand scheme—identification papers signed by the German military governor of Rome hisself!"

"How did you manage that?"

"Ah, there's our Madame Chevalier, a fine Italian citizen who has no truck for the Germans; a grand lady she is, indeed, and one of our most dependable friends. She hides Jews and POWs by the dozens in her apartment. Her lovely daughter, Adrienne, as beautiful as an Irish lass in springtime, she is; could sell ice to Eskimos in the winter. Anyway, I had this opera ticket in the box next to that of the German military governor. What an opportunity! We put our heads together and came up with a plan—give the ticket to Adrienne! Using her considerable feminine wiles and her excellent German, she took advantage of her proximity to the general at the opera to strike up a conversation with the officer. Who could resist a lovely lass like that? Now I ask you? Then she passed him her program and requested his autograph. The general's aide, quite annoyed, pushed her program away, but the flattered general put down the aide quite severely. He took Adrienne's program and signed it before passing it back to her. Now we can forge passes by the thousands with a signature so fine, the good general hisself would swear it was his."

"Good," the friar smiled briefly, "because we expect a large influx of Jewish refugees on their way south to the Allied lines now that the Swiss border is all but closed."

O'Flaherty shook his head in dismay. "Sweet Jesus, have those Swiss no conscience at all? Rest assured, Father, you will have my full cooperation—and that of the Vatican. And that I have on good authority."

"The Holy Father?" Benedetto whispered in wonderment.

"Better than that, me friend, better than that. From the cardinal secretary of state hisself." O'Flaherty laughed uproariously.

October 29, 1943, Genoa, a Convent off Via Roma

They'd practiced it many times. The sisters led the Schwartz family into the secret tunnel under the convent. The tunnel, discovered many years before, would lead them out into the side streets of Genoa, if necessary. Being dressed like sisters, nuns and monks was all well and good, but for non-Italians, their safest course of action was to avoid any interrogation at all by the Germans.

Today, the unthinkable occurred. German soldiers forced their way into the convent in a surprise raid. Joseph and Dora Schwartz and their children barely had time to go into the dark tunnel before the soldiers reached the entrance to the cloister. Standing by the gate leading into the tunnel, but out of sight in the darkness, Dora Schwartz, "Sister Agnes," could see and hear the conversation between the sisters and the German soldiers.

"This is a place of God and a sacred retreat for sisters in His service. Have you men no sense of decency?" It was the mother superior.

"We are looking for Jews," the German sergeant snarled. "And we think you are hiding some here."

"Have you found any, Sergeant?"

"Not yet, but . . ."

"Then get out! Now."

"Shut up you old witch before I take you in for questioning. We must still search the cloister."

Dora watched as German soldiers started to pick up candelabra, chalices and other valuable items of silver as they combed each room.

"What are you doing? Roared the mother superior. That is church property. Leave the cloister at once!"

The sergeant raised his Mauser and pointed it at her. "I would just as soon shoot you if you keep bellowing."

"I am not impressed by your weapons," the mother superior declared, her chin held high.

"The perhaps this'll impress you: you are under arrest. See how mouthy you'll be when the Gestapo gets finished with you."

At the entrance to the tunnel, Dora's knees knocked with fear, loud enough, she feared, to be heard by the Germans close by. But she knew what she had to do. Steeling herself and taking a deep breath, she pushed open the gate and, in the persona of Sister Agnes, walked up to the sergeant, her habit flowing behind her. From the dark tunnel behind her, Joseph and her children looked on in horror at her insane act.

"Who are you?" the German sergeant growled.

"Sister Agnes, and German, like you," she retorted in her native German. "How dare you profane this house of God and abuse this good sister? You make me ashamed to be a German. Did your parents teach you to steal from the church and insult its sisters and nuns?" One by one, she looked at each German soldier. Each turned away from Sister Agnes' blazing eyes.

'Put everything down," the sergeant ordered. The soldiers carefully replaced their loot.

"My apologies, Sister Agnes. Sometimes good manners are a casualty of war. Now if you will excuse us ..." The sergeant did an about-face, walked out of the cloister and left the convent, followed by his men.

Sister Rita grasped her protégé's shoulder. "That was a very brave thing you did. We are forever in your debt."

Dora shook her head. "In your debt? Hardly! You are the brave ones, hiding us and putting yourselves in harm's way. We owe you our lives."

"Nevertheless, you were very courageous."

The mother superior approached Dora. "Sister Agnes, if I may call you that because I feel you are truly one of us in God, please accept this small token of our appreciation." She handed Dora her silver rosary, detaching it from her belt.

"It's beautiful, Reverend Mother, but this is yours," Dora protested. "I couldn't . . ."

"You can and you shall. You will honor me by accepting my rosary. Besides, you will be a more convincing sister fingering this rosary, the next time you have to speak to a German soldier as our representative."

CHAPTER NINETEEN

November 1, 1943, Assisi, the Bishop's Palace
Bishop Giuseppe Placido Nicolini leaned back in his desk chair studying the peasant priest, the angelic-looking yet unassuming Father Rufino Niccacci, sitting in front of him in his brown robes. "I've been speaking to Cardinal Dalla Costa in Florence. From now on, the process will be reversed. Instead of escorting Jewish refugees to Florence, you will take Jews from Florence south to Assisi. The Swiss have closed the border to Jews so we will now try to get them to the south, behind Allied lines."

Perplexed, Niccacci asked, "But what will we do with the Jews once they reach Assisi?"

Nicolini frowned, as if it were the strangest question he'd ever heard. "Why, hide them, of course."

"But, Your Excellency, there is no place to hide so many in Assisi."

"Then we will find places in homes, churches, seminaries and all the convents and religious houses. I am sure the good people of Assisi will provide space in their homes."

"With respect, Your Excellency, you are asking a lot of the citizens of this town. These are quite dangerous undertakings."

The bishop sighed. "Don Rufino, these are trying times, requiring some extraordinary effort from our flock. They are up to the task, you will see."

Niccacci stood up. "Will that be all, Your Excellency?"

"Sit down, Father. There is one more thing."

The friar settled back into his chair.

"Cardinal Dalla Costa and the DELASEM people in Florence are most impressed with the false IDs you've been providing to the refugees who have passed through Assisi. How in the world did you do that?"

"It's the work of Luigi Brizi."

"Brizi," the bishop cogitated. "Do I know him?"

"He's the local printer in Assisi. The one I play checkers with at Café Minerva on Wednesday afternoons. Anyway, I asked Brizi to produce 150 identity cards from various provinces under Allied control—that makes it impossible for the authorities to check their authenticity."

"Yes, yes, I understand that," the bishop said impatiently. "Please, go on."

"So I sent some of the friars to the Central Post Office to find names and addresses of people living in the southern provinces. We have some old battered typewriters. Some Jews hiding in the churches typed the names and addresses onto Brizi's counterfeit cards. We have a real artist among our guests, Paolo Jozsa, a Jewish refugee from Hungary staying at the San Quirico Monastery. Jozsa is a master forger. He's duplicated the signatures of captured or dead German generals in the south, the rubber stamps of each of the southern Italian provinces and even the German seals. Once we complete a false ID, we paste on a photo from the refugee's old papers, stamp it and press on the seal and, like magic, the former Jew is now an upstanding Christian Italian."

Nicolini shook his head. "Amazing! I did not know you had such creative talents, Father."

"We can thank Brizi and Jozsa. Poor Brizi is working nights producing the identification papers—he doesn't dare do it during shop hours. He has his son run the shop during the day. A good thing, too. Last week, two SS officers came into the shop and ransacked it, searching for false IDs or the blanks. They found nothing because Brizi keeps nothing like that in the shop during the day. The SS officers were so embarrassed they ended up buying dozens of postcards."

Nicolini nodded his approval. "Cardinal Dalla Costa would like you to supply him with Brizi's IDs. I told him you would."

"It's difficult, Bishop. We'll have to step up production. I'll speak to Brizi."

November 14, 1943, Salò, Office of Mussolini

Edda was making another protest visit to her father in his new headquarters in Salò in German-held territory. "Papa, what is this order you issued that henceforth, all Jews are the enemy, their property is to be confiscated and they are to be arrested by the Italian police and put in concentration camps? You sound like a junior Hitler."

"Believe me, Edda, I dislike having to do this but I have no choice. I admit it—I'm Hitler's puppet. He considers Italy conquered territory and me a mere convenience to do his bidding. I have protested. He ignores me. He wants me to move against the Jews, I move against the Jews. It's as simple as that. The real governors of northern Italy are Ambassador Rahn and the German generals."

"Then resign, Papa."

Mussolini shook his head. "And be shot at dawn? No thanks."

"What about Gallo, Papa? When are you going to release him?"

"Hitler says Ciano must stand trial. So far I have delayed it, but you have to expect the worst. I'm sorry, Edda."

Edda stood up and faced her father, her feet spread apart, hands on her hips. "Both you and Hitler will be sorry if any harm comes to my husband. I promise you, Papa, I will release the diaries Gallo kept during the time he was foreign minister. They detail all the secret talks and communications between you and Hitler. All your confidential deals. I've read them. I assure you, they're really quite embarrassing for you and the führer." She spit out Hitler's title with obvious distaste.

"It doesn't change anything, Edda. Besides, I don't think you'd do anything to hurt me."

"I don't want to, Papa, but believe me, I will in order to save my husband." Edda turned and started walking out of his office, then looked back at her father. "One more thing, Papa. The diary is well hidden, so don't send any of your Fascist goons to look for it." She slammed the door behind her.

The Same Day, Florence, Office of Cardinal Dalla Costa

Don Leto Casini had volunteered to help Father Ricotti hide Jews in Florence and provide them with false Christian identities. At Cardinal Dalla Costa's invitation, both men took seats in his office.

"Since Mussolini has been installed in Salò, things have gotten much worse, Your Eminence," Casini reported.

Dalla Costa ran his hand lightly over his hair, careful not to disturb the scarlet *zucchetto* sitting precariously on top of his head. "Such as?"

Casini cleared his throat. "Well, my sources inform me he's appointed violent Fascists as his new government leaders. Alessandro Pavolini, that murderous fanatic, is his second-in-command; the corrupt Guido Buffarini-Guidi is his interior minister; and the gunman and racketeer Tullio Tamburini is chief of police. It will be announced shortly."

"You know, Your Eminence," Ricotti interjected, "that Pavolini has already created the Republican Guard as his own terror squad, not answerable to the courts. Mussolini has encouraged all this. Now there are Fascist gangs all over northern Italy. Dr. Pietro Koch's gang—they were notorious for torture and beatings during the old Fascist regime—is in operation again, as is the Muti gang in Milan, and Carità's band and the Brigate Nere here in Florence. The Germans have already started to use these gangs to do their dirty work—torturing and killing Jews."

The cardinal grimaced in disgust. "One thing is obvious: our priority should be to speed up the process of moving Jews from here to the south. Bishop Nicolini in Assisi has promised to send Father Niccacci with a supply of identification cards. The good father will then escort a group of Jews from here to Assisi, where they will be hidden until arrangements can be made to move them south behind Allied lines. Both of you will be responsible for selecting refugees for the first group, those Jews most at risk"

Ricotti and Casini rose to leave.

"One more thing," interjected the cardinal, raising his hand.

The two priests halted.

"Get Rabbi Cassutto into hiding. It's too dangerous for him to be flitting around the city."

"I'll do what I can, Your Eminence," replied Ricotti, "but he's very stubborn—insists on attending all DELASEM's secret meetings. Beside which, he has his own little secret groups of Jewish refugees."

November 22, 1943, Salò, Italian Government Headquarters

A nameless bureaucrat in the government's publicity office picked up the telephone and dialed the number of a municipal police captain in Florence with known sympathies for Jews.

"Never mind who this is," the bureaucrat whispered into the mouthpiece. "If you want to save your friends, warn them to go into hiding and above all, avoid the *Italian Police*. Orders will be issued tomorrow for them and the Fascist gangs to arrest all Jews and throw them into concentration camps."

He hung up, disconnecting the police captain before any questions could be asked.

The Same Day, Florence, the Cardinal's Palace, Father Ricotti's Office

Father Ricotti hung up the telephone. He sighed. His head dropped and his chin rested on his chest.

"What's the matter, Father?" Casini asked, worriedly.

"It's starting. The Italian police were officially ordered to arrest all Jews. They are setting up concentration camps. The government has asked the Fascist gangs to assist the police."

Ricotti wrote some numbers on a piece of paper, tore it off and handed it to his colleague. "Call Rabbi Cassutto. This is the number where he is hiding out. Tell him to stay out of sight. I'm going upstairs to tell the cardinal."

□□□

A few minutes later Rabbi Cassutto put down the receiver. He would have to go into deeper hiding, but before he did so he felt he had to hold just one more meeting of his refugee group, composed of those who stayed in Florence to provide other fugitives with hiding places, money, food and false documents. He called one of the group and asked him to invite the others to a meeting that night.

That man, an affluent Pole, ordered his secretary, Mario Ischia, to spread the word to others. Ischia did as he was told—and more, placing a call to the Gestapo, who were holding Ischia's wife and daughter, threatening to deport them if he did not cooperate.

That Evening, Florence, the Basement of a Building on Via Ricasoli

Four members of Cassutto's refugee group and Don Leto Casini, crowded into the small, dank basement storeroom, piled high with empty wooden crates. Someone had moved the crates around to form a square. The group took seats on the crates and listened intently to the rabbi as he brought them up to date on the new measures to be taken against the Jews. "Perhaps it may be better," the rabbi advised, "if we do not meet again until we see how things work out."

The Polish refugee shrugged. "We've survived this long, Rabbi. I say we continue our work. There are many Jewish fugitives out there who still need our help."

Cassutto nodded. "Well, I just thought that . . ."

Suddenly they heard the outside door being smashed in and the immediately knew. They just sat there, quietly.

"You are all under arrest," the SS captain shouted. The rest of the German squad squeezed into the little, crate-littered basement room, their automatic weapons pointed at the five unarmed men. "Any attempt to escape by any of you and the entire group will be shot."

Rabbi Cassutto looked up at the officer and said quietly, "No one will try to escape, Herr Captain."

The officer smiled grimly. "Ah, the good rabbi of Florence and his accomplice in crime, Don Leto Casini. This is an auspicious day. We have been waiting to catch this priest in the act. And Rabbi, we have been looking for you for months. You have been very elusive—but that's over now."

The Next Day, November 23, 1943, Florence, Gestapo Headquarters

The Gestapo agent handed Mario Ischia the telephone. "The rabbi won't tell us where his family is being hidden. I don't want to waste time, so you will lure the rabbi's wife into a trap. No one knows yet that you're the informer so you can still be effective. Call one of your employer's friends and tell him to get word to the rabbi's wife that if she wants to find out her husband's fate, she should go to Piazza della Signoria at two o'clock this afternoon."

"I—I'm not sure I can get word to her."

The Gestapo agent frowned. "Now that would really be too bad—especially for your wife and daughter . . ."

Several Hours Later, Florence, Piazza della Signoria

At two o'clock, Anna Cassutto entered the great square, accompanied by an agitated Raffaele Cantoni of DELASEM.

"I don't like the smell of this," her escort said dubiously. "If your husband has been taken in by the Gestapo, then this could be a trap."

"But I got word from a reliable source, one that wouldn't set me up for capture. I'm to meet with Ischia, a loyal employee of Nathan's collaborator. I know and trust him. I could never live with myself if I did not take this opportunity."

Cantoni spread his arms helplessly. "Still, it's very dangerous."

"Raffaele, I asked you not to come. You can still leave."

He looked at her. "Anna, for good or evil, we're in this together."

Anna smiled her thanks, then pointed to the other end of the square. "There he is!" She waved to Ischia. He returned the wave.

Anna hurried toward him and Cantoni speeded up to keep pace with her.

"Mario, what's happened to my husband?"

Ischia looked down, not meeting her eyes. "I am sorry Signora, I truly am."

"Why Mario?"

Cantoni's eyes were already sweeping the piazza.

"Because, Signora Cassutto, he has led you and your friend into a trap," a voice behind them said. The Gestapo agent politely introduced himself. Several other agents took up positions nearby, surrounding them.

□□□

Anna was sent to San Vittore Prison in Milan, where she joined her husband. Her only fear was that she could, under torture, reveal the hiding place of her two children and her parents. Fortunately, no one thought to ask. There were few things to be thankful for these days—that was one of them.

November 28, 1943, Florence, Office of Cardinal Dalla Costa
"I suppose it had to happen sooner or later," the cardinal sighed. Rabbi Cassutto has continually flaunted fate these past months. But Don Leto Casini?"

Ricotti shrugged. "I warned him that it was getting too dangerous to attend any meetings now. But he felt it was important to show the rabbi support. And that's not all, Your Eminence. The Nazis, not content with merely catching the Rabbi, set a trap for his wife and took her as well."

"Frightful. What about their children?"

"They're safe. We moved them from the convent, just in case. We set them up with separate Christian families."

"That was wise," approved the cardinal. "What's happening in the streets?"

"Pure anarchy. The Carità band, encouraged I'm afraid, by the Germans, is running wild looking for Jews. They were getting frustrated because they'd found so few of them, so they invaded the Convent of the Franciscan Sisters and the Convent of the Sisters of St. Joseph and discovered a few Jewish women."

The cardinal interlocked his hands together and squeezed. "Dear God, these gangs know no moral bounds. Even the Gestapo largely respected the sanctity of the convents. What about the Italian police?"

Ricotti shrugged. "The police are hanging back. They really haven't tried very hard to arrest Jews."

The Same Day, Florence, Gestapo Headquarters
Captain Dannecker's excuses made SS Major Friedrich Bosshammer, Colonel Eichmann's expert on Italian affairs, livid. Face to face with Captain Dannecker, he shouted, "Colonel Eichmann is

furious with you. You have not gotten the cooperation of the Italian police in rounding up Jews."

Dannecker shrugged. "There's not much we can do. This is a nation of Jew lovers. The Italian police sympathize with the Jews. If you don't believe me, ask Colonel Kappler."

"Never mind Kappler. He'd put them back into the ghetto and feed them! What you must do is pressure the Italian police to arrest Jews. If they do not, made clear to them that we will arrest them also."

Dannecker's tic snapped his face to the side. Bosshammer could barely contain his disgust. "It has been difficult because of all the stories about our concentration camps in Poland," Dannecker whined.

Bosshammer jumped up. "I have an idea. Tell the Italian police that they don't have to turn over their Jews to us. Let them run their own concentration camps free of our influence. That should lull them into a false sense of security. Later, when these camps are full, the Gestapo will take them over and wipe out all of the Jews."

The Same Day, Florence, Convent of the Franciscan Sisters and a Police Station

At the Convent of the Franciscan Sisters, everyone lived in fear of a raid by German SS troops—the sisters and the Jewish women they were hiding. The last thing they expected was the violation of the sanctity of the convent by their own citizens. So a lightning raid by the Carità band took them completely by surprise. The Jewish women, who were not in habits, never had a chance.

The men of the Carità band were vulgar and loutish, smashing the outer gates of the convent and herding the Jews outside and along the street in front of them. Gang members openly selected the Jewish woman they would rape before executing them. Disputes arose over who would have what particular woman. One such conflict arose over Ester Piperno, a buxom, longhaired young brunette. As she and the other victims were pushed along, toward a truck parked in the square, they heard. "Halt," shouted in a threatening tone. Piperno, stopping in her tracks, saw that her captors were just as startled as she. Looking back, she saw a squad of Italian police double-timing up to the group.

The police captain stepped up to the leader of the Carità Band. "We will take possession of these prisoners. You are relieved of responsibility for them."

"Like hell. These are our prisoners and we will damn well do with them what we want."

"If it's a bloodbath you want, well . . ." The captain motioned with his head and the police squad raised their weapons, taking dead aim at the members of the Carità band. "I think, Signore, that most of you will be dead before you can get any shots off—but, of course, that is your decision."

The leader's head swiveled around, first eyeing the police squad, then his own men. His desperation was palpable, trying to maintain the respect of his men and his own self-esteem as leader of this group but not anxious to get himself killed. Self-preservation won out. Waving to his men to move out, he turned to the police captain. "You haven't heard the last of this, Captain," he snarled.

"*Marronne,* you are really full of yourself," the police captain sneered. "Now get out of here before I shoot your balls off!"

□□□

The victorious Italian police marched the women to the police station and locked them up. Ester Piperno looked out from behind the bars of their cell. "What are you going to do with us," she asked the police captain.

"We are not going to turn you over to the Germans, if that's what's worrying you."

"But we are not Jewish. Here, my papers—"

The captain waved the papers away. "Put them away, Signora. We know you are Jewish. Why else would the sisters let you hide in their cloisters? But please, rest assured that you will be treated fairly."

"Just what does that mean, Captain?" asked Piperno, looking him in the eye.

"It means you will be sent to the Fossoli Prison Camp in Modena. Our own people run it; there are no beatings, brutalities or starvation there. I checked on it myself. I know what I am talking about."

"Why are the Italian police arresting us?"

"Orders from our new police chief, Tullio Tamburini. Believe me, I do not enjoy this, but my career has been with the police, so..." He shrugged, not completing his sentence.

December 1, 1943, Modena, Fossoli Prison Camp

Ester Piperno bedded down next to a veteran resident of the camp, a forty-year-old Jewess named Lidia Fiano. Fiano pointed to the sleeping form on the next bunk. "My mother—she's very old. She sleeps most of the time. No one bothers her."

Piperno nodded. "The police captain in Florence said that life in Fossoli wasn't so bad."

"What he told you is true," Fiano confirmed. "The camp commandant, Dr. Avidabile, is very lenient. He has assured us that the Germans will never take over this camp, that he would release us before he would let that happen."

"What do you do all day?" Piperno asked.

"Just light work—sweeping, dusting and some sewing. Look, don't worry, this is an easy imprisonment. The commandant even lets us go into Modena or Carpi to the dentist, the public baths and things like that."

Piperno's eyes widened. "You mean leave the prison?"

Fiano nodded. "But don't get any ideas in that pretty head of yours. If anyone runs away, then all these privileges will be revoked and the commandant will be forced to run Fossoli like a prison. As long as things are quiet here, the Salò government lets him run it any way he wants. And we don't want to change that, *do we?*"

Piperno nodded. "I understand, I won't do anything to endanger the privileges."

CHAPTER TWENTY

December 2, 1943, Florence, Office of Cardinal Dalla Costa

Father Niccacci, summoned from Assisi by Cardinal Dalla Costa, sat in the cardinal's office feeling queasy. Afraid he'd vomit again, he swallowed hard until the feeling of nausea passed.

"It was terrible, Your Eminence. It happened right in front of me as I was walking here. One of the Fascist gangs had found some Jews. They paraded them through the street, then lined them up against the wall and shot them in cold blood." The friar could not control his tears.

Dalla Costa came around his desk and put a comforting arm around the friar's shoulder. Niccacci looked up at him.

"Your Eminence, one of the woman had a baby in her arms. A baby!" he shouted, giving the cardinal a start. "And they shot both of them, can you imagine?"

"This, Father," the cardinal said soothingly, "is precisely why your mission—our mission—is so important. If we get them out of the devil's den, we can spare them all the agony you've just witnessed." He waited while the shaken friar collected himself.

"Your Eminence?"

"Yes, Father?"

"Forgive me for questioning the Holy Father, but why hasn't he spoken out. We've had no instructions from him . . ."

Dalla Costa studied the distraught man. "We do all we do because that is what His Holiness wants us to do."

Niccacci looked up. "He does, Your Eminence?"

"I have been in communication with the cardinal secretary of state and I can assure you that the Holy See is doing everything it can without making matters worse. For example, your Mayor Fortini had written to the Holy Father asking him to protect the holy shrines of Assisi because the presence of a large number of German troops will most certainly invite bombing raids. Fortini has been advised that Assisi will become a German convalescent center for wounded soldiers and nothing more. Other than medical personnel and a small security force, the Germans will be out of Assisi."

"That's wonderful, Your Eminence. But what about the Jews?"

"That's where you come in. As you know, since the Swiss border is closed to Jews, we are now smuggling Jews across the front lines in the south to the safety of Allied-controlled territory."

"That's very dangerous Your Eminence. I'm no smuggler, I wouldn't know what to do."

"On the contrary, Father, you are very good at confronting and confusing Germans. I understand there is a route to the south across the one of the rivers where no smuggler has ever been caught."

Niccacci threw up his arms. "But Assisi is so far from the front lines. How will I ever transport the refugees there without being stopped by the Germans?"

The cardinal sighed. "Have faith, Father Niccacci. You'll figure it out. With God's help, we shall all complete our tasks." He smiled. "Now tell me about your successes—those wonderful false IDs. How did you ever obtain all the official stamps, seals and signatures? My people tell me they are the real thing— or indistinguishable from the real thing—especially the stamps, German seals, and Wehrmacht commander's signatures."

Niccacci nodded. "Our man, Paolo Jozsa, is a real artist at duplicating the signatures of dead or captured German commanders from the south—the ones the authorities can never check up on."

"Excellent work, Father Niccacci. Now we will need you to supply these IDs for our refugees hidden up north."

"If you provide me with their photos, preferably from old identification papers, Your Eminence, we can complete the false IDs and get priests and friars to bring them back here." Niccacci smiled for the first time that day. "They carry back the papers in their shoes."

December 4, 1943, Ancona, a Local Café

Late on Saturday afternoon, Augusto Sonnino sat in a small café sipping a glass of Chianti at an inside table. Since the Fascist gangs had gone on the rampage against the Jews, he'd become more cautious about appearing in the street—or at outside tables. He thought of Joseph Schwartz and his family, who had fled from Rome to Ancona and been taken in by friends of Sonnino. He and Schwartz had become good friends—two Jews with a common problem. Then, the Fascist gangs arrived and the Schwartzes had taken off for the north, hoping eventually to cross the border into Switzerland. But he, a native of Ancona, would not be so easily frightened away. He had taken a job in a winery outside town that provided him with a place to live—actually, a cot in a bunkhouse. The Fascist gangs didn't look for him there. He would come into town on Saturdays when the gang members were home drinking and living it up. Sonnino's musings were interrupted when he spotted Marshal Legnano of the town cabarinieri enter the café. He waved. The marshal ignored him and sat down at the opposite end of the café.

Put out at the snub, Sonnino called over the manager. "What's with Legnano? Am I no longer good enough to be greeted by such a town big shot as the marshal?"

The manager gave him a long look. "Calm down, Signore Sonnino, I'm sure there's a good reason. I'll find out, just stay put."

He watched as the manager conferred with the marshal in low tones. Then he returned to Sonnino's table. He bent down and whispered, "Marshal Legnano says he has orders to arrest you on sight, so—he hasn't seen you. Right? He says his heart bleeds at arresting such an honest person but he has no choice. He suggests that you go to one of the peasant farms in Cuneo, which is out of his jurisdiction. Then, the marshal can report that a thorough search of the town turned up no trace of you."

"But I don't know anyone in Cuneo!"

The manager put his finger to his lips. "Shh, not so loud, you'll get us all in trouble."

"Sorry."

The manager nodded and handed him a small piece of paper. "Here's the name of my cousin and the address of his farm. Mention my name and you will be put up, no questions asked."

Augusto Sonnino stood up, threw some lire on the table for the Chianti and left the café without looking at the marshal. He made a decision: the hell with hiding anymore, he'd join the partisans.

December 6, 1943, Genoa, a Small Church Near the Convent off Via Roma

On Monday morning the old priest of a small church detailed two boys to investigate the bell tower. "Something's wrong," he told them. "I couldn't get the bells to ring for Sunday mass yesterday. Go up and see what the trouble is."

While the two boys were up in the tower, air raid sirens sounded. Working to free the rope, they inadvertently rang one of the bells. The priest heard it and realized the boys were still in the bell tower. He shouted at them to come down immediately.

After a punishing raid, which, fortunately, did not damage the church, the boys started climbing up the tower again. "Halt!" a booming voice rang out in a German accent. An SS officer from the command station across the street came running. "Get down immediately—*schnell*."

The boys hastily climbed down and were at once surrounded by SS troops. "Take these brats in. They have been signaling the Allied bombers from the bell tower. We will show these Italian scum what we do to saboteurs."

Worried about his boys, the old priest shuffled over to the SS officer. "Sir, please, they were only fixing the bell at my instruction. They meant no harm to the Germans."

With one vicious swipe, the SS officer backhanded his gloved fist across the priest's mouth. The priest collapsed at his feet. "Take this lying old fool down to the cells. We'll get the truth out of him—and then we'll execute all three of them."

Same Day, Genoa, The Convent off Via Roma

A few minutes after the bell tower incident, two hysterical priests from the small church ran up to the gate of the convent. A sister immediately opened the gate and let them into the courtyard. Other sisters crowded around.

"We need help, sisters," cried one of the priests. "The SS has arrested Don Luigi and the two boys who were helping him fix the tower bell. They've been accused of sabotage. I heard the SS officer say they will all be shot."

Sister Agnes, née Dora Schwartz, moved closer to listen to the frantic story of the two young priests. The mother superior, who had heard the noise came to investigate, looked pained. "But why did you come here. How can we possibly help?"

One of the young priests cried, "I don't know Reverend Mother. I was hoping you would have some ideas."

The mother superior looked helplessly around the courtyard as if she might find some savior in the wings—and there was one, Sister Agnes.

Dora Schwartz stepped forward. "I have an idea, Reverend Mother." She laid out her plan.

"You cannot do that, my daughter. It's too dangerous. I forbid it."

Dora Schwartz shook her head, swishing her sister's headdress back and forth. She looked directly at the mother superior. "Excuse me, Reverend Mother, there is no other way. I can tell you, it worked before."

Without waiting for an answer, she approached one of the young priests. "Can you show me where this SS command center is?"

"Yes, Sister." Then he put his hand to his mouth in embarrassment and looked over to the mother superior, who gave a slight nod.

"Come, Sister, I will take you," the priest said softly, still intimidated by the mother superior.

□□□

The two left the convent and walked down the street to the steps of the command center. "You wait here," Dora Schwartz told the frightened priest. "If I'm not out in thirty minutes, return to the convent and tell them."

She pushed open the door to the command center and walked up to the desk of the SS sergeant. "Good day, Sergeant. I want to see the commanding officer."

"What is the nature of your business, Sister?"

"That, young man, is between me and your superior."

The SS sergeant shrugged. "Very well, Sister, I will tell him. But my advice to you is to leave now, while you can."

"Are you Catholic?" she said in a low voice so only he could hear.

He nodded.

"I appreciate your concern, Sergeant, but I really need to see the commander."

The sergeant disappeared into the back of the building. He returned and instructed her to follow him. They both entered an office.

An SS officer sat behind his desk, leaning back so that his shined black boots rested on the desk with the soles facing her, showing his disdain.

"Your name?" he ordered gruffly.

What an arrogant bastard, she thought but said, "Sister Agnes."

The SS commander looked at the sergeant. "Throw her in a cell with the other three saboteurs! She has nothing to say that I want to hear."

Gingerly, the sergeant took hold of the sister's arm and turned her toward the door. Shaking him off with a violent jerk, she whirled around to face the commander. "Is this the kind of reception you give to a German sister? And where's my priest and those two innocent boys?" she asked in perfect German. The commander, his feet still perched precariously on the desk, almost fell backwards off his chair. "You're German?"

"Of course, I'm German, but I can't say, at this moment, that I'm proud of it."

His tone changed immediately "What's you real name, please?"

"Gretchen Dengler." She fingered nervously the silver rosary the mother superior had given to her.

"Frau Dengler—"

"My name is *Sister Agnes*."

He nodded. "Sister Agnes, I did not know. Please excuse my behavior."

Oh, that behavior is fine for the Italians and the Jews, but not for good German girls, you animal, she thought. She smiled. "Of course, Commander. Now, about the priest and the two boys."

The commander took his feet off the desk and sat upright. "I'm sorry, Sister, but we can't release saboteurs."

"Commander, I have known Don Luigi for years. I swear to you, he's no spy. He's just a poor priest waiting to retire."

"He sent those boys up to the bell tower."

"Only to repair the bells."

"Or to signal Allied bombers!"

"That's ridiculous," she said crisply, "and you know it! What would ringing the bells do? Rain bombs down on the church?"

"That's not the point, Sister."

"What then is the point? Can you look me in the eye and seriously tell me that Allied bombers one mile up could have heard the ringing bell?"

The SS commander sighed. "You have a good point, Sister Agnes." He turned to the sergeant. "Bring up the priest and the boys."

A minute later the sergeant led in the three prisoners. Dora Schwartz was shocked. The priest's face looked smashed in, covered with blood. She took out a handkerchief and wiped off what blood she could. Turning to the two boys, she said in Italian, "Go home, and take Don Luigi with you and make sure he sees a doctor." Then she turned to the commander and translated it into German.

The boys looked at the commander. He nodded and they left with the old priest.

To the sergeant, the ersatz sister protested, "It's not right for Germans to treat our priests like that. You fight at our side and that is how you act toward us?"

Embarrassed, the sergeant started to back out of the office. The commander came from around his desk and stood face to face with the fake sister. "My deepest apologies, Sister. Here, let me pour you a glass of cognac."

"I don't need a drink, thank you, but a bottle for our hospital would be nice."

"Perhaps you would like some food for the sisters?"

She nodded.

□□□

A few minutes later a very surprised sister opened the gate to Sister Agnes, leading four SS soldiers. The men carried a side of beef and several bottles of cognac into the courtyard, set them down carefully, bowed politely and left.

The mother superior came out to see the amazing sight. "How in heaven . . ."

Dora Schwartz, in her Sister Agnes outfit, smiled and held up the silver rosary. "This convinced them."

In a quite unsisterlike manner, Sister Rita ran up and hugged Dora Schwartz, almost lifting her off her feet.

The Same Day, Rome, the Apartment of Madame Chevalier

Shortly before dinner there was a sharp rap on the door. Madame Chevalier put her eye to the peephole. It was Monsignor O'Flaherty. She slid all the bolts back and threw the door open.

The tall priest stood at the threshold with three people, one dressed in a cassock just like his and two dressed in sister's habits. More refugees.

She spread her arms. "Monsignor O'Flaherty, welcome."

He broke out in a big grin, swept his arms under hers and hugged her affectionately. "As I live and breathe, it's my favorite Irish lass!"

"Oh pooh, you know I'm not Irish."

"I know no such thing and a crime it would be to disabuse me of what meself believes."

She waved away his silliness. "Well, Father, don't stand in the hallway, invite our guests in."

O'Flaherty leaned down, whispering in Madame's ear. "These are not really a priest and sisters, so don't be fooled."

She sighed. "Stop clowning around, Monsignor, and introduce me."

O'Flaherty turned to his guests, shaking his head. "As you can see, Madame Chevalier's a hard lass, she is." He turned to Madame Chevalier. "This is the Divis family—Lev, his wife Zophie, and this lovely lass is their daughter, Bela. They need somewhere to stay."

Madame Chevalier hugged Zophie. "You've come to the right place. You'll be safe here. Where are you coming from?"

"A convent in Trastevere," Divis replied. "We stayed there as long as we could. Then the sisters put us in touch with Monsignor O'Flaherty—and here we are."

"There is plenty of room. I live here only with my daughter, Adrienne. Some POWs are living here now, but there is always room for a few more. Now give the monsignor back his costumes so he can get back to work tweaking the Germans."

□□□

Later, after a full dinner, everyone in the apartment settled in for the evening. Then, a few minutes before the nine o'clock curfew, there were rapid knocks on the door. Madame Chevalier peeped out and opened it. A young Italian boy started to speak excitedly.

Madame Chevalier turned to her visitors. "The Germans are going to raid my apartment tonight. Follow this boy. You can stay in his parents' apartment. But hurry, the curfew starts in a few minutes."

□□□

The heavy pounding on her door an hour later startled her, even though she was expecting it. "Ah, the SS. Only they knocked like that," she said to no one in particular. She didn't bother looking through the peephole but opened the door immediately before they broke it down.

"Who lives here, Signora?" the SS officer thundered.

"Only my daughter and I are in this apartment."

"We must search it."

She shrugged. "Go ahead, if it makes you happy."

A few minutes later, the SS officer returned. "You appear to be right. It does seem, Signora, that you have an enemy who has falsely reported men coming in and out of this apartment. Have you any idea who would say such a thing?"

Chevalier pointed the apartment of her Fascist neighbor on the other side of the living room wall. "In there, next door, they have an awful lot of visitors." She sat in her favorite chair and enjoyed the noise of the SS ransacking the apartment next door.

CHAPTER TWENTY-ONE

December 8, 1943, Assisi, Piazza del Comune

Sitting at an outdoor table at Café Minerva in the main piazza, Father Niccacci enjoyed watching the parade of strollers in the pale noonday sun. He found the sight especially rewarding because many of them, thanks to his false identification papers, were Jews convincingly posing as faithful Catholics. Each of them had been taught some fundamentals of Christian belief. That could be done effectively only for the native Italian refugees. Those with foreign accents could not safely venture out; they were first on the list to be smuggled south across Allied lines.

"Father Niccacci?"

He jerked his head around with a start, looking up into the blue eyes of a lieutenant colonel in the German Army.

"Sorry to disturb you, Father. I'm Lieutenant Colonel Valentin Müller." He offered the friar his hand.

Niccacci shook it. Niccacci thinking to himself that the greeting represented a marked improvement over Captain Ernst Stolmann, the former commander here, who had always heiled Hitler. "Not at all, Colonel, just taking the afternoon sun."

"May I join you?"

Niccacci waved the German to the empty chair. The colonel sat down. "I am the new commandant here. I am also a doctor. This town will become a convalescent center for German soldiers."

Niccacci said a silent prayer of thanks and smiled. "I am very glad to hear that, Colonel. You are most welcome."

The colonel tipped his hat in acknowledgment. "Well, I suppose I am, seeing we're not a combat unit or SS. But to come to the reason for my visit, I understand you are the priest in charge of the Franciscan friary here."

Niccacci nodded, wondering what was coming.

"I am a good Catholic, Father, and I'd like to see all the holy places in Assisi. I have always had a special reverence for Saint Francis. Perhaps you might arrange a private tour for me?"

"Most certainly, Colonel. It will be my pleasure."

The colonel stood up. "Very good. And I assume there will be no problem for you to hear my confession?"

Niccacci also rose to his feet. "None whatsoever, Colonel."

They shook hands and the officer strode away, disappearing across the square.

December 10, 1043, Genoa, Archbishop's Palace, Office of Don Francesco Repetto

"We tried again, and this time fifteen Jews were turned back by the Swiss at the border. They were promptly arrested by the Fascist police," Teglio reported to Repetto.

"How did you find out?"

Teglio smiled. "One woman escaped after they were herded into a tavern."

Repetto's eyes widened. "She was able to escape?"

Teglio nodded. "Quick thinking. The proprietress of the tavern threw her an apron and insisted the young woman was her niece who worked there washing dishes. Then she castigated the 'niece' for leaving the kitchen while there were still dirty dishes to be done."

"God be thanked, but I guess that will just about end the feasibility of sending Jews across that border."

"We shouldn't give up that easily," protested Teglio. Moving a great many refugees so far south is much more difficult—and probably just as dangerous. What I need is a safe system for smuggling our fugitives into Switzerland."

December 15, 1943, Florence, Office of Father Cipriano Ricotti

DELASEM had decided that priority should be given to moving foreign Jewish refugees south and eventually into Allied territory. Native Italian Jews could easily assimilate into the Christian population and, with false IDs, they could exist for months undetected. That was not the case for the foreign Jews.

As foreigners, the Schwartzes, still in their habits, had been moved out of their convent in Genoa and, as pilgrims, escorted by Don Francesco Repetto to Florence and delivered to Father Ricotti. Now Ricotti introduced an unassuming brown-robed friar to the Schwartzes. "Father Niccacci will escort you to Assisi, where you will stay until we can arrange to smuggle you into Allied territory."

Niccacci talked in a soft voice. Joseph Schwartz leaned forward to catch every word. "You will be traveling as Catholic pilgrims—as sisters and priests. It would be very handy if you learned a few prayers."

Dora Schwartz smiled. "Don't worry, Father. We were well instructed by the sisters in the convent in Genoa. They were strict teachers."

"Good. Now give me your old IDs. I need the pictures on them for new ones."

"We already have Christian identification papers," Joseph Schwartz protested.

Niccacci looked at them and shook his head. "Crude. The ones I will give you will be far better—indistinguishable from the real thing."

The Same Day, Hours Later, Assisi, House of the Poor Clares at Santa Chiara

The taxi from the railway station at Assisi pulled up in front of a church near the cathedral. Turning to his "pilgrim" charges, Father Niccacci advised them, "You can stay here until . . ."

"Father, Father," called a friar, who flew out of the church as fast as he could, his brown habit flapping behind him.

Niccacci seized the man's shoulders as the friar tried catching his breath. "Well, what is it, Brother?"

"The—the Germans—they are going to conduct a *razzia* any time now."

"Why, for heaven's sake?"

"It's Mayor Fortini. He refused to hand over hostages. He resigned instead. The Germans are furious. The SS is here. They've already conducted one *razzia*. We expect another today."

Niccacci turned to the Schwartzes, who had just emerged from the cramped taxi and were stretching their legs. "Hurry, follow me. The house of the Poor Clares is just down the street!"

Running, they reached the door of the Poor Clares, adjoining Santa Chiara church, and were admitted into the visitor's parlor. Niccacci rattled the locked gate to the cloister beyond. "Open this immediately," he shouted to a nun on the other side.

"I cannot, Father, not without the approval of the mother abbess."

"My God, then get her. There are lives at stake."

"She is in prayer."

"Call the mother abbess at once, Sister, or I will not be responsible for my actions!" he shouted. It was the first time anyone had ever heard the gentle friar raise his voice.

The startled nun backed away from the cloister gate and disappeared within.

Almost immediately, the abbess, Mother Giuseppina, appeared.

"Reverend Mother, please open this gate, hurry!"

"I cannot, Father, that's the gate to the cloister."

"I know that, Reverend Mother, but these people's lives are in danger. You must let them in."

"You expect me to let men into the cloister? In the seven hundred years since our founding, no man has ever defiled the cloister. And none will now." She crossed herself.

"Reverend Mother, as the guardian in charge of the Franciscans in Assisi, I command you to open this gate!"

Raising her chin and folding her arms across her chest, the abbess declared firmly, "Only the pope can give such an order."

"It's a matter of life or death."

The abbess was not moved.

"What's going on here?"

Niccacci turned around. He recognized the voice. It was Bishop Nicolini, who explained, "I was summoned by one of the friars because of the fracas down here."

Niccacci quickly explained the problem to the bishop.

Glaring at the mother abbess, the bishop ordered, "Open the gate and let these Jews into the enclosure."

Tears streamed down the abbess's face as she wrapped her rosary so tightly around her hand she almost cut off circulation. "I can't, Your Excellency, not without the pope's . . ."

The bishop lowered his voice, his tone softened. "Reverend Mother, I *am* carrying out the pope's orders. Now open up."

She crossed herself. "I—I didn't know, Your Excellency."

"The Holy Father said we must save lives at any cost. Now hurry, the Germans have already started another roundup. They are down the street."

"Another one? Oh, God." She motioned to one of the nuns, who inserted a large key into the gate and opened it. The Schwartz family, Bishop Nicolini and Father Niccacci were ushered into the cloister. Refugee women who had been hidden in the guesthouse joined them.

"This is the safest place," the mother abbess explained. "The Germans wouldn't dare enter here."

Niccacci said a silent amen to that statement.

A minute later they heard banging on the front door. "Do you have any refugees here?" a harsh voice demanded.

"No guests here," replied one of the nuns.

From the cloister the refugees could hear boots clumping across the wooden floor of the visitor's parlor. The same voice announced, "We will check the guesthouse." More clumping boots.

"Now we will check the rest of the house," announced the officer, brushing by the mother abbess, standing at the cloister gate.

"How dare you doubt our word, as daughters of God?" shouted Abbess Giuseppina. "How dare you come in here with weapons? Have you no shame?" Her voice rose louder.

The refugees and the two churchmen in the cloister heard the boots retreating and the front door slammed shut. The abbess came into the cloister and sank down in a chair. She crossed herself. "Thank you, Jesus," she whispered.

Niccacci pulled the Schwartzes aside. "The refugees who are native Italians will be transferred out of here to other hiding places once they have proper identity papers. They can easily melt into the Assisi population. But I'm afraid we cannot do that for foreign Jews. You will have to stay here with the nuns until we move south. You will again have to dress and act like members of the religious order as you did in Genoa. I'm sorry."

Joseph Schwartz laid his hand on the priest's shoulder. "You needn't be. You saved our lives and we are eternally grateful. This is a small price to pay. Thank you."

Niccacci could only nod. He feared his voice would crack if he spoke.

The Same Day, Rome, Lateran Palace
For a few weeks, Attilio Nathan and his son, Michele, rarely ventured far from the sanctuary offered by the church where they were being hidden. But with the false identity papers and baptismal certificates provided by Father Benedetto, Nathan became bolder. Soon he was walking the streets with confidence, often taking Michele with him. But he rarely strayed too far from the church. Mostly, he ventured out to visit his wife, Rosa, at the convent of the Religious Teachers Filippini, located nearby.

Lazzaro Anticoli was another Jewish fugitive given sanctuary in the church. He became friendly with Michele, who looked on the Italian prizefighter in awe and admiration. Bucefalo, as Anticoli was called professionally, soaked up all the adoration he could get, regaling the boy with his feats in the ring. Far more brazen than Attilio Nathan, he ranged far and wide through the streets of Rome. Anticoli offered to take Michele along, but Nathan wouldn't hear of it. Sometimes all of them would walk together in the neighborhood, talking.

□□□

Unknown to the three refugees, an unexpected danger lurked just a few blocks away. It wasn't the Gestapo or a Fascist gang; rather the peril was a beautiful eighteen-year-old Jewish girl, Celeste di Porto, the Black Panther, in the pay of the Gestapo. Di Porto and Bucefalo were acquaintances through the friendship of their parents. Bucefalo would soon regret the connection.

December 18, 1943, Genoa, Office of Don Francesco Repetto

"It worked like a charm," Teglio gushed to his DELASEM colleague. "I used my connection with the Swiss consul in Genoa—he's very sympathetic to the plight of the Jews. He helped me develop the type of fake IDs that would get the refugees asylum in Switzerland. The key is that the Jews who make it into Switzerland should never admit to their Judaism. That was our mistake! As Gentiles, the Swiss won't bother them."

"But the Swiss have closed the border now. How did you get Valobra across the border?" asked Repetto.

"That's the best part! I found two Catholic lawyers of Jewish ancestry. They have a client whose large estate straddles the Italian-Swiss border. I can bring the refugees safely into Switzerland through the estate. I take six to eight at a time, never more. Last night I took seven. One of them was Valobra. He's safely out of the country now."

"Good work. The Gestapo has been going all out to find him. It would have been just a matter of time. It's unfortunate that we can only take over a few a day. We'll have to continue sending most of the Jews south."

Teglio nodded. "I appreciate your assistance with my daughter, Don Francesco. She's being taken care of by the Sisters of the Sacred Heart in Sturla."

The priest smiled. "It's the least I could do. At least it's close enough to Genoa so that you can visit her once in awhile."

CHAPTER TWENTY-TWO

January 9, 1944, Verona, a Small Hotel
Despite her training, SS operative Hildegard Beetz felt sorry for Mussolini's daughter, with whom she shared a room in a small hotel under arrangement with the SS. Assigned to guard Edda Ciano and locate her husband's diary, Beetz had experienced Edda's pain and anguish through most of Ciano's trial by a military court. Ciano, found guilty of treason, had been sentenced to be executed on January 11. Now Edda appealed to her guard in desperation.

"I warn you, Frau Beetz, I will make public the entire contents of the diary if Gallo is executed."

"That would hurt your father, as well, if you do."

"At this point, I don't give a damn for him or Hitler either."

Beetz, standing in front of Edda's chair said, "Calm down Signora, I have an idea. Would you surrender the diaries if we could remove your husband from Verona and take him to safety?"

"Certainly I would. Could you do that?"

"I don't know, but I can try."

Five minutes later Beetz put her hand over the mouthpiece of the telephone and whispered to Edda, "My chief, Kaltenbrunner, is conferring with *Reichsführer* Himmler right now."

After speaking again with Kaltenbrunner, she hung up the telephone. "The *Reichsführer* has approved an SS action to spirit your husband out of Verona and to safety in Germany. But only if you surrender the diary."

Edda folded her arms across her chest. "I will, but not before Gallo is freed and out of danger."

Beetz nodded. "That is acceptable."

"Thank you, Frau Beetz," Edda sobbed.

Beetz put her hand gently in Edda's. "I am glad we could save your husband."

"The Verona proceeding was nothing but a kangaroo court," Edda went on through her tears. "Gallo never had a chance."

Beetz shrugged. "You are undoubtedly correct, Signora Ciano. But you forget this is wartime. All the military courts are alike. For them, there is no such thing as justice."

January 10, 1944, Verona, a Small Hotel

Beetz hung up the telephone. Her long face told Edda the news was not good.

"What's happened, Frau Beetz?"

"I am so sorry, Signora."

"For what? Does it concern Gallo?"

Beetz nodded. "The führer has disapproved of our arrangement. He insists that your husband must be executed on schedule as an example to all traitors."

"But the diaries—I will give them to the press! Doesn't he understand?"

Beetz sighed. "I am sure he does. You must leave Verona immediately, Signora. Get across the border to Switzerland. I'm sure the SS will arrest you before long."

Edda buried her head in her hands. "Is there nothing I can do to save Gallo's life?" she sobbed.

"No, Signora Ciano. What you must now concern yourself with is saving your own life."

"But I am Mussolini's daughter. They wouldn't dare!"

"They would and they will, if you give them a chance. You are a threat and that's how the Nazis deal with threats. You must flee, now, before I receive orders I would not wish to carry out."

"But you are SS! Why are you doing this?"

"I will undoubtedly regret this, but even for a Nazi, there comes a point . . ." Beetz threw up her hands without completing the sentence and walked out of the room.

January 11, 1943, Verona, Forte San Procolo

Ciano jerked forward as the army truck braked to a stop. He looked out the back. They had arrived at Forte San Procolo, a shooting range on the outskirts of Verona. He heard the gates swing open. He wished Marinelli would shut up. He'd been hysterical since the ride began. It was difficult enough to maintain his own composure in the presence of such sniveling and moaning.

The truck rolled into the courtyard. Ciano jumped out with his fellow prisoners. Ahead of him was the proud, erect Marshal Emilio De Bono. Behind Ciano were labor leader Luciano Gottardi and Agriculture Minister Carlo Pareschi. Being dragged by two burly carabinieri was Administrative Secretary Giovanni Marinelli. They were marched to the shooting range where chairs were set up. A guard pushed Ciano down into a wooden chair and bound his arms behind him. Ciano shook his head when offered a hood. He sat quietly, taking himself out of the scene by picturing himself skiing with Edda at Arosa. But tuning out the cries of Marinelli was more difficult. The others sat silently.

The firing squad began taking their positions behind the prisoners. Ciano did not turn to look at them. He focused instead on the twenty people, sitting off to the side, present to witness the executions. Taking a deep breath, he held it as the twenty-five militiamen took aim. He heard the shout, "Long live Italy! Long live the Duce!" It was Pareschi. It was the last voice Ciano ever heard.

□□□

An SS captain was among the witnesses. He was there neither out of curiosity nor as an official representative of the Third Reich. His orders were simple. If for any reason, Ciano was not executed, the SS captain would complete the job on the spot.

How to accomplish that was mooted when the twenty-five riflemen fired. He couldn't believe it. Twenty-five rifles, fifteen paces behind five bound and immobile prisoners, and still they were unable to finish the task. At least two of the prisoners writhed on their overturned chairs, screaming in pain. More shots were fired. Finally, the officer in charge ordered a halt and finished off the remaining prisoners with pistol shots to the head. The SS captain had never seen such a foul-up for such a simple procedure as execution by firing squad. With allies like that, he thought, no wonder we are losing the war!

January 12, 1944, Salò, Residence of Mussolini

Rachele Mussolini burst into the sitting room and strode up to her husband, who was sitting in an easy chair reading the newspaper. Mussolini could see she was seething with anger.

"I had no choice about Gallo," Mussolini pleaded, anticipating the source of her anger. "Sentiment and reasons of state have sharply collided in my spirit."

"That's not what's bothering me," his wife replied. "Gallo got what he deserved, that traitor. But what about Edda? Where is she?"

"She's disappeared with Gallo's diary."

"Disappeared? Where?"

Mussolini shrugged.

"You've got to protect her, Bene. She's our daughter."

"And just how I am I to do that? You know how headstrong she is. You needn't worry, though, she's already in Switzerland—crossed the border yesterday. On my orders, she was not detained."

"Why did you do that?"

"As you so forcefully noted, she's our daughter. In Switzerland she is safe from the SS. Better she should leave with the diary than be assassinated by the Nazis."

"They would go that far?"

Mussolini sighed. "As we have seen in the past few months, there is no depravity they are not capable of or willing to accomplish."

"Then resign!"

"And end up like Gallo?" He grinned cynically. "I don't think so."

Rachele's eyes blazed. "You've brought that whore, Petacci here to Salò, haven't you?"

"Clara? I haven't seen . . ."

"Don't lie to me you philandering bastard!" She plunked herself down in a chair. "I-I thought you were done with all that." Her voice was pleading now.

"Rachele, I assure you, I no longer have such interests. I don't know where you get such ideas."

"Just stop lying, Benito. I know she's living in a chalet in Gargnano. You think I don't have my sources?" Without another word, she stood up and strode out of the room slamming the door hard enough to rattle the glasses at the bar.

At least Clara doesn't bust my balls like Sarfatti, or nag the hell out of me like Rachele, he thought. Rachele simply doesn't understand my needs and never will. Well, I won't change now.

The Same Day, the Hills Outside Ancona

Augusto Sonnino had given up his job in the winery after having been warned in the café that he would be arrested if he appeared in public. Hiding deeper in the countryside, he constantly asked people about the Resistance. Everyone denied any knowledge. It frustrated him and his questions made his hosts very nervous. They did not mind tweaking the Germans by hiding a Jewish refugee or two, but the Resistance—they wanted nothing to do with something so dangerous. So Sonnino moved from farmhouse to farmhouse, continually wearing out his welcome.

He spent his time hiking through the woods. Today was no exception.

"I understand you have been asking a lot of questions about the Resistance." The sudden voice in the quiet of the woods gave him a start. He whirled about and found himself looking at a Mauser automatic rifle pointed at his chest, in the hands of a bearded man who seemed to be around his own age.

"Easy, Signore, no sudden moves."

Sonnino paused to catch his breath. "Are you a partisan?"

The man's eyes narrowed. "Who wants to know?"

"Augusto, Augusto Sonnino, from Ancona."

"Is that supposed to mean something to me?"

"I'm Jewish and I want to fight those Nazi bastards."

"How do I know you're not the secret police?"

"How can I be? They're arresting Jews, not recruiting them."

The partisan seemed unimpressed. "Prove it."

"Here, I still have papers that . . ."

"Put them away, papers don't mean shit. Everyone in Italy has forged papers."

"Then I know only one way to prove it." Sonnino loosened his belt and dropped his pants.

The partisan nodded and lowered his weapon. "Pull up your pants, I'm convinced." He waited until Sonnino was fully dressed and then stuck out his hand. "Vito Volterra, Jewish partisan."

Sonnino shook it. "Thank God. I've finally found a partisan."

"It's a tough and dangerous life, Sonnino. We are often without food and ammunition. And if you're caught, there's no second chance."

"I'm a Jew, Volterra. My second chances have long gone."

The partisan nodded. "Very well, follow me. You will have to convince my commander."

The Same Day, Palestine, Kibbutz Givat Brenner

Well before the war, Enzo Sereni, left the comfortable life in the Rome home of his father, the physician to the king's court, to emigrate, on graduation from the university, to Palestine where he worked as unskilled labor in the fields of the new-formed Givat Brenner kibbutz, located in the southern part of what was then the Jewish Settlement. Later, he joined one of the Jewish resistance organizations, Haganah, in its intelligence operations. Because of his fluent German, he was given the assignment of interviewing German refugees. The horror stories they were telling bordered on the incredulous. Soon he was sent into Germany secretly for a first-hand look. The incredulous turned out to be fact. In 1940, he joined the British Intelligence Service in Palestine. He did not give up his position in the Haganah, but the British did not know that.

When the news reached Palestine of the German occupation of northern Italy the preceding fall, he thought of his family in Rome, either having to hide, or worse, being sent to a concentration camp. Sereni made up his mind. On January 12 he requested an interview with his British commander. "You must let me go into occupied Italy, Sir, to work with partisan units to help escaping British POWs." He did not reveal his true purpose—to rescue Jewish fugitives.

"Why you, Sereni?" the commander wanted to know. "We bloody well have enough agents in Italy as it is."

"But none that know the country the way I do, Sir, or who can pass for a native Italian. I would be able to alternate between the partisans and the Italian Fascists. I can move freely in any Italian setting."

The commander leaned back in his office chair, stroking his handlebar moustache looking curiously at this crazy Jew who wanted to get his head shot off. "Very well, Sereni, but you'll have to learn to parachute. We aren't going to put you in there on a cruise ship."

"I understand, Sir. I'm most anxious to start. The faster I learn, the sooner I can do my job in Italy."

"I'll cut your orders. You speak to Captain Gordon Nelson about arranging the training. He'll wonder what he's doing training a thirty-nine-year-old to parachute. If he gives you trouble, send him in to see me."

CHAPTER TWENTY-THREE

February 3, 1944, Rome, Trastevere

So far Davide Nathan and his family, without assistance, had eluded the Germans and the Fascist militia. Had they sought refuge in any of the havens provided by the church, more than likely the good fathers would have supplied them with false Christian identification papers as they had his brother Attilio. However, the brothers could not compare experiences since neither knew that the other had survived the German *razzia* of October 16. Thus, when disaster struck, the Davide Nathans did not stand a chance.

Nathan was making himself useful, hanging curtains for his hostess, the laundress, when she burst into the small house. "Davide, get your family and leave here. Hurry! One of my neighbors has denounced you to the Fascist militia. They are on their way over right now. A friend of mine in the militia office came to my place of work and warned me."

Nathan raced out of the house and found Elena and Olga browsing around the outdoor market next door. "Hurry," he whispered, "we must go away immediately."

Elena nodded; she needed no explanations.

Walking quickly, but not running so as to attract attention, they headed away from the laundress's house without any clear idea where they were going.

Suddenly, Nathan heard a shout that made his blood run cold. "That's them, that's the Jews I was telling you about."

The Nathans quickened their pace.

Improbable Heroes

"Halt, in the name of the Fascist militia! Halt, or we'll shoot!"

Nathan grabbed the arms of his wife and daughter and stopped them in their tracks. He turned around. "Are you talking to us?"

One militiaman trotted up to them. "Papers, quickly!"

"I'm sorry, officer, we must have left them at home. I'll be glad to bring them down to the—"

"Shut up and come with me. You're all under arrest."

□□□

Across the Tiber, another informer prowled Corso Vittorio Emanuele looking for her next victim and another reward. The Black Panther, Celeste Di Porto, would approach a Jew she recognized and engage him in conversation. That was the signal to Gestapo agents waiting nearby that the person was a Jew and they would move in for the arrest. For this treachery the Gestapo paid her five thousand lire a head. By the end of the war she had identified more than fifty of her fellow Jews. All her victims were caught by these chance encounters with her on the streets.

The day was cold but bright. Squinting into the sun, the Black Panther, shaded her eyes with her hands. A block away, she spotted someone who looked familiar. She quickened her pace to be sure and pulled up alongside Lazzaro Anticoli. "*Ciao,* Lazzaro."

Anticoli looked around at the sound of that sweet voice and stared into the pale blue eyes of the stunning Black Panther. He smiled. "*Ciao,* Celeste." Just as quickly, three Gestapo agents closed in on him. He looked back to Celeste, whose broad smile infuriated him. "Why, Celeste?"

She shrugged. "It's profitable. A girl, too, has to live in these terrible times." She walked away as Anticoli felt the cold metal of the pistol pressed against his temple. Strong hands gripped both his arms. They shoved him roughly into the back seat of a black sedan.

Despite his denials and his false papers, Anticoli could not defeat the sure-fire method of the Gestapo to ascertain his Jewishness— many things could be hidden or altered but not circumcision.

Gestapo men took him from their headquarters directly to Regina Coeli Prison. The heavy iron doors of the old, cavernous building swung open and the black sedan turned into the courtyard.

Anticoli was dragged out of the car and up to the third floor of the prison, the one controlled by the Germans. Thrown into a cell, he took stock of his surroundings. They weren't much. The damp walls were of thick stone, and a bare shining light bulb hung from the ceiling. The only furniture was a small wood bunk without a mattress, and a bucket for excrement.

The cell door clanged shut behind the departing guard. The sound of the key turning the bolt and the lock snapping into place went through him like an electric shock—it signaled the end to his freedom—and perhaps to life itself.

"You bitch," he shouted, kicking the locked door. "Vengeance will be mine, Celeste, I swear it." Overcome with despair, he sat down on the wooden bunk. "Some day, some way," he half sobbed, half growled.

The Same Day, Secchiano

After spending a week with Madame Chevalier in Rome, the Divises were transported in a vegetable truck, arranged by Monsignor O'Flaherty, to the small village of Secchiano in the mountains of central Italy, north of Rome. The village wasn't much, but to the Divises it was paradise. They lived on the second floor of the village schoolhouse.

It wasn't a big village—about 600 residents, and they all participated in harboring and feeding the Divis family. That they were able to fool the Germans was a source of village pride. No one, not a single person in Secchiano, ever thought to turn the Divis family in for the reward.

One day after they had been there for three months, a farmer known to them only as Giuseppe burst into their room over the schoolhouse. "You must leave immediately. German soldiers have entered the village looking for Jews and partisans. Follow me and hurry!"

Divis, Zophie and Bela grabbed their coats and bolted down the stairs after Giuseppe. They used the back door to avoid the main street already occupied by the German soldiers.

Giuseppe took them out to the fields where farm hands were tilling the soil for early planting. He ran into the shed and came out with three hoes, which he shoved at them. "Here, start acting like farmers. Mix with them, imitate them and whatever you do, don't speak. Your accents will give you away."

Divis began to hoe, watching furtively as a squad of German soldiers entered the field and started questioning the farm hands and checking papers. A German soldier approached Divis. "You, where are your papers?"

Giuseppe stepped between the soldier and the Divises. "Excuse me, Sir, but this is a family of deaf-mutes—a very sad story, if you want to hear it."

"I don't have time for your sob stories; just have them show me their papers."

Giuseppe pointed to his own papers and then to Divis's pocket. Divis nodded understandingly and fished out the identification papers for himself and his family, papers prepared by Father Benedetto establishing them as Christians. The soldier checked the papers and handed them back. He looked at Giuseppe and growled, "It's too bad the rest of you Italians are not deaf-mutes like these people. Life in Italy would be so much more pleasant without your babble."

Later, Lev Divis, his wife and daughter returned to the schoolhouse. The village priest had been arrested on suspicion of harboring Jews. But no one ever revealed their presence.

February 8, 1944, Rome

Rosa Nathan felt she could not continue to take food from the convent sisters with making some contribution. Against the advice of the sisters, she left the convent and walked down the street to a grocery shop, a place she'd been to many times before the roundup.

She had a problem. By recent decree, no ration cards would be issued to those who had not lived in Rome for the past year. Because her identification papers had her coming from a city in the south, the authorities in Rome would not give her a ration card.

She looked in the window. The shopkeeper, Erno Celli, poked his head out the door. "Signora Nathan, come in." His greeting terrified her. How could she have been so stupid as to come here? her mind shouted at her. This man knew her as a Jew.

As if he could read her mind, the shopkeeper said, "Signora Nathan, please come in. You looked so worried."

He sounded friendly enough. She stepped inside. She looked only at items that were not rationed, such as pasta.

"You don't have a ration card, do you, Signora Nathan?"

"I—I'm sorry to have bothered you, Signore Celli, I will leave now."

"I understand your concern. But please, I can help you. Come in the back of the shop. I will find you a ration card." He gently led her to the rear.

As he rummaged through a box of cards, he announced, "Here's one. This woman left Rome and won't be back. You can use this."

"Why are you doing this for me?"

"I've known you a long time, Signora, and I like you. Besides I hate the Fascists and the Germans. Anything I can do to undercut them . . ." He shrugged his shoulders.

"I don't know how to thank you, Signore Celli."

"Survive the war, Signora Nathan. Then come back as a good customer again. That will be thanks enough."

February 10, 1944, Genoa, an Apartment, and a Town in Piedmont

Massimo Teglio, having already lost one sister to the Germans, was not about to lose another. He had arranged for his sister Laura to live in a town in the Piedmont province at the home of a retired police marshal. The marshal had no particular love for Jews; he simply saw his lodger as a way to supplement his pension, which he felt, was altogether too low considering his long and faithful service to the city. So Teglio paid the man a hefty fee to board his sister.

Consequently, when Laura appeared at his hiding place one morning, Teglio was surprised—and very distressed—to see her in Genoa. "What are doing here? Are you crazy? You can be picked up at any moment. Do you realize how many people know you and would turn you in for the five-thousand-lire reward?"

"Massimo, I had to see you," said Laura urgently. "The marshal threatened to turn me in. He wants more money."

Seizing her hand, Teglio ordered, "Come with me. I'll find a car and we'll visit this fine, upstanding marshal of yours."

□□□

Several hours later, Teglio, accompanied by Laura, rang the bell of the retired marshal's house. "Signore, I understand you've threatened to turn my sister in." He met the old man's embarrassed smile with steely eyes.

"Well, Signore Teglio, I only meant that with everything costing so much these days, I need a substantial increase in my fee to cover expenses. I mean no harm."

"If you turn my sister out, she will be arrested by either the Fascist militia or the Germans. Do you know what will happen to her then?"

The marshal shrugged. "It has nothing to do with me Signore, I only . . ."

Suddenly Teglio stepped up to the marshal, his face inches away from the old man's, and grabbed his lapels in his fists. "You listen to me, old man. I've already lost one sister to those German swine. Come, let us go to the police station. I guarantee I'll be the one who leaves and you will stay there in jail because I am protected by the Fascists."

"Perhaps, Signore, we have had a misunderstanding," wavered the marshal. "Now that I know your circumstances . . ."

Without letting go, Teglio said menacingly, "Let me make it even clearer. If you do anything to harm a member my family, I promise you, one of us will survive and that one will make you pay dearly."

Teglio let go of the marshal's lapels and the old man stepped back and let out his breath. "Signore Teglio, a thousand pardons. I admire an important man like you with great connections. Believe me, anything I can do to protect your sister I will. Forget anything about an increase in fees. As I said before, it was just a misunderstanding."

□□□

Outside the house, Laura pulled him aside. "Would you really have gone to the police station?"

Teglio laughed. "Not likely. They would have arrested me on the spot and given the old marshal a reward. But he's thoroughly cowed now—and duly impressed with my importance. You'll have no more problems from him. Just keep yourself off the streets."

February 11, 1944, Internment Camp at Servigliano, near Ancona

Davide Nathan settled onto his bunk in the men's barracks at the Servigliano Internment Camp near Mount Sibillini, in the Marches, a few kilometers from Ancona. The occupant of the next bunk held out his hand. "*Ciao*. Levi, Gino Levi from Perugia."

Nathan shook his hand. "Davide Nathan from Rome."

Levi smiled. "Ah, from the big city. You here by yourself?"

"No, they caught my wife and daughter, too. They're in the women's barracks."

"You're lucky you got sent here. No German guards—the entire camp administration is Italian. You're safe for now."

"For now? What does that mean?"

"It means for as long as the Germans stay out of here. Once they come in here, we'll be sent to Poland."

"You think the Germans will take over this camp?"

""I'll be very surprised if they don't. They've been slowly assuming control over everything in Italy."

Nathan looked over Levi. "You look well fed. How do they treat you?"

"They're tough, but not brutal or mean."

"Yes. I've heard that the Italian's are pretty lax in the security of the prisons they run."

Levi raised a warning hand. "That's probably true in a lot of camps but not here. They run a very tight ship. If you're thinking of trying to escape, you'll have a difficult time. Especially if you have to take your wife and daughter."

Nathan got off his bunk and walked to the window, scanning the barbed wire fences. "We'll just have to see."

CHAPTER TWENTY-FOUR

February 20, 1944, Modena, Fossoli Prison Camp
Colonel Adolph Eichmann strode into the camp commandant's office without knocking, followed by an SS sergeant major. Eichmann did not bother to introduce himself. "We will take over this prison tomorrow, Doctor. SS Sergeant Major Hans Haage here will assume the position of adviser to you. In other words, if you want to remain as commandant, you will listen strictly to Sergeant Major Haage."

Dr. Avidabile stood up in protest. "But Colonel, I have been assured by General Stahel that . . ."

"Anything that the general told you is superseded by the orders of the *Reichsführer*," snapped Eichmann.

"Then what do you need me for? Colonel. I'm nothing but a figurehead."

"We want things to look as normal as possible. It will keep the Jews calm until we are ready to act."

"I want nothing to do with this. I promised . . ."

Eichmann smiled thinly. "I know what you promised the Jews, Doctor. We have our informants. You have a choice. Remain the commandant and keep your mouth shut or . . ."

"Or what?"

Eichmann's face clouded over. "Or you will join the Jews when we deport them."

Sergeant Major Haage, his hand on his holstered pistol, moved close to Avidabile, sending an unmistakable message. Eichmann scanned the office and spotted the file cabinets. "Now that we understand each other, I have an immediate need for the list of prisoners at Fossoli. I am sure you must have one in those file drawers. Will you save me the time and get it or do we have to dump out all your files?"

Avidabile shrugged and moved over to one of the file cabinets. He opened the top drawer, pulled out a folder and handed it to Eichmann.

Eichmann opened the folder and flipped through the papers. "Excellent. This is a good start." Handing the file to Haage, he went on. "Understand this, Avidabile, if any prisoners are missing tomorrow, the sergeant major has orders to hold you personally responsible. *Heil* Hitler."

◻◻◻

News traveled quickly in the camp. "Something's happening," Lidia Fiano whispered to her bunkmate, Ester Piperno. "We've never been locked down so early. It's only seven o'clock."

"What do you think it could be?" Piperno asked, frowning.

"I don't know, but whatever it is it won't be good."

Piperno's eyes widened. "The Germans?"

"I think so."

"But Dr. Avidabile told you he'd free the prisoners before he'd let the Germans take over."

Fiano shrugged. "Brave words when there were no Germans around. We'll just have to see. Not that we have much choice."

"Oh God, Lidia, I'm so frightened."

"So am I, Ester, so am I."

Suddenly the loudspeaker blared to life, startling the two women.

"Attention. All inmates will assemble in the courtyard for a roll call. You have five minutes. Anyone not present will be punished severely."

Fiano looked at Piperno. "That's Dr. Avidabile. I never heard such a nasty tone from him. I think we are in trouble, my friend."

◻◻◻

Precisely five minutes later Sergeant Major Haage stood on the raised platform alongside Avidabile as the roll call was taken. Raffaele Cantoni stood in the third row and answered when his name was called. Arrested with Rabbi Cassutto at the ill-fated meeting in Florence, they'd been separated. After beating him several times, the Gestapo was convinced that Cantoni did not know anything else or if he did, the beatings wouldn't get it out of him. They had sent him to Fossoli. Cantoni had no idea what had happened to Cassutto.

The guards reported all prisoners accounted for.

Haage stepped to the front of the platform and barked. "I am SS Sergeant Major Hans Haage. I have been sent here to assist your commandant. That, however, should be of no concern to you. Our plans are to improve the abominable conditions in the prison camp with German efficiency. You have no infirmary here. That is unacceptable. We will open one to treat your illnesses and injuries. We plan to upgrade your recreational facilities and conditions in your cells. If I obtain your cooperation, we will get along just fine and you will receive good treatment from us; life will go on as before. Now, please, go about your usual evening activities."

The prisoners gathered in small groups, discussing the latest development. One woman stopped Fiano. "Lidia, you've been a prisoner here for quite a while. What do you think?" The same question was on Piperno's lips and she cocked her head to hear every word of Fiano's response.

"I don't hold much stock in what that Nazi says. It's their usual approach. Make nice to the Jews to keep us calm, then drop the hammer on our heads."

A voice in the group exclaimed angrily, "Great, that's just what we need, a doomsayer. I'm not going to listen to that hysterical garbage. You heard the sergeant major. He's here to improve conditions. Why can't you just leave it at that?" The group drifted away from Lidia—her views were not what they really wanted to hear.

Then Cantoni, standing in the shadows observing the angry exchange, approached Fiano. "Don't feel bad, Signora. Those people are just frightened and they're striking out at the nearest target. But you're right, of course. It won't be long before the Germans show their true colors."

Piperno put her hand to her mouth. "Oh God, are you suggesting that they will . . ." She covered her eyes with her hands. "I don't want to die," she sobbed.

Fiano didn't appreciate Cantoni's words of support—she'd have preferred to let Piperno down more gently. She threw him a glance of annoyance. He shrugged and walked away.

February 22, 1944, Modena, Fossoli Prison Camp

Yesterday, the day after Haage's announcement, prison security had been tightened. No one was allowed to go into town. But that was to be expected with the Germans in control. Other than that, the day had proceeded normally and the Germans were hardly to be seen. The prisoners took heart. Some even took the occasion to scold Fiano again for her pessimistic attitude. But neither she nor Cantoni had much confidence in the calm that appeared to pervade Fossoli.

This morning the prisoners assembled for roll call, which the Germans called *appell*. This time SS troops were much in evidence. Not a good sign, thought Fiano as she watched. Haage mounted the platform in front of the rows of inmates. "Attention Jews!" He spat out the word with obvious loathing. "Six hundred and fifty of you swine will be deported tomorrow morning at eight o'clock. Your names will be read out at *appell*. Anyone not reporting on time will be shot immediately—no excuses."

Gasps and cries rippled through the rows of Jews.

□□□

The Germans had arrived indeed. Prisoners on work details this morning were beaten severely. Guard dogs attacked some laggard inmates. The prisoners, however, were unaware of the greater horrors yet to come.

At the noon *appell*, the SS guard called out "Rabello, Cesare." No answer. Sergeant Major Haage strode angrily through the rows of prisoners. "Where is the prisoner?" he roared. "Things will go very badly for all of you if he is not identified immediately."

A voice in the back row shouted, "Old man Rabello is deaf. Can't hear a thing. He's in the third row."

Haage moved to the third row, removed his pistol from its holster and held it under an inmate's nose. "Point him out or . . ."

The frightened man immediately pointed to a white-haired old man two places down on his left. Haage moved on to the old man, his pistol lowered to the side of his right leg. "Are you the prisoner Rabello?" he shouted.

Rabello simply looked up at the sergeant major, confused.

"That's him, Sergeant Major, he's stone deaf and can't hear a thing," Rabello's neighbor volunteered.

Haage swiped his pistol across the cheek of the volunteer, who dropped in his tracks, blood spurting from the wound.

"No one speaks in the *appell* unless spoken to," Haage roared. He swiveled around to the old man, raised the pistol to Rabello's head and pulled the trigger. Blood and brains sprayed inmates for two rows back.

Haage strode back to the platform. SS guards dragged forward a semi-conscious inmate. "This is the Jew Pacifico Di Castro," announced Haage. "He did not report for work today, claiming he was 'ill.' You will watch while I make an example of this swine."

An SS guard handed Haage a large truncheon, with which the sergeant major proceeded methodically to beat Di Castro to death. Haage looked up and waited, catching his breath from the unaccustomed exertion. "Any one attempting to escape will meet the same fate as this prisoner." He pointed with the bloodied truncheon to the inert form crumpled at his feet. Then he turned to one of the guards, handing him the truncheon, and ordered, "Get some of these Jews to clean up the mess at my feet and in the courtyard. I cannot abide an untidy facility!"

□□□

Early that evening the women were in their barracks. "It was horrible," Piperno cried. "I have never seen anyone killed, and I just saw two die in the space of a few minutes." She buried her head in the scanty bedding of her bunk.

Fiano shook her. "Come on, my friend, we have an *appell* coming up—and you definitely don't want to be late for it."

"I don't care, I don't care. I can't stand any more scenes like that."

Fiano bent down and slapped Piperno hard with an open palm. "Now get up, you foolish girl, or you will be that scene at the next *appell*!"

Piperno reluctantly pushed herself off the bunk and onto her feet.

Fiano watched Piperno until she was sure the woman would not return to her bunk and then concentrated on rousing her own mother.

"Lidia, how did that deaf man survive the earlier *appell*?" Piperno asked.

"Someone answered for him."

"Who?"

"His nephew, the one Haage beat to death with a truncheon."

"My God!" Piperno said, slowly extending out each word in horror.

□□□

SS Sergeant Elsa Lächert had arrived in Fossoli that morning from an assignment at Auschwitz.

"We have some troublemakers in the camp, Sergeant," Haage had ordered, when she reported in. "Attend to them. I understand you are very good at your job."

At the evening *appell* Lächert identified Lidia Fiano, who was led away by the guards. They threw her into a small dank cell with no windows and no bed.

Fiano was still sitting on the floor of her cell when Lächert entered. "I understand you're a inciter in this camp," accused the sergeant. "I shall teach you a lesson you won't forget."

"I-I've never done anything . . ."

Aiming at Fiano with her right boot, Lächert gave a vicious kick, striking the prisoner on the left temple. Fiano crumpled at the SS Sergeant's feet. "That, Jew Fiano, is one of the problems—you don't know when to keep your mouth shut." Lächert laughed.

Slamming the cell door shut behind her, Lächert turned to the guard and ordered, "Throw ice water on her three times a day. Let's see how long she lasts."

□□□

Some time after the evening appell, Piperno headed toward the center of the courtyard. Cantoni caught her arm. "Don't go out there, Signora. Stay close to the building. Haven't you heard the shots?"

"Yes, I just thought the Germans were taking target practice."

"Only one German is," Cantoni said motioning with his head towards the guard tower.

Piperno looked up. Haage was leaning against the rail, rifle in firing position.

"He's taking target practice all right. He's using Jews walking in the courtyard as the targets. He's killed four, so far."

"I-I feel dizzy."

Cantoni grabbed her under the arm. "Get a hold of yourself. The last thing you need is to call Haage's attention to you."

After a few seconds, she shook her arm free. "Thank you, I'm all right now."

"Good, now go inside and stay there."

"I was looking for Lidia Fiano."

"Forget about her. Just watch out for yourself. There's nothing you can do for her. If they bring her back, fine. If they don't . . ."

The Next Day, Modena, Fossoli Prison Camp

"The following Jews are to be deported today to labor camps in the East. Step forward when your name is called."

Piperno stood stock still in the *appell* line. She felt faint as the guard called one name after the other. She fought the dizziness with all her being, knowing if she collapsed it would be a death sentence. Please God, don't let them call my name, she prayed.

"Cantoni, Raffaele." Piperno watched numbly as the man, who yesterday had probably saved her life, stepped forward. The calling of the names droned on incessantly—more than six hundred names, half the camp. She stiffened as each name resounded throughout the courtyard.

"Ester Piperno." She felt her knees buckle. She could not will herself to move. A sharp poke from her neighbor's elbow galvanized her. She jumped forward.

□□□

A few minutes later the six hundred and fifty inmates selected were marched out of camp to a railroad siding about two kilometers away. Six cattle cars waited, their open doors like gaping maws. One hundred Jews were crammed into each car, packed in so tight many could not sit on the floor. The two water buckets in each car had to suffice for the hundred people. The guards tossed one excrement bucket into each car, almost as an afterthought.

Piperno knew this was the end. She just wished she'd been in the same car with someone she knew, such as Cantoni, even if theirs was a brief acquaintance.

□□□

The train rumbled north for hours. The water was quickly consumed and the single excrement bucket was soon useless. People were forced to foul the area where they sat or stood. Cantoni, one of the first to board the car, had a place by one of its slatted sides. Running his hand over the slats he could reach, he found two fairly splintered ones. He managed to dislodge one slat, which gave him a chance to breathe the outside air. Then it dawned on him. Perhaps he could do more for himself than simply make breathing more enjoyable. He wished he could find Ester Piperno, but he knew there was no chance of that.

February 24, 1944, Modena, Fossoli Prison Camp, Evening

Lächert returned to the cell the day after her attack on the troublemaker. "Is she dead yet?" she asked the guard angrily, as if the prisoner's survival was his fault.

He shook his head. "She's a tough one, Sergeant. No food, nothing to drink, immersed in ice water three times a day, but she still hangs on."

Her eyes blazed with anger. "If that's admiration for the Jewess I hear in your voice . . ."

"No, no, Sergeant, no such thing." She watched him break out into a sweat. She enjoyed terrorizing these strutting SS stallions, taking them down a peg or two. She had to show them she could be more efficient, more heartless and stronger.

"Open the door to the cell."

The guard inserted the key and turned it. He pushed the heavy door open. Lächert entered and approached the still form. She grabbed Fiano's hair and jerked her head up. Fiano moaned.

"Still alive, Jew bitch? Well, I am running out of patience."

She let go of Fiano's hair and the semi-conscious woman's head dropped down to her chest. Lächert kneeled down beside her. "I will remedy that right now." Her powerful hands circled Fiano's neck. She squeezed with all her strength, her thumbs pushing in the windpipe and crushing it. Fiano struggled briefly but had no strength left to offer much resistance.

Lächert left the cell. "The Jew bitch is no more. Go get her mother and throw her in there. No food or water. She can die alongside her dead daughter."

The Same Day, Somewhere in Northern Italy, Aboard the Prison Train

Cantoni worked methodically and slowly, although the crowded cattle car gave him little room to maneuver. Eventually, however, he managed to loosen four rows of slats. It was dark now and the train slowed. Through the slats he'd been able to see the sign at the last station. It read "Vicenza." This was about as close to the Austrian border as he wanted to get. To make some room to extend his legs, he pushed back the people leaning against him. The loud complaints started. They began pushing back. He ignored them. His concentration was focused solely on those loose slats.

He'd have only one chance. He raised his right knee, brought it back to his chest and kicked the leg out with all his strength. The slats gave way with a loud crack—too loud. Would the guards hear it? He pushed the broken slats outward and created a space just large enough, he hoped, to climb out. Gingerly, he put out one leg so that he straddled the slats. Finding a foothold, he pulled his other leg out of the car, slowly. He eased the rest of his body out of the car, hanging on by his hands and feet to the unbroken slats. He wondered briefly how many of the people in the car would follow him out. He dropped the thought and concentrated on only what he could handle, his own escape.

Cantoni, hanging on outside the railroad car, could not, in the dark, really judge the speed of the train, but it did seem to continue to slow down. But the speed didn't matter anymore, he had no choice. He launched himself into the dark void, hoping to clear the track bed without crashing into something solid like a tree or a signal pole.

CHAPTER TWENTY-FIVE

February 26, 1944, Genoa, Office of Don Francesco Repetto
Don Ricotti met Teglio at the entrance to the church.
"He's waiting in my office, Teglio. He's been through a lot." The two men went inside.
Teglio joyfully slapped Cantoni on the back. "Raffaele, you son of a gun, it's good to see you in one piece. You look like hell."
"You'd look like hell too if you leaped off a moving freight train," replied Cantoni without a trace of humor.
Teglio turned serious. "Sorry. Sit down and tell us what happened."
The words spilled out in a torrent. Cantoni hadn't realized how emotionally wracked he'd become until he tried to talk about it. When he reached the part about Haage and the Jews he killed, he broke down. It took several minutes to regain his composure. He had to stop again when he talked about Ester Piperno and Lidia Fiano.
"Jesus, Raffaele, I didn't dream it was that bad." Teglio suddenly realized the priest was sitting next to him. "Sorry Father," he said hastily.
"No matter, Teglio, the story warrants it."
Cantoni bent over in his chair, hands cradling his head. "I can't do this anymore, I'm too frightened. I have to get to Switzerland. I can work for DELASEM there."
"And indeed you should," Teglio agreed. "No man should be put through again what you've endured. I've already taken over

from Valobra. He's in Switzerland now. Don't worry. Between Don Francesco and me the operation is in good hands."

"We've got things running smoothly now," Repetto added.

Cantoni sighed. "I'm sorry, but I'm no good to anyone any more. I'll give you a list of my contacts in Milan, Brescia, Turin and Cuneo."

The Same Day, the Hills near Ancona

Enzo Sereni, in his British captain's uniform, parachuted into the hills just outside of Ancona without incident. Forewarned, members of the Resistance were waiting for him. On his insistence, he was taken to the Jewish partisans. He met with Vito Volterra and Augusto Sonnino.

That night Sereni sat around a small campfire with the two Jews discussing Palestine. Then he turned to the tasks at hand. "Officially, my mission is to assist the Resistance to help the British POWs. But as far as I'm concerned, my first duty is to the Jewish fugitives."

"Well, you've come just in time," Sonnino said. "Another few days and it would have been too late."

Sereni looked questioningly at the partisan.

"The Germans began taking over the camps and deporting all the Jews they found," Volterra explained. "They haven't moved into the Servigliano Camp yet. We have to work fast if we are to save those Jews."

"I have a cache of small arms, mortars and machine guns that were parachuted down at the same time. Not too much though," Sereni offered

Volterra nodded. "That'll help. I have a shipment coming in by truck tomorrow morning, if all goes well." Sereni wondered how a truck loaded with weapons and ammunition could get past the Germans but he didn't ask.

February 27, 1944, At Dawn in the Hills near Ancona

Sereni, leaped for his automatic rifle when he spotted the German military truck in the dawn light rounding the curve at high speed and bearing down on them.

Volterra pushed the weapon down. "It's all right. The driver is one of ours."

Sereni wasn't convinced. "But it's German. How . . .?"

"It's fine, I assure you. Now don't go shooting our comrade."

The German truck screeched to a halt in front of Volterra and Sonnino. The driver started to hop out but stopped cold seeing an unfamiliar figure carrying a rifle.

"It's nothing, Achille, he's one of ours—from Palestine," Volterra explained.

"Tell him to put down that fucking rifle or I drive away!"

Volterra glared at Sereni, who placed the rifle on the ground. Smiling, Volterra said, "Signore Sereni, meet Achille Malcovati, a Christian friend of Massimo Teglio."

Both men shook hands warily.

"How did you get through German checkpoints?" Sereni asked.

Malcovati smiled, finally. "Ah, our Signore Teglio is a daredevil. He's got balls; I'll give him that! He just waltzed into the German embassy in Rome, under the name of Giobatta Triberti, a good Christian Fascist, and offered to supply expensive fabrics at half price from his family's factory to Nazi officials in the embassy *if* they would supply a truck and driver to deliver them. They readily agreed. When we loaded the textiles at the factory, we put the weapons underneath. The driver, a lazy bastard, thank God, just slept in the driver's seat during the loading and was no wiser."

Sereni shook his head in disbelief. "I thought Jews couldn't own businesses in Italy anymore. "

Malcovati laughed. "They can't, but nothing prevents Teglio's Christian friends from running the business for him.

"But what about the German driver? Where's he now?"

Malcovati laughed. "He's sleeping off a hangover in Fabriano, a small town just west of here—with an excellent *tavèrna*, I might add. But enough talk. We have to unload the weapons now. I want to be back before the driver wakes up."

That Night, Just Outside the Servigliano Internment Camp and Rome, the Vatican

Not far from Ancona, ten Jewish partisans, under the cover of darkness, armed with automatic weapons and grenades, led by Enzo Sereni, crept up to the internment camp at Servigliano. Sereni motioned Volterra and Sonnino close to him. "Create a diversion," he whispered, "away from the gate. When the guards open the gate to investigate, we'll disarm them and enter the camp. You follow us in."

Volterra and Sonnino moved away from the group, then began a drunken pushing and shouting match.

Three guards opened the front gate, rushed out to investigate and found themselves looking down the barrels of nine automatic weapons. They quietly laid down their rifles and were quickly bound and gagged. Volterra and Sonnino rejoined the group. The eleven raiders entered the camp and rapidly neutralized the rest of the guards, most of them caught sleeping in their beds. As the Partisans burst into the barracks, someone shrieked "The Germans."

"Calm down, we're Jewish partisans," Sereni assured them. "We have come to free you. But you have to hurry. Follow us out."

The inmates, some uttering prayers of thanks, scrambled to get dressed. One approached Sereni. "I am Davide Nathan. My wife and daughter are in another barracks. I must find them."

"Don't worry, Signore, they're safe," Sonnino assured him. "We're taking all the inmates out of here. You'll see them in a few minutes."

The partisans led the prisoners out of the compound and into the nearby woods. There, Father Benedetto, Monsignor O'Flaherty and Don Francesco Morosini, a priest from Rome, greeted the rescued Jews, introduced themselves and escorted the refugees to a small clearing to waiting trucks.

Davide Nathan spotted his family. "Elena! Olga!" He lifted his daughter off her feet, then kissed his wife.

Father Benedetto gently tugged at Nathan's sleeve. "Come, we must leave. I have arranged for you to go to Assisi. You will be safe there until we can move you behind Allied lines. But first, we must provide you with new identification papers. As native Italians, you should have no problem, even if you're stopped. But we must keep you hidden until then."

Nathan nodded. "That was how we got caught. We had no false IDs. We couldn't talk our way out of it."

"Go with Monsignor O'Flaherty, he will hide you."

◻◻◻

Some hours later, a truck pulled up several blocks short of the Vatican. O'Flaherty looked at his charges. "It wouldn't do to have a bunch of priests and sisters hopping out of a truck in front of the SS guards at the entrance to St. Peter's Square, now would it?"

"Excuse me, Father," asked Nathan, perplexed. "Did you say a 'bunch of priests and sisters'?"

"Ah, me boy, tis fine hearing you have. Now let's see how clever you are at getting dressed quickly." O'Flaherty handed him a monsignor's cassock and Elena and Olga, sister's habits. He did the same for a second Jewish family, a man and wife with a seven-year-old boy.

When they were all costumed and assembled on the street, O'Flaherty checked over his charges. "Monsignor" Nathan looked the smartest in his low-crowned hat, long black cassock with purple-red buttons and sash and silver-buckled shoes. Ah, the Lord was with me today, he thought. The shoes I brought actually fit!

"We are going into the Vatican," he explained. "You follow me, but not too close—and appear to be praying until we clear the SS men and the German paratroopers patrolling the entrance and we are well into St. Peter's Square. O'Flaherty picked up the young boy. You and I, my young man, are going in together. We are going to be best friends now, aren't we? After all, even a priest can have a laddie for a nephew, can't he?"

Nathan wasn't sure how a priest looked when he prayed so he folded his hands together, cast his eyes heavenward and mumbled a few Hebrew prayers—one for drinking wine, another for eating bread, a third for lighting the Sabbath candles and whatever else he could remember. The group passed the German guards without incident and followed O'Flaherty into the Vatican to his office.

"Monsignor O'Flaherty?"

Nathan looked up. It was the father of the young boy. Nathan hadn't caught his name.

The Irishman smiled. Nathan figured that it was his favorite expression because he seemed never to be without one. "Yes, Signore Coen?"

Coen unbuttoned part of the front of his cassock. O'Flaherty stared in surprise as the fake priest began unwinding a solid gold chain that wound twice around his waist. "If we are captured by the Germans we will die in the Nazi gas chambers, we know that. But our son is too young to meet such a fate. Please, Monsignor, take our son until the war is over and take this gold chain. Each link you sell should bring enough to keep him alive for a month."

"I'll tell you what, Signore Coen. I have a better plan. I will place the boy somewhere safe and I will keep the chain for you. I will not use it unless I have to." O'Flaherty opened the drawer to his desk and dropped the gold chain in. "Then I will get you and your wife new papers, Italian Christian papers. Those will keep you safe. Come with me, I have found space at Hospice Santa Maria until other suitable arrangements can be made. But continue to wear your religious dress because the entrance to the Hospice is in full view of the German patrols."

February 28, 1944, Rome, Hotel Excelsior and the Palace of Prince Filippo Doria Pamphili

SS Colonel Kappler watched General Kurt Maelzer across the lunch table in the hotel dining room. The general had assumed command of the German garrison in Rome from General Stahel.

"Have you caught that renegade priest yet?" Maelzer asked.

Kappler threw up his hands. "Like a cat, Monsignor O'Flaherty has nine lives—or more! We send spies and informants into the Vatican to trap him—and nothing. I even sent some SS operatives undercover into the Vatican to kidnap him and what happens? They get beaten up and thrown out. I tell you, I put informers in there, but it seems he has better informers at Gestapo headquarters."

"Why do you bother so much about him? He's only one priest."

"O'Flaherty—he's the center of a ring that hides Jews and provides them with false papers. Why the priest cares about those Jews, I'll never understand."

"It's part of the contest of war," Maelzer said dismissively. "The game's the thing. Danger sharpens the game and your priest finds that exciting and fulfilling. Especially since he appears to be very good at it. I can understand that very well." He waved the waiter over and ordered another drink.

Kappler studied him speculatively. *This fat, 55-year-old, carousing ass will be drunk again by the end of the lunch. Why must he suffer these fools? First Stahel, now this one.*

Kappler had given orders to catch O'Flaherty in the act, but so far the SS hadn't been able to do so. Looking up, he spotted his aide entering the dining room, obviously looking for him. He waved, catching his attention.

"Colonel, one of our operatives thinks he spotted the priest entering the palace of Prince Filippo. What are your orders?"

Kappler jumped up. "Sorry, General, business calls. If I can catch O'Flaherty meeting with the prince, I'll get two birds with one stone. I know that Prince Filippo has been funding a lot of the Jew-protecting activities. Nabbing them together will prove it!"

□□□

A few minutes later, Prince Filippo Doria Pamphili, of one of the great Roman families with a history of anti-fascist leanings, passed a large envelope containing lire to O'Flaherty. As the priest nodded his thanks, the prince's valet rushed in.

"Forgive the intrusion, Sir, but there is a squad of SS at the front door."

The prince jumped to his feet. "That'll be the end of both of us if you're caught here! Follow me." The priest and the prince raced down the stairs to the basement.

"Can you manage the coal chute, Monsignor?"

"Ah, me boy, it wouldn't be the first time, no indeed. You go up and greet your visitors. I'll scoot up and out." As his host returned upstairs, O'Flaherty immediately set his feet and hands on the sides of the chute and began climbing. Halfway up, he was met by lumps of coal cascading down the chute. Hanging on tight he struggled to keep above the coal flowing in the other direction. By the time he reached the access window at the top, his face and hands were pitch black with coal dust, which is what the astonished coalman saw—an apparition of eyes rising out of the coal chute.

"Sweet Jesus, who—or what—are you?" the coalman squealed, backing up a few steps.

"Just a representative of Him, me son" whispered Monsignor O'Flaherty. "I'd surely appreciate a ride in your truck." Without waiting for an answer from the dumbstruck coalman, he leaped into the back of the coal truck, nestling among the lumps of coal.

◻◻◻

By that time, Kappler was confronting the prince in the marble entrance hall. "I know that priest is here," he shouted angrily.

"You are mistaken, Herr Colonel. Look for yourself."

"One of these days," Kappler snarled, as he turned away, "I'll see both of you in the cellars of my headquarters where I will entertain you. Tell that to your stinking priest!"

CHAPTER TWENTY-SIX

March 1, 1944, Late Afternoon, Assisi

Had they been Italians, the Divis family probably could have blended in safely with the citizenry of Secchiano until the end of the war. But acting the part of deaf-mutes could carry them only so far before they put themselves, and the villagers, in mortal danger.

Recalling Monsignor O'Flaherty's words about the safe haven provided by the church in Assisi, Lev Divis asked villagers to put him in touch with the Jewish partisans who might take them there. Augusto Sonnino, a partisan from Ancona, offered to do so. He assured them Assisi was not more than a day's brisk walk away. Would they want to leave this morning? They would.

For hours the three Jews and their guide trudged over the hills, working their way around the town of Foligno, south of Assisi, to approach Assisi from the southeast. They arrived late in the afternoon. As they entered the Porto Nuovo gate and plodded wearily up Via Borgio Aretino, Sonnino pointed to the looming Romanesque tower ahead and to the right. "My information is that we can find a priest at that church to help you."

□□□

Don Aldo Brunacci, a professor canon at San Rufino Cathedral, was standing in a dark corner of the nave as the four travelers entered and looked around warily. He noticed that none crossed themselves.

They waited hesitatingly by the font, just inside the entrance. He guessed these were more Jews, seeking shelter.

Brunacci stepped out of the shadows, startling the visitors. He smiled. "Saint Francis and Saint Clare were baptized in that font."

The visitors looked blankly at Brunacci, then at the font.

"How can I help you?" the canon asked.

"Father," replied Sonnino, "this family needs the church's help. They are foreign Jews and unless they are hidden they will be . . ."

"Yes, my son, I am well aware of the problem. Rest assured, they have come to the right place. And what about you?"

"No thanks, Father. I'll just go back into the hills after I eat something, if you have a little food for me."

Brunacci nodded. He understood immediately that he was talking to a partisan.

Pointing to the large door of the cathedral, he said, "If you follow me, I will escort you to the friars at San Quirico. The women will stay with the sisters in the convent adjoining the monastery. I am sure you will find the accommodations quite comfortable. They will provide a good meal for your friends."

Don Brunacci, Sonnino and the Divis family began walking through the streets of Assisi to the monastery. "Don Aldo," a voice shouted out, about a block away. Brunacci turned. He saw ex-Mayor Fortini running to catch up.

"What's the emergency, Mayor?"

Fortini pointed down the street. "I have a Jewish professor . . ." He caught his breath. ". . .Just arrived from Padua. He needs help. He's sitting in the café, just down the street."

"Well, bring him along. We're on our way to the brothers at the San Quirico monastery. We'll wait for him right here."

A minute later Fortini made introductions. "Father Brunacci, this is Ernesto Varelli."

"Brunacci smiled and held out his hand. "Signore Varelli?"

The man looked embarrassed. "Actually, Father, I'm Emilio Viterbi. Varelli is the name on my false papers."

"Come, Signore Viterbi. We can talk on our way. Come along with us, Arnaldo." Fortini and his companion fell in behind the priest.

Brunacci pointed to Lev Divis. "This is the Divis family. Where are you from Signore Divis?"

"Originally from Prague, Father."

Brunacci clucked, "It's a shame what they did to the Czechs—totally unprovoked." The priest turned to Viterbi. "You are a professor, Signore? Where?"

"Yes, in Padua—a research physicist. I was fired because I'm a Jew."

Brunacci shook his head in dismay. "Doesn't Italy need people like you?"

"More than they'll ever know, Father. I worked with a brilliant man, Enrico Fermi, who fled to the United States because the Fascists persecuted his wife." He held up a briefcase. "I have research papers on atomic physics that Fermi and I worked on that should never fall into Nazi hands."

Brunacci's brow creased. "I am not familiar with that branch of science."

Viterbi smiled. "Someday you will know all about it, I assure you."

"I can hide those papers for you," offered Fortini, holding out his hand. "They will be safe until you need them." Viterbi did not move to hand over the briefcase. Instead, he looked searchingly at Brunacci.

"Do not worry, Signore Viterbi," the priest assured him. "Our ex-mayor hates the Germans with a passion. That is why he resigned as mayor. You can trust him with your papers."

□□□

By this time the four Jews with Sonnino, the priest, and the mayor had reached San Quirico, where they were kindly received. Once inside the gate, Lev Divis couldn't believe his eyes. Paolo Jozsa, a fellow refugee he had left in Trieste, stood in the courtyard. "You left Trieste?" was the only thing he could think of to say.

"As usual, you were right." Jozsa smiled. "I should have left with you. I barely got out of there after the Germans annexed the city."

"How . . .?"

"After I made my way to Florence, a priest there hid me in the cardinal's residence! Father Niccacci, a Franciscan friar in Assisi, brought me down here"

"And a good thing it was for us, indeed!" Brunacci added.

Divis, puzzled, looked at Jozsa, who laughed. "These people have turned a fine artist into a master forger. All those false IDs with German generals' signatures? They're mine!"

Sonnino, standing in the background, overheard the exchange. He motioned to Jozsa. Divis caught it. "Paolo, this is the Jewish partisan who saved us." He looked at Sonnino. "Augusto, meet Paolo Jozsa."

The friars quickly produced some bread and cheese and soup for Sonnino. As he ate, he and Jozsa talked. After Sonnino finished he bid the Divises goodbye and disappeared. So did Jozsa.

The Same Day, Evening, Assisi

"Head for the monastery of San Quirico," Father Rufino Niccacci, ordered the taxi driver, pointing to the direction.

Sitting in the front passenger seat, he turned around to face the Davide Nathan family, sitting in the back. "I put the Italian Jews up with the brothers. It's not immune from a *razzia* but, as Italians, you will blend in nicely with brothers in the monastery and the sisters at the convent. You will be quite safe, even if the Germans surprise us and raid the monastery or the convent before we can evacuate you. They are not likely, however, to violate the sanctity of the cloisters of the Poor Clares, so we put the Jews with foreign accents there."

Nathan smiled appreciatively at his escort. "Thank you, Father. It's been a harrowing few days—being rescued from the camp by the partisans, being hidden under the noses of the SS by Monsignor O'Flaherty and now the taxi ride to Assisi. It will be nice to stay put for awhile."

"You were very fortunate, Signore Nathan. If the Germans had arrived at that camp first—I've heard horrible stories."

"Pray for a rapid end to the war and Nazism, Father."

The friar sighed. "Amen."

Minutes later the taxi reached the monastery and the visitors were welcomed and taken to the guesthouse. "Lev Divis! I am so happy to see you." Nathan spread his arms and engulfed the Czech doctor in a bear hug. Divis returned the affection, slapping Nathan on the back.

Niccacci watched the reunion. "I see you know this man, Signore Nathan."

"Know him? He was my doctor in Rome. Saved my nephew, Michele, when none of the hospitals would admit a Jew."

Divis turned to Nathan. "How is your brother, Attilio? Did he get out before the *razzia?*"

Nathan spread his arms in frustration. "I don't know. I called his apartment during the roundup and there was no answer. I have no idea whether he and family escaped or were shipped out to the concentration camps."

Divis took Nathan's hand. "Take heart, Davide, I heard most of the Jews in the ghetto escaped."

Nathan didn't answer.

March 2, 1944, Assisi, the Convent at San Quirico

Five peals of the bells in the cathedral tower—the signal meant an imminent German raid on the village—galvanized Don Niccacci into action. He knew Mother Abbess Giuseppina would be forcefully herding her Jewish charges into the cloisters of the sisters Poor Clares. He could depend on the ferocious abbess to keep the SS at bay until the Schwartzes and the sister's other guests were safely concealed. He could attend to the more pressing problem of the Jews in the monastery.

He ran up the hill and burst unceremoniously through the gate. Brunacci, who had already arrived from the cathedral, met him just inside. "Hurry," Niccacci gasped. "We have to get the Jews out."

"I have already told them to gather their belongings," Brunacci reassured him. "We'll be ready to go in a few minutes."

A young boy ran through the still open gate toward Niccacci. "Father, Signore Fortini sent me to tell you the Germans are already in the main square."

"Hurry, there is no time to lose," Niccacci shouted to the Jewish refugees who were crowding around. "Follow me."

"Father, where's Paolo Jozsa?" Lev Divis asked.

"He hasn't been seen since yesterday. We don't have time to look for him now." Niccacci raced across the courtyard and down the steps to the cellar. The Nathans, Divises and the other Jews were hard on his heels. Brunacci brought up the rear.

"Where the hell is he going?" Nathan whispered to Divis. "We'll be trapped down here."

"He hasn't let us down yet," Divis whispered back.

Niccacci led the group hurriedly through dim, dungeon-like rooms until they came to a large metal gate. He produced a key from his pocket and turned it in the lock. He pushed hard, but the gate would not budge. Nathan and Divis rushed forward and pushed with him. The rusty portal hadn't been used for years. Straining harder, they could feel the gate beginning to give. Suddenly it surrendered so completely that the three of them tumbled through.

Niccacci picked himself up first. He thrust the flashlight into Nathan's hand. "Take it and go through that tunnel. I'll lock the gate."

The Jews, followed by Brunacci and Niccacci, streamed through the tunnel and came out into the woods outside of town. Brunacci took over the head of the column and led them into the dense oak forest on the slopes of Monte Subasio, where St. Francis and his companions lived as hermits.

By morning, Niccacci had guided some of the refugees, including the Divis and Nathan families, to caves deep in the forest. Some were hidden in the homes of peasants in the surrounding hills, well out of Assisi.

□□□

Back in the convent, the ferocious Mother Giuseppina kept the SS at bay while the Jews, including the Schwartz family, hid in the remote reaches of the cloister.

Thanks to the efforts of the abbess, the priest, the friar and courageous peasants, the SS did not find a single Jew in the town of Assisi. The *razzia* was not a success.

March 4, 1944, Assisi, Late Afternoon, Café Minerva

Niccacci moved his queen. "Check," he called out.

Colonel Müller, sitting opposite the friar at an outside table at Café Minerva, parried the threat easily, moving the king directly behind his bishop. He smiled. "You see? I, too, can hide behind a bishop for protection."

Niccacci continued to look at the board, showing no reaction.

"I'm just joking, Father. Don't be so serious."

Now Niccacci looked directly at his opponent. "How can I not be, Colonel? After we were treated to that Gestapo party two days ago. I thought you, as commander, would spare Assisi such indignities."

"I'm sorry, Father, I truly am. You must understand that the SS and the Gestapo act independently of the commanders in the field, even independently of our own courts. They are going through all the towns like this, looking for Jews. It was Assisi's turn. They found nothing. I am sure they are finished with Assisi."

"You don't inspire much confidence, Colonel."

Colonel Müller sighed. "That's obvious. How can I make it up to you?"

Niccacci looked at the chessboard, then at the colonel. "Perhaps there is something . . ."

"Yes? Yes? Please, tell me."

"Well, I have a problem. I can't figure out how to get a group of pilgrims, who came to honor St. Francis, back to San Ambrogio."

"To where?"

"San Ambrogio, a town in the south, near the Rapido River."

The colonel leaned back in his chair, thinking. He looked at Niccacci. "Perhaps I could spare a military truck and driver. It's not according to the rules, but I owe you something."

"That would be most appreciated, Colonel. I will mention you in my prayers to the good saint."

Niccacci looked down at the board. He saw the move he could make for checkmate. Instead, he swept the pieces off the board. "Why don't we quit now? It is getting late and I have to prepare the pilgrims for the trip."

Müller threw his pieces in the box, pushed back his chair and rose to his feet. "*Ciao*, Father. I enjoyed the game."

"*Ciao,* Colonel—and thank you."

March 8, 1944, Assisi, House of the Poor Clares

After a couple of uncomfortable days hidden in a cave, Divis and his family were led back to Assisi and installed this time with the Poor Clares. There Dr. Divis had set up a small infirmary to treat the various ailments of the nuns. He'd just prescribed for one of them when Mother Abbess Giuseppina hastily entered.

"You must come quickly, Dr. Divis. It's one of the refugees—we can't wake her up!"

Divis followed the abbess into the guesthouse. "Is there anything you can tell me about her, Mother Abbess?"

"It's Clara Weiss. I know she's a diabetic—been ill since she's been here."

The attending nuns watched anxiously as Divis bent over and examined the unconscious woman.

He straightened up, shaking his head. "I'm sorry, but she's in a deep coma. There's not much I can do for her. She's almost gone."

Clara Weiss died later in the day. After much discussion, the refugees agreed to a Catholic burial with a priest presiding to avoid arousing suspicion. After ten Jewish males hidden in the monastery gathered and said a secret Kaddish, the mourner's prayer, in the nun's chapel, she was taken to the cemetery in a two-horse carriage draped in black. The priest read from the New Testament and prayed. The cross on Clara Weiss's grave bore the name, Clara Bianchi.

March 12, 1944, Approaching San Ambrogio and Crossing the Front Line

The truck ride, several days later, was a reunion of sorts. Niccacci had collected most of the foreign Jews for transport since they were most vulnerable to arrest. It brought together the Schwartz and Divis families. They and the other refugees were dressed as priests, friars and sisters on pilgrimage. The German military truck, with a German military escort sailed through most of the checkpoints, hardly slowing down. As it approached San Ambrogio, a sergeant in the German military police and an agent of the Italian Secret Police, waved the truck to a stop. A German soldier climbed into the back of the truck. "A bunch of religious people, Sergeant," he shouted.

The sergeant questioned the driver, who pulled out a letter from Colonel Müller. Niccacci, in the front seat with the driver, prayed silently but fervently.

Standing among the "pilgrims" in the back of the truck, the German soldier approached a rabbi dressed in a priest's suit. "Father, I am Catholic. Could I have your blessing?"

He bent his head to be blessed. Had he looked closely, he would have seen that the priest's ring had Hebrew lettering, disquieting, to say the least. The rabbi placed his hand on the young soldier's head and intoned a benediction, unlike any the recipient would have heard before, if he could have understood the mumbling of the rabbi.

The sergeant handed the letter back to the driver and waved him on. Soon after, the truck pulled into San Ambrogio. "Get a good night's sleep," Niccacci told the driver, "we will return to Assisi the first thing in the morning." He slipped the driver a roll of lire. The driver nodded and hopped out of the cab.

The "pilgrims" piled out of the back of the truck and stretched their legs. The relief of having survived the German checkpoints was palpable. Much danger, however, still lay ahead. They still had to get through the front lines and into Allied territory. The front lines were close. They could hear the pounding of the artillery over the hills to the south.

Niccacci depended on two well-paid smugglers to conduct the refugees across the Rapido River and then along trails that would take them away from the fighting and to safety. His assurance that the smugglers hadn't lost a refugee yet hardly calmed Lev Divis and Joseph Schwartz, whose fears for their families increased with each artillery barrage. They were wondering if they'd made a mistake ever leaving Assisi.

□□□

That night the "pilgrims" crossed the river to the south side in two rowboats. Arriving on the other side of the river, they jumped out of the boats and trudged on foot closely behind the smugglers, so close to the enemy that they could actually hear some of the conversations of the German troops. Schwartz tried to be as quiet as possible as second thoughts continued to nag him. This is stupid, he thought. We're at the front lines. Both the Allies and the Germans will fire first and ask questions later. Silently, he kept repeating, like a mantra, Niccacci's assurance that the smugglers had successfully done this dozens of times.

The lead smuggler stopped suddenly, putting up his hand. "Wait here," he whispered. Only those close to him could hear it. Others passed back the word through gestures and hand signals.

Schwartz looked at his watch. Ten minutes had passed. The Germans must have captured him. *They are surrounding us as we wait!* Frustrated and helpless to protect his family, he could only think to recite the Shema in Hebrew—silently so as not to panic anyone. "Hear, oh Israel. The Lord is God, the Lord is One."

The smuggler's sudden appearance gave Schwartz such a start, he barely avoiding wetting himself. The smuggler whispered, "I've made contact with the British. Follow me."

About three kilometers along the trail the "pilgrims" came upon an open field. The smuggler pointed. "The right side of the clearing—see that tent?' Schwartz nodded. "It's a command center for a British company. They know you're out here. Just enter the tent slowly with your hands on top of your heads. Don't be alarmed by the weapons. They are very skittish near the front lines." The two smugglers disappeared back down the trail toward the river.

Schwartz crossed the clearing and slowly opened the flap of the tent. He stepped in and immediately placed his hands on his head. Several British soldiers drew their weapons.

"Speak English?" the captain at the desk asked.

"Only a little, Sir."

The captain switched languages. "Understand me now?'

Startled, Schwartz dropped his hands and stared in surprise. *Yiddish!* He responded affirmatively—also in Yiddish.

The captain rose and came over to Schwartz. "Welcome. Get everyone in the tent. There is the threat of snipers."

Schwartz nodded, opened the flap and waved the rest of the refugees inside. "But how…?"

The captain smiled. He thrust out his hand. "Avram Levine, with the British Jewish Brigade in Palestine."

Dumbfounded, Schwartz tentatively stuck out his own hand. "Joseph Schwartz," he stuttered. The captain grasped it.

"Did I hear right? Schwartz asked in disbelief. "Jews from Palestine—fighting in the war?"

The captain laughed. "From *Eretz Israel*—and killing those Nazi bastards as fast as we can! Now, let's get you back to the rear and feed you. And smile, you're out of the clutches of those monsters for good."

CHAPTER TWENTY-SEVEN

March 18, 1944, Rome, House near the Ruins of Theater of Marcellus

Attilio Nathan, in the company of his son, Michele, met his wife, Rosa, a few times a week at the ruins, close to the convent where she was hiding. While Rosa's stay with the sisters remained uneventful, the same could not be said for her husband and son.

Two weeks ago, while Nathan and Michele had been taking one of their daily strolls, a direct bomb hit had collapsed the Church of San Giovanni in Lateran, which had sheltered them. They'd arrived back to a pile of rubble in the streets. Nathan had managed to find nearby, room and board run by a seamstress. It had the advantage of being close to the convent and the ruins of the Theater of Marcellus.

Today, as usual, they escorted Rosa back to the convent, then walked slowly home to their room. Climbing the front steps, Nathan noticed a large black sedan parked at the curb. Unusual for this neighborhood, he thought. He and Michele climbed the front steps and entered the house, passing the parlor, where the seamstress had two male visitors. She pointed to her two lodgers, exclaiming, "There they are!"

The two men stepped forward. "Gestapo," one barked. "You will come with us."

Nathan glared at the seamstress. She looked away, somewhat embarrassed but ten thousand lire richer.

The Gestapo agents shoved the two Jews into the back of the black sedan and drove them to Regina Coeli Prison, situated on the west bank of the Tiber. Father and son were placed in the same cell; they soon discovered that their old friend, Lazzaro "Bucefalo" Anticoli, the prizefighter, occupied an adjoining cell.

March 23, 1944, Rome, Via Rasella

Augusto Sonnino had been sent to Rome, assigned by the partisans the task of monitoring a particular German SS military police contingent, the 11th Company of the 3rd Bosen SS Battalion. He did so for over two weeks, carefully recording the time it marched past each landmark. Finally, he was getting his chance to strike back at the Nazi beast.

He looked at his watch. Like clockwork, the SS marchers, 150 strong, armed with rifles and pistols, reached the intersection of Via del Traford and Via Rasella every day at precisely 2 P.M. Thank God for German efficiency, he thought. At 1:58 P.M., just before they rounded the corner onto Via Rasella, a narrow street lined with tall apartment houses, Sonnino, looking down the street, tipped his hat. Halfway down the block, a man dressed as a janitor rolled his cart to the curb. He quickly walked into the building and out a back entrance. When the entire SS contingent filled Via Rasella, the feared death head and double lightning symbols standing out on their helmets and uniforms, the powerful bomb, filled with shrapnel, nails and pellets, detonated. The walls of the apartment houses enclosing the street magnified the effects of the blast. The resulting carnage left thirty-two German soldiers dead and the rest of the contingent, to some degree, wounded.

By two in the afternoon, General Maelzer was usually drunk. Today was no exception. Arriving at the scene with Colonel Kappler and Ambassador Rahn to investigate the explosion, Maelzer had lost all control, raging that German bombers would level a forty-block area around Via Rasella. Rahn, well aware that the general was in no condition to take command, finally convinced him, after much loud arguing, that Berlin would not stand for his acting without orders on such a momentous decision as leveling a large portion of Rome.

Later the Same Day, Rome, Office of Colonel Kappler

At his desk Kappler squeezed the corners of his eyes with his hand. It was shortly after four and he had just heard from Berlin. It might have been easier if Maelzer had gone ahead and flattened part of Rome. Instead, Berlin had placed the monkey squarely on Kappler's back. An outraged führer had ordered ten Romans shot for every German killed by the bomb—and it had to be accomplished within twenty-four hours. Hitler had made it clear that the order was unalterable and that he, the führer, would hold Kappler personally responsible if his order was not carried out to the letter. Everyone backed away from this demand—the diplomats, Dannecker, Kesselring and even the outraged Maelzer. They were just as happy to leave that burden to the SS colonel.

Kappler had sent enough people to their deaths—he could live with that. But never had he ever killed anyone by his own hand. He expected that would change now and he was not looking forward to the prospect.

Hitler had originally ordered fifty Italians killed for every German, but even Berlin realized that was not feasible and finally persuaded Hitler to reduce the figure to ten to one. That was bad enough. Where would Kappler find 320 Italians by tomorrow? Sweep them off the streets? Even the SS had to draw the line somewhere.

Then he had an idea. Why not empty the prisons of those prisoners who had committed, or were accused of committing, capital offenses? Under German martial law, most crimes fit into that category. He rang for his aide. "Get me a list of everyone held in Regina Coeli Prison and the crime each has committed—and make it fast."

□□□

When the list arrived on hour or so later, Kappler counted 270 prisoners who, if convicted, would have been sentenced to death. But even that fell 50 prisoners short. He looked at his watch—ten o'clock in the evening. He had to finish the job either by two the next afternoon, the time when the bomb went off, or by four, when the order was received. He didn't know which time applied and he was not about to ask. He would aim for two o'clock. That left sixteen hours. As he was going over the list again, it hit him, The Jews, of course! They were going to die anyway—eventually.

After he checked off the fiftieth Jew imprisoned in Regina Coeli, he put the list down. Now he needed help to carry out the actual executions. Telephoning the commanding officer of an SS attack battalion stationed in the center of Rome, he asked, "Could you supply a company to assist in the executions?"

The officer turned him down in a reply laced with obscenities.

Kappler then attempted to call General Mackensen. He reached the general's chief of staff, Colonel Wolfgang Hauser, who replied, "The general's not available and there is no way *I* would issue such an order to my troops."

Kappler called in his aide again and ordered, "Get hold of all the SS and Gestapo men attached to this office and have them here by one this morning."

He had one more possibility. He telephoned Major Hellmuth Dobbrick, commanding officer of the Third Battalion, the unit that had been bombed.

"Major, Colonel Kappler here. I am pleased to give you this opportunity to avenge the deaths of your men. I need forty of your soldiers to carry out the executions ordered by the führer."

"Is that an order, Colonel?"

"Yes, it's an order."

"Then I must respectfully refuse, I'm sorry." Kappler heard the distinctive click of a receiver being hung up. Incredulous, he looked at his own receiver, as if it could provide an answer, then placed it back on the cradle. It was a problem he'd never considered—who would carry out the killings. He'd not killed anyone with his own hand and was loathe to start now.

He telephoned General Maelzer.

"You must carry out the führer's orders," Maelzer demanded.

Kappler looked at the receiver. "I will put my men at you're your disposal to carry out the task."

"That," Maelzer replied tartly, "is not an option. You must set an example for your men if you expect them to carry out the führer's orders."

Kappler sighed. "I suppose your right. I have no right to order my men to do what I am not willing to do."

□□□

At one in the morning Kappler paced in front of the group of SS and Gestapo men the aide had been able to assemble. "It is up to us to carry out the führer's orders," he told them. "Being executioners is not a pleasant task and the officers of this unit, including myself, will set an example by firing the first shots at the beginning and the last shots at the conclusion of the executions. We must avenge the deaths of thirty-two of our comrades. After careful study, I have selected the ideal site to conduct the executions—the Ardeatine Caves, just outside of the city, in the southeast. Early in this century, the caves had been mined for raw material to make cement. It's exhausted and abandoned now with hundreds of feet of tunnels—an ideal spot for our project. We can clear the area of civilians for a mile in every direction. Using the Caves will permit us to accomplish the plan out of the sight of the Italians. Afterwards, we will seal every entrance to the caves with dynamite so that no one can ever gain entrance. Remember, the location of the executions must remain secret."

March 24, 1944, Rome, Regina Coeli Prison
Early in the morning, the fifty Jews on Kappler's list were herded into the prison courtyard. An SS sergeant moved through the lines of prisoners. "You Jewish scum will be ready to leave in two hours. You will pay dearly for the slaughter of our brave SS soldiers. You will be returned to your cells until then."

"Sergeant," Attilio Nathan called out.

The SS man whipped around angrily. "Who said that?" he screamed.

Nathan raised his hand. "I did, Sir. My son here is only fourteen years old and I was wondering . . ."

"Shut the hell up, you filthy Yid, or I will finish off you and your brat right here, right now." In a fury, the sergeant stomped away.

Back in his cell, Lazzaro Anticoli knew this was the end; that he'd be deported to Auschwitz and gassed. He found the pencil and scrap of paper he'd had in his pocket at the time of arrest and had stashed away in the cell. He leaned the paper against the wall and printed carefully:

IF I NEVER SEE MY FAMILY AGAIN, IT'S THE FAULT OF THE SELLOUT BY CELESTE DI PORTO. AVENGE ME. BUCEFALO, THE PRIZEFIGHTER

He folded the paper and inserted it in a space between the stones lining the cell walls.

Bucefalo did not know it, but his cry for vengeance had application to a far broader group. Of the fifty Jews Di Porto identified in all, thirty-five of them were among those taken to the Ardeatine Caves.

The Same Day, Rome, Office of Colonel Kappler

General Maelzer threw the *Osservatore Romano* on Kappler's desk. "Did you see the Vatican rag today?"

"I don't have the time for this, General. Why don't you just tell me what it says?"

"The pope wrote a short piece. He blames the bombing on the work of the Communists and asked us for no 'ill-judged' acts in reprisal."

Kappler laughed harshly. "I just wish it were that easy to place blame. The partisans represent a much broader base of the Italian population than merely the Communists. But this pope seems to want to blame everything on the Bolsheviks."

"The hell with that," Maelzer growled. "I was referring to his 'no ill-judged reprisals' language. Does he expect us to 'turn the other cheek' and do nothing? Does he think we will act like one of his priests, or worse, like the Italian Army?" Maelzer raised his voice. "We are Germans, and by God, we will act like Germans and teach the Resistance a lesson they will not soon forget."

"By saying 'we', General, I take it you are here to provide me with at least some of the troops to carry out the 'lesson.'"

Maelzer shook his head. "That is your job, Colonel. See that you carry it out. You objected to my solution. Had we bombed Rome as I suggested, then it would have been my responsibility. *Heil* Hitler!" The general turned and stomped out of the office slamming the door behind him.

"And thank you for your help, Herr General," Kappler muttered to the closed door.

The Same Day, a Few Hours Later, Rome, Approaching the Ardeatine Cave Area

Attilio Nathan put his arm around his son while the truck bounced over the rough pavement and rocked from side to side, speeding to its destination. He felt the boy shiver. "Soon, Michele, Passover will be upon us. Suppose we do a Seder ahead of everyone else. Let's tell the story of the exodus from Egypt."

Without a *Hagadah*, the Passover prayer book, Nathan had to go through the Seder service by memory. He looked around the truck. "Michele, you appear to be the youngest here. Why don't you recite the four questions?"

Michele nodded. He'd done it often enough so that he could remember the gist of the questions if not the exact wording. "Why is this night different from all others?"

"On all other nights we eat leavened or unleavened bread, on this night we eat only matzos," Nathan responded softly. And so Michele proceeded through each question, and his father gave the appropriate response.

They had just finished singing *Dayenu* ("That Would Have Been Enough") when the truck began slowing down. The irony of the lyrics was not lost on Michele. "Papa, we have just thanked God for all the good things he has provided, including our freedom, but we are not free."

Nathan sighed. "True, my dear Michele, but we were also thanking Him for giving us the Torah and the Sabbath—and he did free our people from the yoke of Egyptian slavery. Unfortunately, we are now oppressed by another, modern-day pharaoh."

The squealing of the brakes interrupted the improvised Seder. "Every one out, *schnell!*"

Nathan looked around. They were in a large square surrounded by a high wall. Hundreds of prisoners were jumping out of the rear of the German trucks. He recognized the area, the Ardeatine Caves. He'd been here before.

Nathan held on to Michele until the German guards bound their hands behind them. "Stay right next to me," he whispered to his son as the prisoners were pushed into a long line, five people across. The first group of five was led to the entrance to the caves.

◻◻◻

Kappler commanded the first group. He had to set an example for his men if they were to accomplish this gruesome task. He led the group deeper and deeper into the caves until satisfied they were in far enough away to muffle the sounds of the gunshots. He didn't want a riot on his hands back in the square.

His men did as instructed; each stood behind a kneeling prisoner. Kappler went first. Unholstering his pistol, he pressed its barrel behind the neck of the prisoner and pulled the trigger. Now, by his own hand, he'd killed his first human being. In the confined space, the noise from the pistol hit like a shock wave, immediately followed by four other shots.

The rest of the 320 prisoners were led in, five at a time, followed by five SS men. Slowly, the tunnel began filling up with bodies. The horror multiplied for each succeeding group of victims, who were led up to the growing pile of bodies, a pile to which they would be added.

◻◻◻

Their turn finally came. Nathan had seen Bucefalo led away two rows earlier. Now an SS man stood behind Nathan, another behind Michele. Pushed forward they approached the mouth of the cave.

"Papa, I'm frightened."

"I know, son. And you are being very brave."

The SS men behind them did nothing to restrict the verbal exchange.

"Michele, do you remember the last thing we say at the conclusion of the Seder?"

Michele nodded. *"L'shanah haba-ah bi-rushalayim!"*

"Exactly, 'Next year in Jerusalem!' We shall be there together from now on. Just keep that thought in mind."

□□□

Kappler had taken his turn again. He stood behind Attilio Nathan. Kappler, of course, didn't know the victim's name—he was just another hostage. The young SS officer next to Kappler, standing behind the boy, wavered. Kappler noticed it and ordered a halt. He took the young SS man aside. "What is the matter?"

"I can't do it, Colonel. He's such a young boy! I have a brother his age."

"Nothing to be ashamed of," Kappler said softly. "I understand. Would it help if we switched hostages?" The SS officer nodded. "Good, then let's get this over with."

□□□

Just before two o'clock the SS captain reported to Kappler. "We had trouble finding room for the last group of prisoners. We had to throw them on the pile after they were shot."

"Have all the executions have been carried out?"

"Yes, Colonel."

Kappler nodded. "Very good. Instruct the demolition teams to seal off every entrance. Just make sure no one can ever get into the caves again."

March 26, 1944, the Outskirts of Rome and the Ardeatine Caves

Two days later Don Giorgi Fernando was puttering in the church garden at St. Calixtus in southeastern Rome when young Paolo, one of his parishioners, interrupted him with an unbelievable tale. The insistent young pig herder grabbed the priest's arm. "Please, come with me, Don Giorgi. I will take you there."

"Not so fast, Paolo. Are you sure about all this?" he asked soothingly. He called over two colleagues standing nearby, who had been engaged in conversation. "Tell them what you told me."

The youngster hopped up and down impatiently. "I was in the hills above the caves tending my pigs when I saw the Germans take hundreds of people into the tunnels. The Germans came out but the people didn't."

The two priests Don Giorgio called over looked horrified.

"Why did you wait two days to tell us?" Don Giorgio asked.

"I was afraid, Father, and I really did not know who to tell."

Don Giorgi nodded. "Stay here, I'll be right back." He disappeared into the church and returned with a flashlight.

◻◻◻

After a twenty-minute walk, the three priests and the boy came to the now deserted square and approached the caves. They checked—every entrance blocked by rocks and boulders. Paolo scrambled up one pile of rocks. "Over here, Father, a small opening."

The three priests climbed gingerly up the rocks in their cassocks. They were neither dressed for, nor accustomed to, such vigorous activity. Don Giorgi reached the top first and caught his breath. He turned to the other priests. "Let's see if we can move some of these rocks."

Laboriously lugging them off the pile, they eventually created a hole large enough for one person, Don Giorgio, to stick in his head. First he thrust his arm into the hole holding the flashlight. When he looked in, he jerked upward at the smell of putrefaction, banging his head against the rocks. The stench drove him back from the opening.

"What's the matter, Father?" one of the priests called out.

"I'm afraid to say." Don Giorgi pulled out a handkerchief and tied it around his face, covering his nose. It didn't help much, but now prepared, he forced his head into the opening.

He switched on the flashlight and swept the site with the beam. "Sweet Jesus in Heaven!" He withdrew his head from the hole. "There are bodies piled up all over the place—hundreds of them." He crossed himself and began crying. "I've never seen anything like it. Who could believe . . . ?" He could not continue.

Later that Day, Rome, Vatican, Office of the Cardinal Secretary of State

Monsignor Montini picked up the single sheet of paper and waved it in the air. "This is all His Holiness authorized us to say?"

Cardinal Maglione gestured helplessly. "I told him what Don Giorgi reported. His first reaction was not to issue any statement at all. This was all I could convince the Holy Father to say."

Montini shook his head. "My God, there were 320 of our own Italian people that they slaughtered—and I doubt if any of them were 'Communists.'"

The cardinal did not respond.

March 27, 1944, Rome, Office of Colonel Kappler

"The priest did what?" Kappler raged at his visitor.

"He removed some of the rocks and was able to look into the Caves," the SS captain repeated.

"Who is 'he'?"

"Don Giorgi Fernando, a priest from a church nearby."

"Well arrest him before he causes trouble."

"Too late," said the SS captain flatly. "Our agents report he's already been to the Vatican."

"Shit. Arrest him anyway and ship him to Auschwitz."

March 27, 1944, Rome, a Partisan Hideout

Sonnino paced angrily around the room in a working-class quarter where a few partisans were gathered. "I am not a Communist! I am a Jew seeking revenge for my people. Why does the pope call us Communists?"

The leader shrugged. "What's the difference? Isn't it better for the Germans to be looking for the Communists than for us? Besides, we are fighting on the same side and have the same objectives—killing Germans."

"But does the pope blame the Germans for slaughtering 320 innocent civilians? No. Just listen to what he said in the *Osservatore Romano* yesterday: 'Thirty-two victims on the one hand, and on the other three hundred and twenty persons sacrificed for the guilty parties who escaped arrest. We call upon the irresponsible elements to respect human life.' And he calls us 'the guilty parties who escaped arrest.'"

"It's politics, Sonnino. After all, the Vatican is a nation in its own right—and obviously, it fears the Communists more than the Nazis. But rest assured, Augusto, we will not be dissuaded."

The Same Day, Salò, Mussolini's Office
Mussolini's eyes bulged more that usual at the shocking news. "How many Italians?"

Count Serafini Mazzolini, the Duce's new foreign minister, leaned forward. "You heard me correctly, Sir. The SS slaughtered 320 Italian citizens—not soldiers but *civilians*. And one of my friends, a young diplomat, Consul Filippo de Grenet, was among those shot at the Ardeatine Caves."

"What was he doing in prison?"

"The SS arrested him on suspicion of cooperating with the Badoglio government, but no charges had ever been filed against him. After I found out about the slaughter, I made a furious protest to Ambassador Rahn, but it is clear he doesn't give a damn."

Mussolini raised his chin folded his arms across his chest and declared with determination, "I shall order the release of all political prisoners in Italian jails and camps, before the Germans can get to them."

The foreign minister looked intently at his superior. "Duce, I'm afraid it's too late for that. The Germans have already taken over the prisons."

CHAPTER TWENTY-EIGHT

April 4, 1944, Assisi, Bishop's Palace

Bishop Nicolini listened to his activist friar, Father Niccacci, making one of his periodic reports.

"SS Captain von den Velde paid me a visit. He told me that German military trucks may be used only for the war effort and not to transport pilgrims," Niccacci advised the bishop. "So I checked with Colonel Müller. He apologized but said we both knew he was breaking the rules. He can no longer provide us with trucks."

The bishop scratched his head. "How are we going to get the refugees to the Allied lines?"

"We're not, Your Excellency. I have just received more bad news. You know the two smugglers who have been guiding our groups to safety?"

The bishop nodded.

"They were caught by the Germans returning from a smuggling trip and shot. Without the trucks and the guides, we no longer have the resources to smuggle people out of German-occupied territory."

"Very well," Nicolini said grimly. "We will just have to keep them hidden here until liberation."

"I have already gone house to house asking residents to take in more Jews. Most have agreed."

The bishop raised his eyebrows. "Why don't we use the church of San Andrea in Porta di Santa Susanna. It's not too far from here. I will speak to Don Vincenti. We have the room to hide quite a few there."

"Your Excellency?"

The bishop looked up. "Yes?"

"Colonel Müller told me something else: Captain von den Velde is investigating my activity concerning the so-called pilgrims. Since the Gestapo is involved, Müller said he could not protect me."

The bishop stood up and leaned against the desk. "Then you must go into hiding—with your Jews."

Niccacci shook his head. "There's too much to do, Your Excellency. But I will be careful."

April 12, 1944, Assisi, Bishop's Palace

"Your Excellency, Father Niccacci's gone!" Brunacci cried, bursting into the bishop's office unannounced.

"Calm yourself, Don Aldo, sit down and give me the facts."

Brunacci dropped into a chair. "He's been arrested by Gestapo. They took him away—to Perugia."

The bishop leaped up and grabbed his cape. "Come with me."

A Few Minutes Later, Assisi, Office of Colonel Müller

Colonel Müller was doing his best to calm the irate bishop before him. "Your Excellency, I assure you, I did everything in my power to protect your Father Niccacci. Believe me when I say he is a good friend of mine and I am greatly distressed."

The steely-eyed bishop persisted. "But surely, you as a colonel could order von den Velde, a captain, to release my priest and bring him back from Perugia."

Colonel Müller spread his arms wide. "Against the Gestapo, I couldn't even protect my own family! They are a law unto themselves. I have no authority over them."

Nicolini stood up. "Understand this, Colonel. If anything happens to Father Niccacci, I shall hold you personally responsible."

"I assure you, Your Excellency, I will do everything in my power, but it is not my responsibility, it is . . ."

But the bishop had already swept out of the room.

□□□

Back in his office, Nicolini picked up the telephone and dialed his friend, Vincenzo Texeira, a lawyer in Perugia with connections. When it came to accomplishing legal objectives, it was said Texeira could accomplish miracles. The bishop certainly needed one about now.

April 14, 1944, Assisi, Bishop's Palace

Niccacci looked drawn but otherwise in one piece as he reported to the bishop. "Captain von de Velde threw me in a cell and said I would be shot if I didn't confess."

"To what?" Nicolini asked.

"He wouldn't tell me; he said I knew well enough. Anyway, I wasn't given food or water for three days. He made me watch as they shot prisoners, saying I would be next if I didn't confess. It was terrible, Your Excellency, innocents shot without a second thought." groaned Niccacci, shaking his head. "They kept shooting people and forcing me to watch." His voice cracked.

The bishop waited until the friar had recovered his composure. "But they ultimately freed you?"

Niccacci nodded. "A lawyer came to see me. He said he had spoken to you. He'd gone before the German chief judge for Perugia and obtained my release. The priest at the Church of San Andrea in Perugia picked me up, took me to the church and fed me. He knew the lawyer—said I wasn't the first one whose release he'd obtained. The lawyer apparently has some sort of relationship with the mistress of the German judge."

The bishop smiled. "Mistress, eh? A relationship we normally frown on—but it did save our priest. The Lord does indeed work in mysterious ways."

April 15, 1944, Milan

Seeking an ally in his efforts to save Jews, the Capuchin friar, Father Benedetto, had teamed up with Stefan Schwamm, a Jewish lawyer from Vienna, who was posing as a representative of the International Red Cross in Geneva. So effective was Schwamm in his role that the Germans had willingly provided the "Red

Cross"—Schwamm—with the gasoline that he and Benedetto used to transport Jews to the Swiss border and safety.

On the way back from one such trip, Schwamm pulled over to the curb at the entrance to a hotel in Milan. "Father Benedetto, please wait in the lobby. I have to meet a contact in the bar."

From his seat in the lobby, Benedetto watched Schwamm stroll up to the bar and shake hands with a short man wearing a gray Borsolino hat. The friar stiffened as he saw two burly men follow Schwamm into the bar. He had learned long ago to recognize the Fascist secret police from OVRA. He felt helpless; there was no way to warn Schwamm. The OVRA agents and Schwamm exchanged loud words that Benedetto couldn't quite make out. One of the men grabbed Schwamm's arm and pushed him out of the bar, through the lobby, and out into the street.

Stifling the urge to run, Father Benedetto slowly followed them out of the lobby. The OVRA men were already searching the car. If they had Schwamm under surveillance, they undoubtedly already knew he had a passenger and probably knew what that passenger looked like. Quickly, the friar ducked back into the lobby and headed for the rear of the hotel. Behind him he heard shouts in the lobby. OVRA was looking for him! Trying several locked doors, he finally found one that opened into an alley. He rushed out and spotted a church across the street. He heard the door being opened in the alley. This time he ran—straight into the church. OVRA agents would search the church, but they would be unlikely to take on the sisters in the adjoining convent.

◻◻◻

Over the next five days, Father Benedetto, with the help of Idlefonso Cardinal Schuster of Milan, cautiously made his way back to Rome. Since it was clear that both OVRA and the Gestapo were looking for him, Cardinal Maglione ordered him into hiding in the Vatican, thus ending his years of clandestine activities.

April 20, 1944, Assisi, the Basilica of San Francesco
The suddenness of the raid caught them off guard. Captain von den Velde and a squad of SS, accompanied by Colonel Müller, had

burst into the Franciscan friary near the Basilica of San Francesco before Niccacci had a chance to evacuate the Jews or take them to the cloister of the Poor Clares. He was thankful that his guests wore the brother's habits at all times. The best he could do was to lead all the "brothers" into the church to say mass.

Colonel Müller observed the proceedings from the doorway. Velde strode up to Niccacci as he knelt in prayer at the altar, and barked, "Stop this charade, at once!"

Niccacci ceased chanting and slowly rose to his feet. Ignoring Velde, the friar walked past him to the back of the church and confronted the colonel. "Are you going to permit this invasion of our privacy in the middle of a mass?"

Embarrassed, Müller averted his eyes. "Sorry, Father, but the captain *claims* that you have been hiding Jews in this town and that you've abused my trust. There is nothing I can do."

Niccacci wasn't fooled. The colonel was talking for the benefit of the SS captain.

Hands on his hips, the captain glared Niccacci. "Priest," he shouted, "I want to quiz these friars, monks, priests or whatever else they claim to be."

Niccacci knew, of course, that was out of the question. A few answers would reveal their identities. "That's impossible, Captain. These *friars* have taken vows of silence and they will not violate them for you, for me or for anyone else."

The captain snapped his riding crop in his gloved hand. "That is unacceptable," he shouted. He motioned to the SS squad. "Take these people in for questioning."

"Now wait just a minute, Captain," intervened Müller. "You may not like it, but I'm a practicing Catholic. I cannot permit you to force these pious friars to break their religious vows. As a colonel in the Wehrmacht, I can command a lot more troops than you have at your disposal. If I have to butt heads with the Gestapo, so be it, but I will not countenance profanation of a holy place in the city of St. Francis. Do I make myself clear?"

Captain von den Velde looked around. "Very clear, Colonel." Stalking out of the church, he waved his squad to follow. Before he cleared the door, he turned. "This is not the end. I promise you. Assisi will suffer for this!"

May 20, 1944, Assisi, Café Minerva and Office of the Chief of Police

Luigi Brizi, the printer, and Father Niccacci were enjoying a quiet game of chess at an outdoor table at the café in the Piazza del Comune. Brizi jumped his black knight and took Niccacci's white queen. A small smile of triumph formed on his lips. Niccacci, usually the master of Brizi at chess, had been distracted. He'd just heard the BBC broadcast reporting that the Allies had finally taken Monte Cassino and were driving toward Rome. That was the good news but it did not lessen his worries. His sense of anxiety stemmed from Captain von de Velde's threat against Assisi last month. If the captain was going to do anything, it would have to be soon.

He looked up and spotted Father Brunacci hurrying across the square toward the café. "Father Niccacci," the usually taciturn priest shouted.

Niccacci left the chess table and went to meet Brunacci. "What's the matter, Father?" he asked.

"The chief of police . . ." Brunacci gasped, trying to catch his breath.

"Bertolucci?"

Brunacci nodded. "He's arrested a young Jewish boy and threatens to turn him over to the Gestapo."

"May the good Lord help us. That's all the excuse Velde needs. Everyone in hiding will be at risk!"

Since Jews had arrived in Assisi, the Fascist chief of police had been a problem. A Mussolini man, he strutted around looking for anti-Fascists and partisans to arrest. So far, he'd left the Jews alone, but lately Alessandro Pavolini, Mussolini's second in command and a long-time virulent anti-Semite, had been railing against those incompetent Fascist police who hadn't searched out the Jews. Niccacci feared this would happen. He jumped up.

"What about our game?" Brizi protested. "I am two moves away from checkmate." But Niccacci was already halfway across the square.

Without a moment's hesitation, he swept into the police station, past the reception desk, and into Bertolucci's office. "Release that boy, Bertolucci," he demanded. "Have you gone out of your mind?"

"This is out of your jurisdiction, Father," replied the police chief. "Go back to your church and save souls. Leave the enforcement of the law to me. I have my orders and I intend to carry them out. The boy will be turned over to the Gestapo."

"Your soul is my jurisdiction and you will be damned to eternal hell if you murder that young boy."

Bertolucci shook his head. "Father, you're overreacting. I will murder no one."

"Turning that boy over to the Gestapo is the same thing, and you know it."

Bertolucci shrugged. "I have my duty . . ."

'You dare speak of duty? What of your duty as a good Christian?"

"Father Niccacci, the subject is closed," declared Bertolucci, rising from his chair. "So if you will please . . ."

Niccacci interrupted. "You fail to understand, Signore Bertolucci. You are already the most hated man in town. Surely, you must realize that as part of the Fascist militia, your position is already very precarious. The Allies have broken through at Monte Cassino and will shortly be in Rome, just a few kilometers south of here. Before you know it, they'll be in Assisi. If you do not release that boy, I, *personally*, will see that the Allies are aware of your Fascist activities. They'll deal harshly with you, I promise. And I am sure I'll be supported by most of the citizens of Assisi." Niccacci paused to examine his fingertips. "On the other hand, if you release the boy, I will stand up for you. Believe me, Signore Bertolucci, you will need all the help you can get."

Bertolucci flopped back down into his chair. He shouted for his assistant, who stuck his head in the door. "Release the Jewish boy to the custody of Father Niccacci." He turned to the priest. "I don't want to see that boy on the streets of Assisi again."

Niccacci got to his feet and bowed slightly. "Thank you, Chief Bertolucci. You've made a wise and compassionate decision."

Bertolucci grunted an inaudible reply.

May 29, 1944, Assisi, Office of the Chief of Police

Some days later, Niccacci knocked on the door of the chief of police and entered. "You wanted to see me, Chief Bertolucci?"

"Yes. Please sit down, Father. You remember our last conversation in this office?"

"I do."

"Well, to show my good faith, I must warn you: I have just heard that Captain von de Velde has ordered German sappers into Assisi to blow up the major structures in town before the Allies arrive."

"When is this supposed to happen?"

"I heard they are arriving today."

□□□

It was not much of a warning. As Niccacci left the police station, he saw German military trucks roar into the Piazza del Comune. They stopped and Captain von de Velde leaped out of the cab of the lead vehicle. He watched Niccacci approach. "Before you say anything you'll regret, Father, any attempt to interfere with *my* sappers will be met with a most severe response."

"Even Nazis like you must have some respect for these old buildings, imbued with the history of St. Francis..."

Velde turned his back and shouted orders. The sappers dragged boxes out of the trucks. Teams headed for the town hall and various other buildings to lay the charges. Niccacci saw Colonel Müller watching the activity from the other end of the square. The friar approached and urged, "Colonel, you must do something. You, who revere St. Francis so, cannot let them destroy Assisi—and the saint's legacy!"

The colonel cast his eyes toward the pavement, refusing to meet the priest's imploring gaze. "I've seen his written orders. I'm powerless to override them. I'm sorry, Father Niccacci, there is nothing I can do unless those orders are countermanded. At this moment, I am not particularly proud of being German."

May 31, 1944, Assisi

Niccacci had run out of options. The sappers were almost finished laying down the charges throughout the town. Colonel Müller could do nothing, a situation in which Captain von den Velde took obvious relish. Appealing to the captain's conscience and morals had proven fruitless, as Niccacci had expected. There would be little left of Assisi after the Velde gave the order. At this point, prayer seemed to be Niccacci's only recourse.

Bishop Nicolini decided to make one last plea to Colonel Müller. Niccacci held out no hope but accompanied his bishop. As they approached the commandant's headquarters, just off Piazza del Comune, a small German military vehicle screeched to a halt in front of them. A German soldier jumped out.

Niccacci's jaw dropped as recognition dawned. It was Paolo Jozsa, the artist who had disappeared over a month ago!

Jozsa spotted Niccacci and waved the white envelope in his hand. He was grinning from ear to ear as he disappeared into headquarters.

Niccacci and Nicolini looked at each other uncomprehendingly.

A moment later, Colonel Müller emerged from the building, ignoring the two churchmen, and ran into the square. Niccacci and Nicolini watched in fascination as Müller gestured wildly at Velde with a sheet of paper. Niccacci listened in vain to hear what Müller was saying. Velde grabbed the sheet and read it.

When Jozsa emerged from headquarters, Niccacci accosted him. "What's happening? Where have you been?"

Jozsa smiled. "I just delivered orders from General Kesselring declaring Assisi an open city."

The bishop uttered a prayer of thanks. "I knew the Holy Father would not permit this to happen. When did His Holiness intercede?'

Jozsa shrugged. "To tell you the truth, Your Excellency, the pope had nothing to do with this."

"Then how . . .?"

"When the Jewish partisan Sonnino found out that I did the forgeries here, he asked for my help. It seems the Resistance had gotten hold of stationery from Kesselring's headquarters already stamped for an emergency. Using that stationery, I simply prepared an order declaring Assisi an open city and signed Kesselring's name. With all the orders he'd already issued to the population, there were plenty of samples around of his handwriting." Jozsa swept the square with his eyes. "I'd better get out of here and get rid of this uniform." He disappeared behind the building.

"Father Niccacci, Your Excellency."

They looked over in the direction of the shout. It was Müller.

"Good news! General Kesselring has declared Assisi an open city. I have ordered the sappers to dismantle the charges and leave the city. Velde is furious, but he does not relish a run-in with my troops for disobeying the commanding general's orders. Apparently, the Gestapo is courageous only against people who are unable to fight back. Assisi will not be blown up."

Niccacci held out his hand. "May I see the order?"

Müller handed it to him. "Signed by the General Kesselring himself. It's all in order. By now, I know Kesselring's signature very well."

PART VI

Liberation

CHAPTER TWENTY-NINE

June 1, 1944, Genoa, Cathedral of San Lorenzo
Massimo Teglio burst into the cathedral in the middle of a mass. Don Francesco Repetto turned from the altar, annoyed at the impudent interruption.

"Don Francesco, the Gestapo is on the way here to arrest you," Teglio whispered urgently. "You must leave at once."

Repetto hastily whispered to one of the other priests to continue the mass while he walked Teglio to the entrance of the cathedral. He heard the service resuming behind him. "How did you find out?" Repetto asked in a low voice.

"One of my sources overheard two Gestapo agents asking questions about you. I'm sure they're on their way over here." Teglio thrust papers into Repetto's hands. "Here, take these."

Repetto glanced at the identification papers; his own photo stared back at him.

"I had these made up in a hurry, but they should suffice. I've got to leave now. You have a back door?"

Repetto pointed up a side aisle. Teglio headed for it. "Thank you," Repetto called out to the retreating figure. Teglio waved acknowledgment without turning around.

□□□

Shortly after the mass ended, two Gestapo agents entered the cathedral.

Repetto met them at the entrance. "Can I help you?"

"Are you Francesco Repetto?" one demanded.

Repetto shook his head. "He's not here right now."

The other agent thrust out his hand. "Papers!"

Repetto reached into his cassock and pulled out his false papers, identifying him as Sabastiano Donatelli. The agent looked quickly and handed them back. "We must see the cardinal—immediately."

"Follow me, gentlemen. I will see if the cardinal is available."

□□□

Calmly Repetto led the two Gestapo agents across the street to the residence of Cardinal Boetto. "Your Eminence, two Gestapo agents are right outside wanting to question you."

"About what, Don Francesco?"

"About me, Your Eminence. They are here to arrest me. Teglio prepared some false identification for me."

"That's not good enough," said the cardinal, frowning. "They may be playing with you. You must leave at once and go into hiding. Go out my private door," he directed, motioning with his head. "I will keep the Gestapo busy until you're well away from here."

Repetto nodded and disappeared through the door. The cardinal walked into the reception area. With an ingratiating smile, he greeted the two agents in fluent German.

June 2, 1944, Highway Outside Genoa

The Catholic friend who provided Teglio with a hiding place owned a transport company. He had hired Teglio as an employee, permitting the Genoese Jew to use one of the company cars to deliver food and money to refugees, and to drive them to the Swiss border, where he arranged for their safe crossing as "Christians."

Repetto fidgeted in the passenger seat as Teglio headed north out of Genoa. Reaching the Swiss border by car, 160 kilometers away, seemed to the hunted priest like a dangerous and impossible goal, what with all the German checkpoints and roadblocks between here and their destination. But Teglio was insistent and inexplicably confident. His only comment: "Leave it up to me," was hardly reassuring.

Two German officers on the side of the road outside the city watched expectantly as the traffic flowed north. Teglio slowed down and pulled off the road, heading for the officers.

"What are you doing, Teglio?" Repetto cried, clearly alarmed.

"Don't fret, Don Francesco, I know what I'm doing. Here's our passport to the border."

"Are you crazy?" It was too late. Teglio had stopped the car and the German officers were already opening the rear door.

"Need a ride, gentlemen?" Teglio shouted out.

"Yes," one officer responded. "We are trying to get to Como."

"Get in, we're going that way." Repetto stiffened as the officers scrambled into the back seat.

When they reached the first German roadblock, a German soldier approached the car, his Mauser machine pistol at the ready. "Papers please." Then he noticed the two German officers, a captain and a major, in the back seat and waved Teglio through the barrier without inspecting their papers. And so it went at each checkpoint until the officers were let off in Como.

"You could have warned me, I almost had a heart attack," Repetto groused.

Teglio grinned. "If I had you'd probably have gotten out of the car and refused to go. It was better this way."

"How did you know they'd wave you through the checkpoints?"

Teglio laughed. "Don Francesco, I have been doing this for weeks, delivering food and funds to the refugees. I always pick up German officers—and I've never been stopped, much less searched!"

Repetto uttered a short prayer.

June 4, 1944, Rome

Augusto Sonnino sat at a fourth-floor window of the apartment, giving him a sweeping view of the Porta Maggiore, the entrance in the wall in the western part of the city. He peered down the street looking for more retreating Germans to shoot. The street was empty now so he rested his sniper rifle on the windowsill. Mixed emotions assailed him. Ecstatic that the Germans were in full retreat, he nevertheless found killing other human beings traumatic—even if they were Germans bent on annihilating his people. He couldn't wait for the moment of revenge, but when it arrived . . ."

His thoughts were interrupted by a rumbling sound. First barely perceptible, it now grew into a roar—*Tanks! German?*

He lifted his rifle, checked the ammunition clip and hefted the weapon into the firing position, aiming at the opening in the wall.

He couldn't believe it. A tank with an American star lumbered into view followed by another, and another. *Liberation!*

□□□

As the American Fifth Army rolled into Rome, Allied POWs, Western diplomats and Jews streamed out of the Vatican, flinging themselves at, and hugging, the American troops. At the same time they were leaving, Germans and Fascists were streaming in the other direction *into* the Vatican to seek asylum. The reversal of fortunes had begun. Not surprisingly, Monsignor O'Flaherty was there to greet the new refugees and provide them with accommodations and, of course, priestly garments.

St. Peter's Square began filling up with people weeping, dancing and cheering. Within an hour, crowds packed the enormous square from end to end while the church bells pealed. The cheering and noise died down when a lone figure in a white cassock appeared on the balcony overlooking the square. Pope Pius XII raised his arms in benediction. "Today we give thanks to God and all the saints that both contending armies collaborated to preserve the Eternal City. I give my blessings to this city and to the world."

June 16, 1944, Morning, Assisi, Café Minerva

Colonel Müller strode up to Father Niccacci, who was watching the loading of the German trucks from his table at the Café Minerva.

"It's time for me to leave Assisi," Müller announced. "I have left all the medical supplies in the hospital for the people of this town—bandages, medicines, things like that."

Niccacci stood up and shook the colonel's hand. "You are a good man, Colonel Müller. Assisi owes you an enormous debt of gratitude. The bishop has asked me to bestow his blessing on you."

"And Assisi gave me the opportunity to assuage my conscience. I hope you and your Jews prosper." It was the first time the colonel openly acknowledged the presence of Jews in Assisi.

"Thank you, Colonel. The bishop has spoken with the partisans. They have agreed to take no action against you or your men."

A young captain strode up to Müller and snapped to attention. "Colonel, Sir, the convoy is ready to leave."

Müller nodded. "Very well, Captain, I'll be along in a few minutes."

The captain clicked his heels. "Yes, Colonel, *Heil* Hitler!"

A look of annoyance flickered on Müller's face. *"Grüss Gott,"* he responded.

Niccacci smiled. "Come visit after the war, Colonel, and we can explore the life of St. Francis in much greater detail."

"Oh, I will, Father. Rest assured, I'll be back."

That Afternoon, Assisi

From his vantage point in the street, Davide Nathan had watched the German trucks pull out of Assisi. For the first time since arriving in Assisi three months ago, he did not have to look over his shoulder and he wore his own clothes.

Now he could see the dust rising from the road a distance south of Assisi. Fascinated, he watched as the tanks and military vehicles of the British Army came into view. As they approached, he couldn't believe his eyes. That jeep—the soldiers—they all wore yellow Star of David patches!

"Shalom!" Nathan shouted.

The jeep braked to a halt. "Shalom!" One soldier responded. "You Jewish?"

"Yes, and this is the first day in seven months I have not been in hiding," Nathan said, half laughing, half crying. "But why are you wearing those horrible yellow stars?"

A sergeant climbed out of the jeep. He touched the star. "The Nazis made you wear it as a star of shame. We have elected to wear the same star with pride. We are the Jewish Brigade of Palestine."

"Jews, fighting the Germans in Italy?" asked Nathan in disbelief.

"Jews are killing the German pigs all along the front—Palestine Jews, American Jews, British Jews."

Nathan smiled. "And I know some Jewish partisans fighting in the hills."

The sergeant nodded. "We've been in contact with them." He tossed Nathan pack of cigarettes. "Is there anything you need?"

"We could use a ride back to our home in Rome."

"How many?"

"Myself, my wife and my daughter."

The sergeant turned to the others. "Hop out, boys. I'll take this man and his family to Rome and pick you up later. Have a ball in Assisi!"

Later that Day, Rome, Trastevere

After the joyful ride from Assisi the Nathans entered their ransacked home. Elena flicked the switch—no lights. She went to the kitchen and turned the faucet handle in the sink—no water. She turned around and looked at her husband. Their eyes met. "We survived, Davide, and we avoided the concentration camps. So you think *I'm* going to complain now?"

He hunched his shoulders quizzically.

She answered the rhetorical question with a shake of her head. "Not me, not with all of us still alive."

The old sofa was still where they left it. They sat down, Elena resting her head on Nathan's shoulder. Both watched quietly as their most prized possession, Olga, moved gracefully around the apartment. Her survival said it all.

EPILOGUE

Of the 45,000 Jews in Italy when the German occupation began in 1943, about 6,000 were deported to the death camps. Another 300 were murdered outright in Italy. As a percentage, the rate of survival was among the highest in Europe. Considering the brevity of the German occupation, however, many would consider those losses high. About 1,000 Jews fought in the resistance, 5,000 to 6,000 crossed into Switzerland and 4,000 reached Allied lines in the south. Of the 1023 Jews rounded up in Rome and shipped to Auschwitz, only sixteen returned.

Italy's aid to the Jews did not stop with the end of the war. Of all the countries in Europe, Italy did the most to promote clandestine emigration to Palestine, notwithstanding the difficulties this policy caused in Italy's relations with the British.

Actually, most of the Jews, particularly the Italian Jews, were able to hide without the aid of any organized effort, thanks to their assimilation in the Italian population and to the disdain of ordinary Italians for the racial laws and anti-Semitism and, above all, to the Italians' willingness to put themselves at risk to help the Jews.

General Giuseppe Pièche, commander of the carabinieri and head of intelligence in Croatia, who warned the Italians of what the Germans were doing to the Jews as early as 1942, was honored by the Jewish community in 1955 for his rescue work.

Father Rufino Niccacci, in 1974, fulfilled a long-held dream, making a pilgrimage to the Holy Land. There, he received a hero's welcome, receiving the highest honor Israel could bestow, that of the Righteous Gentile. The Jewish Community of Italy, in 1955, awarded him a gold medal adorned with the Ten Commandments and the seven-armed candelabrum with the words, "From the Jews of Italy—In Gratitude." He returned to his home in Montenero, founding the Ecumenical House, a place to which Christians and Jews could discuss closer relations between the two great religions. He died in Montenero in 1977.

The Italian Jewish community also honored Father Maria Benedetto with the gold medal for his rescue efforts. So did the State of Israel, which awarded him, in 1967, the Medal of the Righteous. On it was inscribed, "He who saves a single life, saves the whole world."

Father Francesco Repetto returned to Italy from Switzerland after the war. He was made a monsignor. In 1980, Israel honored Repetto with the gold metal of valor. He died in Genoa in 1984.

After the war, Monsignor Hugh O'Flaherty turned to helping Italian and German POWs and notifying their families. Herbert Kappler, the SS colonel who tried to have the O'Flaherty assassinated, had only one visitor in prison, Monsignor O'Flaherty, who saw him once a month. O'Flaherty pleaded with the Allies to free Kappler after six years but was denied. Britain, the United States, Canada, Australia, Haiti, San Domingo and Italy honored O'Flaherty for his rescue efforts of POWs and Allied soldiers. British General Alexander, impressed with O'Flaherty's rescue efforts, provided him with military air transportation to South Africa to arrange for the repatriation of Italian POWs and then to Jerusalem, where the Monsignor helped with arrangements to transfer to Israel many of the Jews he had saved. Suffering from arteriosclerosis and after several strokes, O'Flaherty died in 1963 in his beloved Ireland. His obituary, in part, reads, "And above all, one could say of him that, without ostentation, his life was always ordered to using his powers in fair weather or foul for the glory of God. Can any of us hope to achieve any more?"

In 1946, the Italian citizens voted to eliminate the Savoy monarchy.

Pope Pius XII died on October 9, 1958 and was buried in the crypt of St. Peter's Basilica. Procedure was begun in 1965 for his possible beatification.

Monsignor Giovanni Battista Montini, one of the Vatican officials who was instrumental in opening churches, monasteries and convents to hide Jews, became Pope Paul VI on June 21, 1963. When the Jewish community attempted to honor him, he said, "I acted in the line of duty, and for that I am not entitled to a medal."

On April 27, 1945, Mussolini, uniformed as a German soldier, left Salò with a German column withdrawing from Italy. At Dongo, a Communist partisan band stopped the column. The partisans agreed to let the Germans proceed if they allowed the partisans to search the trucks for Italians. A partisan recognized Mussolini, despite his disguise, and he was taken prisoner along with Clara Petacci, who refused to leave his side. At a farmhouse in Bonzanigo, the partisans executed them. The next day their bodies, along with those of several other Fascist leaders, were taken to Milan and strung up by their ankles on a steel girder at a filling station.

After Mussolini's downfall, Gino Preziosi, the brutal and anti-Semitic second in command in the Salò government, with his wife, leaped to their deaths from their fifth-floor apartment in Milan.

General Italo Balbo, whose popularity caused Mussolini to remove him from the limelight by appointing him governor of Libya, was killed when his plane, it was alleged, failed to give correct recognition signals and was shot down by *Italian* gunners in Tobruk harbor.

The note written by Lazzaro Anticoli (Bucefalo, the prizefighter) was found in his cell. After liberation, a group of Jews seized Celeste Di Porto, the Black Panther, and dragged her through the streets of the ghetto. She was tried and sentenced to twelve years in prison. She served eight of those years.

Rudy Lercoz, the guide who betrayed the Ovazzas, was captured by Italian partisans and executed.

Of the Germans, Colonel Herbert Kappler extorted fifty kilograms of gold from the Jews on the false promise of safety. He shipped the precious metal to Ernst Kaltenbrunner, his superior and the highest-ranking figure in the SS command, save for *Reichsführer*

Himmler himself. If Kappler expected praise for his efforts, he was disappointed. The receipt of the crate of gold was not even acknowledged by Kaltenbrunner. The crate, found after the war in a corner of Kaltenbrunner's office, had never been opened! Kappler, captured by the British, was turned over to the Italians, who tried him as a war criminal for the Ardeatine Caves massacre and for extorting gold from the Jews. He was sentenced to life imprisonment (Italy did not have a death penalty) and apparently escaped in 1977 and died shortly thereafter in his home city of Stuttgart.

Ambassador Eitel von Weizsäcker was sentenced to seven years in prison. His sentence was reduced shortly thereafter and he was released.

As far as can be determined, Major Hellmuth Dobbrick was never punished for refusing to obey Colonel Kappler's order to participate in the executions at the Ardeatine Caves.

Of the Jews, Rabbi Nathan Cassuto and his wife, Anna, were sent on the same train to Auschwitz on January 30, 1944. She survived, he did not. Their two boys were placed with separate non-Jewish families and survived. Anna Cassuto emigrated to Israel. Several years later Arab terrorists murdered her.

Ugo Foà survived the concentration camps and resumed his life in Rome.

Arminio Wachsberger survived both Auschwitz and Dr. Mengele, and returned to Italy.

Rabbi Israel Zolli and his family never left Rome. They hid in the homes of Catholic friends. After the war, much to the chagrin of the Italian Jewish community, Rabbi Zolli converted to Catholicism, receiving baptism on February 13, 1945 under the baptismal name of Eugenio, in honor of Pope Pius XII. Zolli died in 1956.

Massimo Teglio resumed his life where he left off at the time of the German occupation—as a playboy and aviator.

The Jew Coen reclaimed his son hidden by Monsignor O'Flaherty. He also received back his gold chain, untouched, from the drawer into which the Monsignor had tossed it.

□□□

Adolph Eichmann fled to Argentina where Israeli agents captured him and spirited him off to Israel. After a lengthy trial in Jerusalem, he was hanged in 1961.

The West German government reported that Theodor Dannecker, a right-hand man of Eichmann's in rounding up and deporting Jews, committed suicide. Many question the truth of that claim.

Field Marshal Albert Kesselring and General Kurt Maelzer were sentenced to death; their sentences were commuted to life imprisonment. Kesselring was released in 1952 and died in 1960; Maelzer died in prison.

◻◻◻

Many times in their history, Jews have been martyred for refusing to give up their faith. Under the Nazis, they had no such option. They were slaughtered simply because they were Jews. It didn't matter if they renounced their religion, were baptized or married Christians; they were murdered unmercifully—shot, gassed, burned or starved to death. Books like this must continue to be written. We must not forget what the Nazis, what ordinary German citizens, did; we must not forget what cruelty human beings are capable of inflicting on other humans. Nor should we forget what heroics *other* ordinary people are capable of, such as the Italian citizens, lay people, sisters, nuns, friars, bishops, cardinals and priests, who, at great risk to themselves, saved so many Jews.

AUTHOR'S NOTE

In 1942, when SS *Obsturmführer* (Lieutenant) Kurt Gerstein, who served in the death camps attempted to tell the world about the gassings, he allegedly left his report with Catholic authorities in Berlin. It is not clear how that information was passed on to the Vatican. Therefore, I decided to use the vehicle of Bishop Preysing's meeting with Cardinal Secretary of State Maglione as the channel of delivery to the Vatican. I selected Preysing because he was among those German Catholic prelates who desired the church to speak out against Nazi atrocities. During the time the concordat between the Vatican and Germany was under consideration, Preysing reminded a conference of bishops, "We owe it to the Catholic people to open their eyes to the dangers for faith and morals that emerge from National Socialist [Nazi] ideology." His determined campaign against the Nazis, culminating in a meeting with Cardinal Pacelli when Pacelli was Vatican secretary of state and later, with the very ill Pope Pius XI, was undoubtedly a factor in the issuance of the encyclical *Mit brennender Sorge*. Preysing, who was archbishop of Berlin at the time of the Gerstein report, would have been a likely transmitter of such information. Gerstein's 1942 report is not in the public domain, but his 1945 report on the murder of the Jews in the concentration camps is. A fair assumption, I believe, is that the information in the 1942 report is set forth in the 1945 report.

The experiences of the character Attilio Nathan and his family were based in large part on the real-life family of Attilio Di Veroli.

The real Attilio and his son, Michele, died in the Caves massacre, as described above.

The character Augusto Sonnino of Ancona was based in part on some of the experiences of the real-life Augusto Seppili, who fled the town in a manner similar to Sonnino. Seppili joined the partisans, fought the Germans and survived the war.

The Schwartz family portrayed in the book did not exist, as such, but their travails are based on the actual experiences of many real families of foreign Jews who fled to Italy from Czechoslovakia, Austria, Romania and other German-occupied countries in Europe. Dora Schwartz's heroic use of her native German to stand down the SS troops in the convent in Genoa and later, in the SS offices in Florence, are based on a reported interview with a woman identified only as "K.L. from Galicia." At the time of the roundup, she was living in Merano, Italy.

A Fascist gang raided the Convent of the Franciscan Sisters in Florence. While there was no Ester Piperno hiding in that convent, as such, many of the Jewish women captured there, like portrayed in the Piperno character, were sent to Fossoli Prison Camp and later deported to Auschwitz. Piperno's experiences set forth in the book were representative of those of many Italian Jewish women. Piperno represents the women of Fossoli killed in the German extermination camps.

Similarly, there was no Lidia Fiano, Piperno's friend. The brutal strangulation committed by SS prison guard Elsa Lächert in Fossoli Prison actually occurred. However, the woman she murdered was not identified.

The character Professor Dino Frascati of Florence, helped by Rabbi Cassutto and Father Cipriano Ricotti to obtain a false ID, is based loosely on the experience of Neppi Modona, a Jewish professor from Florence.

There are undoubtedly both those who would criticize my treatment of Pope Pius XII and his policy of silence as too lenient and those who would say that I denigrated the efforts of the pontiff in the help he extended to the Jews. I can only say that I entered into this project, admittedly, with a negative view of the pope, but my research found cogent arguments on both sides of the issue of his policy of silence, with little middle ground. Many of the hard facts might still reside in the secret archives of the Vatican. Certainly, the most conclusive evidence died with Pope Pius XII, who, for the most part, kept his own counsel as to his motives and thinking. I tried simply to present the facts known to me. Readers will have to make up their own minds.

Let me just say that the pope's silence is certainly fair game for criticism but his people did, in secret, help the Jews of Italy with, I am sure, his knowledge. On the other hand, Roosevelt did precisely the opposite. He went about quite publicly condemning Nazi persecution of the Jews but his State Department's secret policy prevented Jews in Europe from escaping to the United States through draconian immigration restrictions. So where is the greater hypocrisy?

SOURCES

Aarons, Mark and John Loftus. *Unholy Trinity.* New York: St. Martin's Press, 1998.

Adams, Henry. *Italy At War (World War II).* Alexandria VA: Time-Life Books, 1982.

Barnett, Correlli, ed. *Hitler's Generals.* New York: Grove Weidenfeld, 1989.

Barzini, Luigi. *The Italians.* New York: Simon & Shuster, 1964.

Bassani, Giorgio. *The Garden of Finzi Continis.* New York: Harcourt Brace Jovanovich, 1977.

Berenbaum, Michael. *Witness to the Holocaust (An Illustrated Documentary History of the Holocaust in the Words of its Victims, Perpetrators and Bystanders).* New York: HarperCollins, 1997.

Bessel, Richard, ed. *Fascist Italy and Nazi Germany, Comparisons and Contrasts.* Cambridge: Cambridge University Press, 1996.

Blet, Pierre. *Pius XII and the Second World War.* New York: Paulist Press, 1999.

Bondy, Ruth. *The Emissary.* Boston: Little, Brown and Company, 1973.

Bowlby, Alex. *Countdown to Cassino.* London: Leo Cooper, 1995.

Cannistraro, Philip and Brian Sullivan. *Il Duce's Other Woman.* New York: William Morrow, 1993.

Caracciolo, Nicola, translated and edited by Florette and Richard Koffler. *Uncertain Refuge-Italy and the Jews during the Holocaust.* Chicago: University of Illinois Press, 1985.
Cheetham, Nicholas. *A History of the Popes.* New York: Barnes & Noble, 1982.
Churchill, Winston S. *Closing the Ring.* Boston: Houghton Mifflin, 1951.
------*The Hinge of Fate.* Boston: Houghton Mifflin, 1950.
------*Their Finest Hour.* Boston: Houghton Mifflin, 1949.
Cohen, Kate. *The Neppi Modona Diaries.* Hanover, NH: University Press of New England, 1997.
Conot, Robert E. *Justice at Nuremberg.* New York: Carroll & Graf, 1983.
Cornwall, John. *Hitler's Pope.* New York: Viking, 1999.
Davis, Melton S. *Who Defends Rome?* New York: The Dial Press, 1972.
De Lange, Nicholas, ed. *The Illustrated History of the Jewish People.* New York: Harcourt Brace, 1997.
Deakin, F. W. *The Brutal Friendship.* New York: Harper & Row, 1962.
Dear, I.C.B. and M.R.D. Foot, editors. *The Oxford Companion to World War II.* Oxford: Oxford University Press, 1995.
Di Scala, Spencer M. *Italy from Revolution to Republic (1700 to the Present).* Boulder, CO: Westview Press, 1995.
Einstein, Stephen and Lydia Kukoff. *Every Person's Guide to Judaism.* New York: UAHC Press, 1989.
Eisenhower, Dwight D. *Crusade in Europe.* New York: Doubleday, 1948.
Falconi, Carlo. *The Silence of Pius XII.* Boston: Little, Brown, 1970.
Fargion, Maria Luisa. *Beside Still Waters.* Ashfield, MA: Paideia, 1991.
Fein, Helen. *Accounting for Genocide.* Chicago: University of Chicago Press, 1979.
Fermi, Laura. *Mussolini.* Chicago: University of Chicago Press, 1961.
Fest, Joachim C. *Hitler.* New York: Vintage Books, 1974.

------Speer, *The Final Verdict.* New York: Harcourt, 2001.
Fogelman, Eva. *Conscience & Courage (Rescuers of Jews during the Holocaust).* New York: Doubleday, 1994.
Friedländer, Saul. *Nazi Germany and the Jews (Vol. 1, The Years of Persecution, 1933-1939).* New York: Harper Collins, 1997.
------*Pius XII and the Third Reich.* New York: Alfred Knopf, 1966.
Gallagher, J. P. *Scarlet Pimpernel of the Vatican.* New York: Coward-McCann, 1968.
Geier, Arnold. *Heroes of the Holocaust.* New York: Berkley Books, 1998.
Gelb, Alan. *Mussolini, the Untold Story.* New York: Pocket Books, 1985.
Gibson, Hugh, ed. *The Ciano Diaries.* New York: Doubleday, 1945.
Godman, Peter. *Hitler and the Vatican.* New York: The Free Press, 2004.
Gunther, John. *Inside Europe (1940 War Edition).* New York: Harper & Brothers, 1940.
Hansen, Ron. *Hitler's Niece.* New York: HarperCollins, 1999.
Hearder, H. and D.P. Waley, editors. *A Short History of Italy.* Cambridge: Cambridge University Press, 1963.
Hitler, Adolf. *Mein Kampf.* Boston: Houghton Mifflin Company, 1962.
Hochhuth, Rolf. *The Deputy.* New York: Grove Press, 1964.
Hutchinson, Robert J. *When in Rome (A Journal of Life in Vatican City).* New York: Doubleday, 1998.
Irving, David. *Hitler's War.* New York: Avon Books, 1990.
Katz, Robert. *Black Sabbath.* Toronto: The Macmillan Company, 1969.
------*Massacre in Rome.* New York, Ballantine Books, 1967.
------*The Battle for Rome.* New York: Simon & Shuster, 2003.
Kelly, J. N. D. *Oxford Dictionary of Popes.* New York: Oxford University Press, 1986.
Kogos, Fred. *1001 Yiddish Proverbs.* Secaucus, NJ: Citadel Press, 1997.

Laing, Stuart, editor. *The Illustrated Hitler Diary*. New York: Galahad Books, 1980.

Lamb, Richard. *War in Italy, 1943-1945*. New York: St. Martin's Press, 1993.

Langer, Lawrence L. *Holocaust Testimonies (Or the Ruins of Memory)*. New Haven: Yale University Press, 1991.

Lapide, Pinchas E. *Three Popes and the Jews*. New York: Hawthorne Books, 1987.

Laqueur, Walter and Richard Breitman. *Breaking the Silence*. New York: Simon & Schuster, 1986.

Leckie, Robert. *The Holocaust*. New York: Harper & Row, 1987.

Levi, Primo and Tullio Regge. *Dialogo*. Princeton, NJ: Princeton University Press, 1984.

Levi, Primo. *If This Be Man (Remembering Auschwitz)*. New York, Summit Books, 1960.

Levin, Nora. *The Holocaust The Destruction of European Jewry, 1933-1945)*. New York: Thomas Y. Crowell Co., 1968.

Lowry, Thomas P. and John W. G. Wellham. *The Attack on Taranto*. Mechanicsburg, PA: Stackpole Books, 1995.

Ludwig, Emil. *Talks with Mussolini*. Boston: Little, Brown & Co., 1933.

MacGregor-Hastie, Roy. *The Day of the Lion, The Rise and Fall of Fascist Italy (1922-1945)*. New York: Coward-MacCann, 1964.

Marchione, Margherita. *Yours is a Precious Witness*. Mahwah, NJ: Paulist Press, 1997.

McBrien, Richard P. *Lives of the Popes*. San Francisco: Harper San Francisco, 1997.

McDowell, Bart. *Inside the Vatican*. Washington: National Geographic Society, 1991.

Meltzer, Milton. *Rescue (The Story of How Gentiles Saved Jews in the Holocaust)*. New York: Harper Collins, 1988.

Menen, Aubrey. *Four Days of Naples*. New York: Seaview Books, 1979.

Michaelis, Meir, *Mussolini and the Jews*. Oxford: The Clarendon Press, 1978.

Moody, Sidney C., Jr. *Associated Press War In Europe*. Novato, CA.: Presidio Press, 1993.

Morris, Charles R. *American Catholic*. New York: Times Books, 1997.

Morse, Arthur D. *While Six Million Died (A Chronicle of American Apathy)*. Woodstock, NY: The Overlook Press, 1967.

Murray, William. *The Last Italian (Portrait of a People)*. New York: Prentice Hall Press, 1991.

Neal, Patricia. *Harder Than War*. New Brunswick, NJ: Rutgers University Press, 1992.

Origo, Iris. *The War in Val D'Orica*. Boston: David R. Godine, 1947.

Passelecq, Georges and Bernard Suchecky. *The Hidden Encyclical of Pius XI.* New York: Harcourt Brace & Company, 1997.

Paul, Wolfgang. *Hermann Göring (Hitler Paladin or Puppet?)*. London: Brockhampton Press, 1998.

Pepper, Curtis G. *The Pope's Backyard*. New York: Farrar, Straus & Giroux, 1966.

Ramati, Alexander (as told by Padre Rufino Niccacci). *The Assisi Underground, The Priests Who Rescued Jews*. New York: Stein and Day, 1978.

Reader's Digest. *Reader's Digest Illustrated History of World War II.* Pleasantville, NY: The Reader's Digest Association, 1969.

Rosenbaum, Alan S. *Prosecuting Nazi War Criminals*. Boulder, CO: Westview Press, 1993.

Roth, John K. and Michael Berenbaum, editors. *Holocaust (Religious and Philosophical Implications)*. New York: Paragon House, 1989.

Runes, Dagobert D. The War Against the Jew. New York: Philosophical Library, 1968.

Russell (Lord, of Liverpool). *The Record (The Trial of Adolf Eichmann)*. New York: Alfred A. Knopf, 1963.

Sachar, Howard M. *A History of Jews in America*. New York: Vintage Books, 1992.

Salwak, David, ed. *The Wisdom of Judaism*. Novato, CA: New Old Library, 1997.

Scrivener, Jane. *Inside Rome with the Germans*. New York: Macmillan Co, 1945.
Silver, Eric. *The Book of the Just (Unsung Heroes Who Rescued Jews from Hitler)*. New York: Grove Press, 1992.
Smith, Dennis Mack. *Mussolini*. New York: Alfred A. Knopf, 1982.
Smyth, Howard McGaw. *Secrets of the Fascist Era (How Uncle Sam Obtained Some of the Top-Level Documents of Mussolini's Period)*. Carbondale, IL: Southern Illinois University Press, 1975.
Spalding, Henry D. ed. *Encyclopedia of Jewish Humor (Biblical Times to the Modern Age)*. New York: Jonathan David, 1969.
Speer, Albert. *Inside the Third Reich (Memoirs)*. New York: Galahad Books, 1970.
Starkie, Walter. *The Waveless Plain*. New York: E. F. Dutton & Co., 1938.
Stein, George H. ed. *Hitler*. Englewood Cliffs, N.J.: Prentice-Hall, 1968.
Steinberg, Jonathan. *All or Nothing*. New York: Routledge, 1990.
Stille, Alexander. *Benevolence and Betrayal*. New York: Summit Books, 1991.
Sulzberger, C. L. (text by). *American Heritage New History of World War II*. New York: Viking, 1997.
Taylor, Telford. *The Anatomy of the Nuremberg Trials*. New York: Alfred A. Knopf, 1992.
Toland, John. *Adolf Hitler (Vol. II)*. New York: Doubleday, 1976.
Trunk, Isaiah. *Jewish Responses to Nazi Persecution*. New York: Stein and Day, 1979.
Trye, Rex. *Mussolini's Soldiers*. Osceola, WI: Motorbooks International, 1995.
Waagenaar, Sam. *The Pope's Jews*. La Salle, IL: Library Press, 1974.
Wallace, Robert. *The Italian Campaign (World War II)*. Alexandria VA: Time-Life Books, 1981.

Wheal, Elizabeth-Anne, Stephen Pole and James Taylor. *Encyclopedia of the Second World War*. Edison, NJ: Castle Books, 1989.

Wiskemann, Elizabeth. *Italy*. London: Oxford University Press, 1947.

Wyman, David S. *The Abandonment of the Jews (America and the Holocaust, 1941-1945)*. New York: Pantheon Books, 1985.

Yahl, Leni. *The Holocaust (The Fate of European Jewry, 1932-1945)*. New York: Oxford University Press, 1987.

Zolli, Eugenio (alias Israel). *Before the Dawn*. New York: Sheet and Ward, 1954.

Zuccotti, Susan. *The Holocaust, the French, and the Jews*. New York: Basic Books, 1993.

------The *Italians and the Holocaust*. Lincoln: U. of Nebraska Press, 1988.

ABOUT THE AUTHOR

Carl Steinhouse had been a federal prosecutor for the United States Department of Justice and then entered into private practice specializing in class actions, white-collar crime, and antitrust investigations and trials. He served in the U.S. Army Counterintelligence Corps, with a tour of duty overseas during the Korean War. He spent a year living in Trieste.

Mr. Steinhouse wrote and edited books on grand jury practice, criminal trial practice, criminal jury instructions and model criminal jury instructions for the American Bar Association. He was a frequent lecturer and participant in the ABA National Institutes.

At the time of the crisis for Soviet Jewry, he was active on an international level for the National Conference on Soviet Jewry, making several trips to Jerusalem and Helsinki on fact-finding missions and to the Soviet Union, aiding Refusniks (those Jews the Soviets refused to let emigrate). A former member of board of the Cleveland Anti-Defamation League and ADL's National Legal Affairs and National Fact Finding Committees, he remains active in ADL matters, including monitoring activities of hate groups.

Mr. Steinhouse, who had family in German-occupied territory during World War II, and had been personally affected by the Holocaust, became interested in research on the rescuers of Jews after a visit to Budapest where he spoke with survivors of the Holocaust who related stories of how they were saved by the brave righteous Gentiles in adventures rivaling those in the imagination of any fiction writer. This resulted in his first two published books, *Wallenberg is Here!* and *Righteous and Courageous* that received rave reviews from Holocaust scholars and authors. Steinhouse used his considerable research skills, honed by thirty-five years in law enforcement and litigation practice, to marshal the facts surrounding improbable saviors of Jews.

The author is happily married and lives in Naples, Florida, where he does his writing.

Printed in the United States
152058LV00001B/252/A